Brave
New
Church

Published by:
Clear Faith Publishing LLC
22 Lafayette Road
Princeton, NJ 08540

ISBN 978-1-940414-09-6

Printed in the United States of America

First Clear Faith Publishing edition: January, 2015

Cover & Interior Design by Doug Cordes

Brave New Church is typeset in Source Sans Pro and Mercury.

Brave
New
Church

William J. Bausch

Published by:
Clear Faith Publishing LLC
Princeton, New Jersey
2015

Contents

PREFACE

At the beginning of the last century, in 1903, Giuseppe Sarto became pope. He took the name of Pius X and was later canonized. Politically naive, somewhat narrow-minded, conservative, he sided with his equally conservative Curia to confront what was known at the time as "Modernism."

Modernism was more of an attitude than a specific doctrine, an attitude that was trying to come to terms with the biblical, archeological, and linguistic discoveries of that time. It ended up with an appreciation of the development of dogma and the historical method of dealing with Scripture (a method endorsed by the Church some seventy-five years later). The so-called modernists—prominent names were Alfred Loisy, a biblical scholar, George Tyrrell, a Protestant turned Catholic Jesuit, and the famous Baron von Hugel—were trying to align the Church's then-current teaching with modern scholarship.

But their approach got them into trouble, for they treated the Bible simply as a work of literature and left out the supernatural and traditional Church interpretations. Alarmed, Pius X issued a scathing encyclical against Modernism and its practitioners, kicking off a veritable intellectual witch hunt whereby suspected professors, teachers, and theologians were scrutinized and relieved of their positions. A secret service organization was set up (not formally dissolved until 1921), with a thousand informers and a thousand agents, to keep files on those with Modernist leanings—one of them being Angelo Roncalli, the future Pope John XXII. Further, all theologians, bishops, and pastors had to take an oath against Modernism.

There is no doubt that some of the Modernists were blinded by the intellectual fashions of their time, and that some of their views could not be reconciled with traditional Christianity. But our concern is with the way the Modernists were treated by the Catholic hierarchy. The condemnations and witch hunts of the official Church wound up suppressing and alienating those very theologians who could have helped forge a middle ground. As history has shown, forbidding discussion, suppressing dialogue, and censoring speech have never worked. This was especially true during the start of the twentieth century, a time when the systems of modern communications were just beginning to emerge. In her book *Prophets and Guardians*, historian Meriol Trevor says some sensible words, for then and for now:

> The usual defense of Pius X and his advisers is that they were acting on behalf of the "little ones" whose faith was threatened by the Modernists. Christ's warning, addressed to those who mistreat children, was taken by ecclesiastical rulers to include adult but simple members of the church. But were Loisy's exegetical studies a terrible danger to the fishermen of Brittany? Would Blondel's philosophy, almost incomprehensible to his friends, upset the peasants of Provence? If the little ones were the bourgeois capable of reading books of criticism, was a condemnation the best way of answering the questions raised? If it was necessary to crush Modernism in order to preserve the faith, what sort of faith, what sort of faithful were envisaged?

> When Cardinal Richard censured L'Evangile et L'Eglise (The Gospel and the Church), Loisy's sales doubled. After Tyrrell was dismissed from the Society of Jesus, his books commanded a wider public than before. People wanted to know what the fuss was about—they always do. Suppression of criticism and of new ideas, never easy since the invention of printing, was quite impossible by the beginning of the twentieth century. No one

in authority would admit the questions, let alone provide what could have subdued Loisy's influence with better answers, than his. Persistent refusals to face these questions surely meant that it would become harder for educated Catholics to remain believing Christians. And if Rome was willing to jettison the educated in order to preserve the faith of the simple, it was short-sighted not to realize that as more and more received education, so the problems would be revived on a wider scale and would not be less difficult to solve for the passage of time.[1]

Trevor has hit the nail right on the head, and she underscores the point of this brief excursion into history. If the process of stifling discussion was counterproductive in the days of printing and at the beginning of mass education, how much more is this so today when the laity are fully educated? Most of all, we must realize that the Internet, with its resources, information, and networking connections, has subverted all authority, creating a wide-open, censor-free vehicle for every and any subject, from hardcore pornography to the overheated environment.

In this book, topics that usually are not openly raised or, in some instances, officially off-limits—for example, bishops privately acknowledge that Pope John Paul II has explicitly forbidden them to discuss matters such as homosexuality or a married priesthood, other than to defend the Church's official teaching[2]—are explored. Though few, these topics are important and are in need of open discussion. For the most part, I take a moderately conservative position as we examine the post-Christian era in which we live, an era that poses a dozen challenges to the Church in general and to the parish in particular.

The post-Christian era

No one denies that in a relatively short time, since the 1960s, there has been a vast cultural meltdown. The old communal order, along with the system of Judeo-Christian morals and values, has broken down. It has been replaced by unbridled individualism for which any barrier, any check, any moral teaching is considered an assault, a constriction, and a violation of human freedom. As a result, we find ourselves easily in a post-Christian, postmodern world. How could this happen so quickly, within the short space of some thirty or forty years? James Q. Wilson, reviewing Francis Fukuyama's book, *The Great Disruption: Human Nature and the Reconstitution of the Social Order in Public Interest*, says:

> The reason culture can change quickly is that much of it is produced by social elites who are easily drawn to new ideas and adventuresome practices. In England and America, changes had begun around the turn of the century and had come into full flower by the end of the First World War....
>
> At first, ordinary people continued in their customary cultural patterns. They flirted with sexual expression and personal liberation in the 1920s, but soon the Great Depression and the Second World War put an end to those adventures. Those two decades—the 1930s and the 1940s—could be called the Great Timeout: a two-decade interruption in the process of self-liberation. But when the war ended, and as the children of the Baby Boom reached adolescence, self-liberation returned with a vengeance and the Great Disruption was born. This produced many good things—for example, a concern for civil rights—but many bad ones, too. The tragedy for ordinary people, as Myron Magnet has pointed out in *The Dream and the Nightmare*, is that they often lack the resources with which to fight back against decadence. The rich can afford psychotherapy and drug treatment programs; the poor cannot. The rich can use gates and guards to protect their homes; the poor cannot. The rich can send their children to good private schools; the poor cannot. And so social elites can more readily cope with the defects of contemporary society while the poor, and much of the middle class, must await the slow reemergence of a more virtuous culture.[3]

We must indeed await the emergence of "a more virtuous cul-ture." Meanwhile, we must identify the vices, so to speak, of our current culture. We must take a critical look at the twelve challenges wrought by this "Great Disruption," both for society and for a brave new Church that seeks to move from turmoil to truth.

INTRODUCTION

The brave new Church finds itself in the midst of a postmodern, post-Christian world. To most people, these slippery terms mean that we are in a different world—very different. The traditional Judeo-Christian storylines are muted and have faded into one chapter in a book with many chapters.

Life today, on all levels, has changed. At one time doctors used leeches to draw "bad" blood; now they can replace hearts. At one time we inherited our looks and family resemblances; now cosmetic surgeons can erase any trace of them. At one time we were Earth-bound; now we are planning to go to Mars. At one time we were the center of the universe; now we know we are but an infinitesimal speck in countless galaxies, and likely not the only place where life exists. Cloning, the ability to create life in a test tube, watching revolutions as they happen on the other side of the world, technologies that develop far too quickly for us to think about them and draw ethical conclusions—all of these have no precedents against which to judge them.

A scholastic, medieval religion based on a static chain-of-life hierarchy is no longer viable. Marriage between a man and a woman for the purpose of children is merely one choice among many, as unions between anyone are deemed acceptable, and designer children can be bought from the eggs and sperm in your latest catalogue. In a word, the past is no longer a guide, and ancient wisdom is no longer in demand. The older generation, befuddled by the world around it, is asking the younger generation for guidance.

We are all as awed by technology as we are affected by it. Medical and ethical questions are coming at us faster than we can handle them. New configurations in human relationships present profound challenges. Secularism and affluence have dulled the soul. Pluralism has created unspecified diversity that undermines the polis, the community. Life is moving faster, faster, faster. Organized religion, under the pressure of a glorified individualism—I make my own god—is declining. The old solutions, the old guideposts, are insufficient. We are beyond the images, the vocabulary, the mindset, the theology that anchored us in the past as we moved along on our human journey. We are afloat in an uncharted, new, postmodern, post-Christian world.

Yet paradoxically, more than ever, there is a great hunger for the Divine. There is a fierce hunger for meaning and purpose, especially among the young. They have inherited the fractured world of their Baby Boomer parents, who often have left a legacy of broken homes and religious illiteracy. A world of easy money, easy sex, and easy drugs has left the young unfulfilled, and they are searching—often in the wrong places, but searching nonetheless.

The Catholic Church, in the throes of its own internal cultural war, has a strong residue of tradition and spirituality to offer these post-modern, post-Christian era folk. Underneath all the losses, in-fighting, and scandals lies the basic substratum of the Eucharist, a faith community, a long litany of scandalous yet creative saints, a historic ability for self-reform, and flowering greatness. If only we can get off the ground, if only we can identify and meet the challenges.

This book attempts to give a perspective and direction concerning the Catholic Church today. As the reader will learn, it is much concerned with balancing the tensions between diverse groups such as a lay ministry and the diminishing priesthood, straight and gay clergy, men and women, conservatives and liberals, those who favor authority and those who favor freedom.

Part One offers twelve basic challenges to the Church as it struggles in this time of history. In Part Two, we look critically at the current stopgap measures being used to address these challenges. Then, in Part Three, we move on to responses and approaches that we, the Church, might consider.

Brave New Church: From Turmoil to Trust might be regarded as an end to the trilogy that began with the books *The Parish of the Next Millennium* and *Catholics in Crisis?*, for it repeats (minimally) some of the basic material and tone of those books and uses the parish as a lens by which to consider the larger problems of the Church. But this book then goes on to what I see as a far richer analysis, and to far more practical considerations.

I dearly hope this book might be read communally; it works best that way. As such, this is a book for study groups, small faith-sharing communities, parish staffs and councils, seminary staffs, and groups of seminarians—any group that might take each chapter, read it, study it, critique it, agree or disagree with it, and then apply it to local circumstances.

The Church is no stranger to controversy. Unfortunately, it is also no stranger to corruption, division, and stifling bureaucracy. Above all, it is no stranger to renewal and revival. This pilgrim Church has been around for two thousand years and has survived. Lucky, some might say; the time of dissolution has finally come, others might say. We say, the Spirit of Jesus is alive in this Church. And we have to prove ourselves right.

A New Introduction

Since I first wrote this book, about a dozen years ago, there have been continuous social and moral changes. In a dramatically rapid turn-about, for example, in four short years, homosexuality has gone from pariah status to mainstream respectability. Gay marriage is commonplace, legal in many states and soon to be federally sanctioned for the whole county. The two-parent household has declined, having a special economic impact on males and affecting the 10% of America's grandparents who have taken in their grandchildren. In recent years, more couples are living together than married, and for the first time there are more children born outside of wedlock than within, from 12% in 2002 to 22% in 2010.

Family life continues to be loosely defined. As one headline announces, "And Baby Makes Four; How a woman, her son, her sperm donor and his lover are helping to redefine the American family" (*New York Times.* June 19, 2011, p. 25). Two-thirds of married mothers are employed or the sole breadwinner in 40% of households. More people are staying single than marrying. Men are so behind women in education, status and opportunity that articles asking "Are Men Necessary?" are commonplace, with the more radical feminists reducing them to occasional sex partners rather than life partners. The men themselves have opted for perpetual adolescence. They are simply dropping out of society: no college, no jobs, no marriage, no fatherhood.

In 20-30 more years, whites in America will be in the minority and the official Church seems ill prepared for this demographic fact. Finally, we still, Catholics and non-Catholics alike, in a kind of collective Stockholm Syndrome, are held willing captives to a pervasive, all-embracing secular consumerism that continues to sap our souls.

On the Catholic religious front, an ever-vigilant secular press keeps the focus on the open wound of clerical sexual abuse. Catholic schools, once the bedrock of vocations and passing on the faith, are closing at alarming rates: more than one third of parochial schools have closed between 1965 and 1990, and enrollment has fallen by half. Religious illiteracy is the proven norm.

Church membership is hemorrhaging. Of the 34% of Americans raised Catholic, only 24% still identify themselves as such. Three out of every 5 Christians disconnect after age 15. One-third of the 20-30-40 year olds describe themselves as having "no religion"—the "Nones". The "spiritual but not religious" attitude dominates. In fact, those with no religious affiliation—including atheists and agnostics—are now the third-largest "religious" group in the world. According to Vatican statistics over the past ten years, Catholic marriages have declined drastically, and a little-observed and appreciated fact is that Catholic baptisms have similarly declined, both absolutely and in proportion to the number of births. The Center for Applied Research in the Apostolate (CARA) finds a reason: "Catholics are just as likely as non-Catholics to have children but are less likely to baptize these children than in the past" (Vol 1. No 1, Summer, 2013). Obviously, the Catholic population percentage will decline in the coming years, threatening the long-term health and stability of the Church.

For Catholics, the Church is no longer the primary place they turn for answers. They have no connection with any "magisterium", and are limited in what they are willing to accept. They live in a very diverse, open, and tolerant society, and are impatient with "fixed", churchy answers. The fact is that most young adults, heirs to a severe recession, terrorism, numbing wars and broken families, no longer follow the old path of leaving home, getting an education, finding a job, getting married, and having kids by the time they're 30. These events are likely to be delayed or bypassed altogether, and that's the "new normal" the Church has to deal with.

As the male clergy shortage grows and overworked clergy steadily age, the call for women deacons and priests continues. Vocations decline. Parishes continue to merge. Mass attendance continues to drop. The schism between right- and left-wing Catholics widens. Meanwhile, we have had two new popes: Benedict XVI, who resigned in 2012—the first pope to do so in six hundred years—and Pope Francis, elected in that same year. Pope Francis, departing from the usual image of pomp and circumstance, presenting a more humble and compassionate face to the world, has raised hopes that he can initiate some much needed reform to the Vatican bureaucracy (the Curia) and deal decisively with the scandals of the Vatican Bank and the blight of a predatory clergy.

None of these developments negate the arguments of this book, where some references may be dated, but rather enhance them. In fact, so much do all these expansive contemporary issues find echoes in *Brave New Church* that it was felt that such timeliness justifies a reissue. Here it is, intact, with some occasional revisions, plus a new final chapter of what the Church might be like during the pontificate of Pope Francis.

William J. Bausch
Feast of St. Joseph, 2014

PART ONE

The Twelve Challenges

1

The First Challenge

Secularism and the Assault on Faith

"Secularism" can be a slippery term. It can be taken to mean that the Church has lost its central place as the mover and shaker of society. Other institutions have taken over what the Church once controlled: law, medicine, the university, and so on. Truth be told, most of us accept this as a fact of life, especially in a complex, ever-growing society such as ours. In fact, with the teachings of Vatican II, we may embrace this loss of control. Some see this broader, secular culture as being in opposition to the Gospel, requiring a "Christ against culture" stance. Others, more fruitfully, I think, see the culture as an ally to be in dialogue with.

In this chapter we will use the term "secularism" both in the more fashionable sense of popular or "pop" culture, and in the sense of a hostile culture that connotes a certain attitude toward life and religion. This attitude can range from an outright public disdain of religion to support for privatizing belief; that is, successfully ushering belief out of the public square into the deep and quiet inner sanctuary of personal opinion, where one belief is no better or worse than any other.

Secularism comes from the Latin *saeculum*, meaning "generation", "spirit of the age", or "fashion." In our modern understanding, secular basically means that the physical world, nature, is all that exists. There is no other reality, and we must make our own way without any help from a non-existent deity. Moreover, this sense of the word posits the concept that a God who hears and answer prayers is unproven and antiquated. There is no divine purpose being worked out in the universe. All that we are and have is here and now. We, not some remote God, are in control of our own destiny. (Besides, who can believe in God after the Holocaust, Pol Pot, Stalin, AIDS, and the suffering of the innocent?) In this sense secularism is a practical denial of anything beyond the here and now.

Several contemporary steams feed into this attitude. First, there is scientism. Scientism preaches that only what is observable and provable is real, is true. The rest is false, misleading, irrational. Religion is a collection of myths, hostile to reason and common sense. Faith, in the words of Richard Dawkins (*The Selfish Gene*), is "blind trust, in the absent of evidence, even in the teeth of evidence". A. C. Grayling (*Against All Gods*) says that "faith is a commitment to belief contrary to evidence and reason". A photo of a young adult shows him wearing a T-shirt where the cross is crossed out and the logo is "in science we trust".

Scientism reigns in our schools, colleges, and universities in proportion as the humanities have been dropped even in Catholic colleges. Half a century ago, in a famous "Two Cultures" lecture, C.P. Snow lamented the growing rift between science and the humanities. Today that rift is a chasm, as science dominates. Science is where the action is, where the jobs are, and education's task is to produce workers, not thinkers about the human condition. The liberal arts, storytelling, poetry, philosophy have no part in a scientific world. Religion, that depository of poetry, myth, and storytelling, has no place in a digital world. Twelve or more years of "scientific" education produces minds unable to see beyond their iPads, to think about the deep questions about life's meaning, human existence, and how we are to act in this world. That absence of reflection leads to secularism.

Next, there is downfall (except among the most fundamentalist) of the literal Bible. For decades now, the public has been used to the major weekly magazines like *Newsweek*, *TIME*, and *US News & World*

Report, and the monthlies like *The Atlantic, Harpers*, etc. and the TV documentaries. Particularly around the religious holiday times, they routinely display on their covers the latest lead story of a new artifact found, a manuscript discovered, a novel theory proposed that shows or "proves" something in the Bible as faked, forged, or fabricated. Sprinkled over all, like confectioner's sugar, are thin suggestions of duplicity and deceit, cunning and conspiracy. We have come to expect several slick pages of text and artwork undermining the traditional interpretation of the Bible, pages ending with a few sentences indicating that, yes, other reputable scholars disagree.

Although there has been some shameless jockeying for ratings and profit—one thing the *National Geographic* showcasing of the discredited Gospel of Judas showed was the fact that scholars *have* found an incredible amount of new materials that have shed light on the Bible. Ever since the cracking of the Near Eastern languages in the late 1800s, the startling discoveries of Gnostic writings at Nag Hammadi in Egypt in 1945, and the unearthing of the Dead Sea Scrolls between 1946 and 1956 along with discoveries of new manuscripts (some still awaiting translation) and artifacts, the Bible will never be the same, and the skepticism this has engendered and the questions this has raised have fed into the secular mind.

Finally, there is diversity (which we will treat in chapter seven) and its fallout: the confusion of faith as belief in propositions and faith as trust in something more. From the infighting of the early Church emerged a dangerous trend: the primacy of "faith" as believing correct dogma. Dogma, necessarily enshrined in culture-bound formulations and language, became universal for all times and places. Eventually, as must happen, when those formulations, the language, could no longer bear studious scrutiny or common sense application or give spiritual nourishment, it was still clung to as dissidents burned at the stake, or reinterpreted into the opposite of what it said, or just left to wither away. A more educated age became skeptical.

A secular age became disdainful, especially when faith as belief in doctrine began to have little or no relation to faith as lived. The

Church, it was observed, ignored the public sinner and excommunicated the public dissenter. The hierarchy flattered and groomed the Coreleones of *The Godfather*. By any chance were they to publicly deny the Trinity, excommunication would be swift.

These, along with the new public face of a very vocal atheism, are silent steams that feed the secular spirit. At this point, let me list six characteristics of secularism as we meet it in everyday life.

First: Secularism downplays humanity

In this regard, it is implicitly (and sometimes explicitly) declared that the only real meaning our lives have is the meaning we create. Humankind is but a part of nature and has clearly emerged as a result of continuous, natural evolutionary forces. We are ultimately, as Carl Sagan once said, the product of the stars; that is, the same primal material cooked up in the Big Bang has slowly found its way to produce us. And we are latecomers, at that. Again, according to Carl Sagan, if the fifteen billion years this universe has existed were compressed into a single calendar year, all recorded human history would occur during the last ten seconds of December 31—and the birth of Jesus would have occurred just two seconds before midnight!

Our planet itself is but a single ecosystem, and if there is any such thing as moral value, it is the proper use of nature. Nor are we unique in the universe. Years from now, we might well launch another spacecraft to Mars. There, we hope to find signs that will indicate—in this endless universe of which we are but one minor planet in one minor solar system in one minor galaxy in literally countless systems—there may be other life forms lesser or greater than our own.

Furthermore, it is maintained, we are but evolving, high-grade animals who share 98% of our genes with chimpanzees, and who are going nowhere in particular. We are a compilation of mechanical parts with a brain, and we have the technology to replace everything from knees to hearts. Cloning has gone mainstream, with companies offering to store the DNA of your aging pet so that someday one just like it can be cloned for you. In 1998 Joan Hawthorne and John Sperling founded the Missyplicity Project. This couple gave $2.3 million dollars to Texas A&M University to remake the couple's pet dog, thereby offering the world the fantasy that those we love can be replaced by genetic copies.

The point of mentioning this revolutionary technology is to reveal how, in a very short time, the cloning of living things has been normalized and marketed. Soon we will not only be able to manufacture children as consumer goods—in February of 2000, the European Patent Office issued a patent that could include human cloning—but concoct them ourselves in a petri dish out of chemicals we mix up. We will be as gods. Even now, human eggs sell on the Internet for $150,000, and sperm banks offer designer babies—blue eyes being in short supply, at the moment.

Universities are starting to offer law courses on animal rights, the novel (and very lucrative) category used by lawyers to sue on behalf of animals. What is intriguing and unsettling is the official nomenclature that describes the subject of this interest as "non-human animals". Seriously. So what we have is that Hitler killed lots of human animals and slaughterhouses kill lots of non-human animals, but both are classified as animals. From being made in the image and likeness of God to being made out of star mix, from being a little less than the angels to a category of animal species, human beings have been downplayed and redefined.

Finally, the historical sequencing of the entire human genome—that is, laying out the biological code for the more than 50,000 human genes that make up human DNA—is one of the most dramatic discoveries since the beginning of time. With this information, the possibilities for identifying and curing potential diseases and for improving human life are endless. On the other hand, the further commodification of humans is also possible. While ruled unconstitutional in 2013, corporations once applied for patents on human genes to be later sold at a profit. Without that ruling our genetic information would have been subjected to the open market as interested parties (such as insurance companies) attempted to pry into our genetic history.

The mapping of the human genome is a major step toward controlling our environment and well-being, offering the possibility that someday we will know whether we are genetically predetermined to certain types of development and behavior. Yet already eugenics is operative, as parents dispose of fetuses diagnosed with some undesirable trait, or put in their order for a blue-eyed boy. We are well on the road to designing the body traits and behavior of future generations. This can be unsettling. Since the foundation of our moral conduct and legal system is that we can choose between right and wrong, to find out that, even before we are born, our decisions are predetermined or limited makes humanity less human, more mechanistic, and fosters the tendency to see human beings simply as products of manufacture.

Second: Secularism celebrates the individual

Perhaps secularism's most notable effect is the loss of community, of a communal sense. In a way, this is a logical development. Since one of the tenets of hard secularism is that there is no outside referee and no absolutes, then the self becomes the measurement of all things. Thus is born one of its fruits: individualism. Like art being whatever the artist says it is, truth is whatever I think it is or want it to be, and self-interest is right and proper.

The Triumph of the Therapeutic, Philip Reiff's groundbreaking book of 1986, has captured the modern secular mood. He reminds us that in the therapeutic world of psychology, what is good for the individual becomes an entitlement one is free to pursue directly and fully. In fact, one is not only free to pursue it, one has a responsibility to pursue it, and so we see countless people declare they will settle for nothing less than the good life. No longer does the notion of the ancient *polis*, the commitment to public life, prevail; no longer is the model of the early Christian community put forth as an ideal. Rather, we have the emancipation of the individual "I" from the communal "we".

It is no accident that, in a few short years, the focus of the magazines on our newsstands has gone from People to Self. Or as United BMW of Duluth, Georgia advertises, "It's all about you," and Day-Timers' online store also proclaims, "It's all about you". This sentiment is echoed in dietary guidelines which urge you to make healthy choices that "fit your lifestyle"—as long as those choices include eating beef. eBay, the online auction site, encourages "about me" pages. An advertisement for New York University pictures a pretty young girl with a self-satisfied look next to the blurb, "I am the president of me, inc." In case we don't get the message, there is a billboard which reads, "Now the world really does revolve around you," put out by the computer industry. The computer, that quintessential shrine of the solitary, becomes both the conduit and the metaphor for individualism as it offers a self-enclosed world where we can all click for our individual joys.

It is to be noted that often even religion has adopted the individualistic, therapeutic stance. A brochure handed out at the Grace Episcopal Cathedral in San Francisco is a good example of secular individualism, what we might call "Christianity lite":

> You know from the past about inquisitions and crusades and witch hunts. You live in a time of religious military zealots, abortion clinic bombings, and TV evangelists attempting to take power in our land. [Grace Cathedral is] a place of religious immunity [from such horrors]....Here operates an unconditional surrender to the freedom of God to speak to whomever in whatever language is understandable. In this space you can walk the labyrinth of life to the tune of the Spirit which you uniquely hear. Immunity from religious control is granted you upon entry. Grace offers "sanctuary" to everyone and promises this glorious freedom of God as the climate to explore the healthiest living that religion affords.

"Speak what you like," "march to your own tune," be "free from control" (i.e., no rules), "enjoy healthy living," the "Spirit you uniquely hear"—sounds like pure New Age talk. No community, no cross here. Seek your own happiness. As one commentator writes:

> Lately the pursuit of happiness has become a mainly private activity. Americans take mood drugs to fire up the happiness circuits of the brain and go to the gym to release happiness endorphins. Phrases like "job satisfaction" and "personal growth," by which we assess our careers and marriages, have become part of the language, while terms like commonweal and even citizenship—in which there lingers a residual sense of public good and private obligation—sound archaic. This succession from public to private notions of happiness is the culmination of a long historical process.[1]

But who are we to criticize? Let's back up a minute. In spite of a strong tradition of community, Catholics have not been exempt from rampant individualism. They, too, have bought into what had previously been a longstanding Protestant tradition, and we ought to take a look at that. A recent survey of American Catholics, for example, quite clearly shows that they are in fact becoming more individualistic and less institutional in their religious beliefs and practices, especially, as we might guess, the younger generation.[2] For example, the findings show that while 88% of pre-Vatican II Catholics were married in the Church, only 59% of post-Vatican II Catholics are. In 1988, 68% of women surveyed and 62% of men said they would never leave the Church, but today only 56% of the women and 57% of the men would not leave. In 1987, 70% claimed they could be good Catholics without attending community Mass, but in 1999 that figure rose to 77%. In 1997, 51% said they could be good Catholics without marrying in the Church, while in 1999, 69% said so. Finally, in 1977, 39% said they could be good Catholics without obeying the Church's teaching on abortion; in 1999 that number rose to 53%.

Further, for many younger Catholics, the Church itself has become but one denomination among others, one religion among many, no better or no worse. They can easily slide into another religion if the person they marry has a stronger faith than theirs. Also, the non-Catholic partners of Catholics are not converting to Catholicism as often as they once did.

There are other signs, too: routine shopping on Sunday, catechetical classes that bow before the soccer schedule, Catholics who send out Christmas cards with snowmen or dogs on them, and who spend the most sacred, solemn time of their faith, Holy Week, at Disneyland with the children or grandchildren. From this evidence and from all polls that have ever been taken, there is no difference whatsoever between Catholics and the rest of the population in consumerism, attitudes toward premarital sex, divorce, capital punishment, churchgoing practices, and abortion rates. Indeed, Catholics are a testimony to the triumph and pervasiveness of individualism and the secular spirit among us.

That is why George Gallup could say to a November 5, 1999 gathering of the Catholic Broadcast group:

> Today, Catholics are as upscale as the rest of the population. Catholics reflect the views of the entire country....The majority disagree with [Church] teaching on social issues such as sexuality, the role of women, and celibacy...[and since Humane Vitae, Catholics regard Church teaching as] "a norm, or ideal from which to deviate."

These facts and figures demonstrate the individualistic trend, the homogenization of Catholics into the pervading American culture, and the steady drift away from the teachings of the institutional Church.

Third: Secularism commodifies people

Unscrupulous funeral directors sell the gold on our bodies, from the rings on our fingers to the fillings from our teeth, and donated human remains are harvested for profit. People who are urged to donate bodies are nobly told that vital organs, such as kidneys and hearts, will save lives; but in fact most of the body parts are sold for commercial use—to the tune of nearly one billion dollars in profits to these companies. Human skin, for example, is used to heal burn victims; but it is also used to puff up the lips of models, enlarge genitalia, or smooth out wrinkles. A single body can provide material that is worth up to $40,000. This is indeed a revolution.

Up to now, all cultures, from the ancient Mesopotamians and Egyptians to the Incas and North American Indians, paid special respect to the dead. They honored their spirits and were wary of disturbing their bodies. Elaborate funeral rites and tombs testify to that respect. Christians were especially reverent, imbued as they were with a sense of St. Paul's question, "Do you not know that you are temples of the Holy Spirit who dwells within you?" Catholics paid special attention to the rites of Christian burial and interred bodies with deep respect.

Today, the secular marketplace and mentality have co-opted even the dead. There is a deepening sense that, from before birth, when our fetal remains are used to make cosmetics, to after death, when our bodies are sold openly on the market, we are merely a commodity. This is indeed a shift from the sacred to the secular. And there is more. As the 100,000 human genes are rapidly being identified, sorted out, catalogued, and patented, scientists are even now trying to rearrange them into something we can perhaps no longer call human beings. (Defining who and what "they" are will be an unspeakable challenge to society and the Church.) There are pills, relentlessly pushed, to control every mood, from behavior control for two- and three-year-olds to Viagra for an improved sex life. Serial marriage, private and corporate greed, abortion, assisted suicide, and killing deformed babies (as utilitarian professor Peter Singer of Princeton advocates) are logical extensions of the secular outlook. Eminent Biblical scholar Walter Brueggemann sums it up:

> Everyone knows that we are in the midst of a huge techno-logical revolution that has the potential of deeply impacting all social relationships. Since the publication of Jacques Ellul's *Technological Society* in 1967, people of faith have been on notice that the technological revolution is an urgent issue in theological reflection and critique. Technological advances range, of course, from the seemingly innocuous to the obviously ominous, from home computers to the capability of war by stealth. As Ellul has made clear, the threat of all such technical advances is the pursuit of control and the reduction of life to human management. We can see this development everywhere...control of information, concentration of wealth, reduction of reality to imagery, and the seemingly endless capacity for surveillance. Many would not follow Ellul all the way in his dire assessment; but none can resist his connection of technology to control, and with control, to a flattening and closing of the mystery that keeps life human.[3]

Fourth: Secularism encourages consumption

That we live in a consumer culture is a given. A consumer culture is one in which people define themselves in terms of their visible wealth and possessions rather than their personal significance. When people define themselves as what they have or don't have they are no longer subjects; as we have seen above, they become objects, commodities. And, what's more, they do so willingly. So argues James Twitchell in his book, *Lead Us into Temptation: The Triumph of American Materialism*. He says that although we are seduced by advertising, we have nonetheless freely embraced it and have succumbed to consumerism. Indeed, we have become addicted to it. Consumption has become a kind of secular religion as people who used to organize themselves around the cathedral now organize themselves around the mall. (Where else can you go on Sunday?)

So we enter the addictive consumerist cycle: we work hard so we can play hard. We earn more so we can spend more. We drive ourselves—Americans are true workaholics—so we can drive our cars. A paycheck is something that enables us to spend more. We are in a vicious cycle of production and consumption. With such rampant consumerism, we have become blind to human relationships, especially those with our children, and to the harsh reality of need and poverty. Consumerism is an addiction indulged in at the expense of the poor and weak. But we don't want to see that; we don't want to be reminded of it. As Michael Crosby tells us:

> With its obsession for increased production and consumption, our society rarely concerns itself with issues related to distribution. However, domestically the consequences of our consumer-driven economic system witness to an ever-increasing disparity between rich and poor to the point where the wealthiest 2.7 million have as many after-tax dollars to spend as the poorest 100 million. The ratio has more than doubled since 1977, when the top 1 percent had as much as the bottom 49 million people. This means that the richest 2.7 million people and the 100 million at the other end of the scale will each have about $620 billion to spend. Since the $620 billion that must be shared by the 100 million comes to $6,200 per person, we know the consumer lifestyle is not a viable option for the poor—although poor people are as tempted to "buy into" the consumer culture as are the rich. Thus when we speak of "consumerism" we are actually speaking about the lifestyle that is promoted for everyone yet is available only to the top 40 percent of the population who have 71.7 percent of the income.

> When we consider the international scene, the disparity between the rich and the poor is increasing, as well. A 1999 World Bank study showed that the number of people living on less than $1 a day appears to be rising. It reached 1.5 billion people by the end of 1999. The bank noted that, while 1.2

billion people lived on less than $1 a day in 1987, this figure had risen to 1.3 billion by 1993. Assuming the proportion of people living in poverty will remain unchanged, the bank reached its figure of abjectly poor people at 1.5 billion as we start the new millennium. At the same time one in every three citizens of the U.S. describe themselves as heavily or moderately in debt because of their consumer choices.[4]

Income inequality is a searing and crippling fact of life, but consumerism makes us blind to that. Understandably. Take a typical day in the life of your child or grandchild. He rises from a comfortable bed in his own room, which has its own bathroom, telephone, television, VCR, and computer. He puts on his designer clothes, grabs his cell phone, checks his pocketful of disposable income, is driven to school, plays soccer, comes home to an empty house, watches TV, snacks, eats, does homework, and goes to bed. (OK, so for some children this is an exaggeration—but for many others, it is not.)

Like his parents or guardians living in a cocooned life, this child never, ever has to meet a poor person. That most of the kids in the world do not have a telephone or a TV or enough to eat is simply beyond his comprehension. That the Nike baseball cap he's wearing and for which he paid around twenty dollars was made somewhere in Asia by workers earning a dollar or less never arises in his consciousness. That he is an integral part of a secular, consumerist culture which has little regard for the ecology; that so much of the consumption he takes for granted is dependent on the destruction of rainforests, or affects water pollution and water rights, is never raised.

He and we don't want to be reminded that we who make up but 5% of the world's population consume close to 30% of its oil supply, or that we produce 290 million tons of toxic waste yearly. Like the casinos—which have no windows, so they can screen out local poverty, and no clocks, so all time is now, and use specially weighted coins so they make more noise when falling out of the slot machines—a consumer society keeps the focus on the secular, consuming self and away from "the cry of the poor."

Fifth: Secularism is spread by evangelization

Three elements stand out in this regard. First, for some reason known only to themselves, most university professors eventually morph into evangelists who preach the secular outlook on life. They do this by deconstructing the old certainties as they indoctrinate their students. Given as sacred writ in halls of learning are principles such as these: anything outside oneself is suspect, and there is no objective "other" such as God—or, for that matter, any objective reality or any objective standards. All truth remains subjective. There is no common nature to us at all. Human nature in only a "social construct"; who we are and what we become is entirely shaped by our cultural and social context. We are, in short, creatures of our environment, and there is nothing "essential" to us at all. There are no great stories—that is, no overarching or coherent way of understanding ourselves. We move through life piece by piece.

It is drummed into the students that no one, no religion or morality, has a right to place limits on them, to curtail their freedom. This is why there must always be a radical suspicion of authority of any kind, much less religious authority. There is no truth, only what you construct. History is going nowhere. It has no goal. There is no solid ground beneath us; rather, we are marooned on a raft, tossed about by the tides of fate and history. There is no transcendent meaning. There is only the utilitarian meaning of life, which is to cope as best you can. Each of us, as atheistic philosopher Jean-Paul Sartre said, is just "a vain passion" doomed to lifelong frustration. This secular underpinning in what is taught to students sets them up for self-defining participation in an atomistic society. Catholic students, taking their cues from the schools, the marketplace, and the entertainment industry, have similarly constructed their identities far distant from the Church.

Second, secularism has found the most bountiful, practical platform for its evangelists in the marketplace and its three all-embracing outlets: television, the Internet, and the entertainment field. Like all celebrity evangelists, the media have become the most powerful spokespersons in the world, reaching deep down into the very recesses of each person's psyche with their images and messages of consumption. Indeed, what else is commercial (the adjective is significant) television but a way to provide a meeting place for advertisers and consumers?

In a marketplace such as this, literally everything is for sale, from babies to political office to universities and sports. I'm glancing at the newspaper headline on my desk: the National Collegiate Athletic Association has just signed a $6 billion, eleven-year television contract. And consider the multimillion dollar salaries offered to certain baseball players or the fact that the New York Yankees have become the first baseball team in history with a payroll above $100 million. Youthfulness is also a big market item, evidenced by the fact that one of the most common operations in America today is cosmetic surgery. Money and profit, with all of their inequities are the driving forces of this culture—the average corporate chieftain now makes more in a single day than the typical American worker makes in a year.

In a secular culture, morality comes in second—if that. Here is a case in point: Recently, Playboy.com was placed on the Nasdaq index. Prior to this, Wall Street had kept its distance from online porn. But the money is just too fabulous, too enticing. Wall Street knows that, overall, Web-surfers have spent some $970 million for access to adult-content sites, a figure projected to reach $3 billion in two years. The combined outlets for pornography have spawned a $10 billion annual industry, which is growing with no end in sight. Porn money is so plentiful that the industry even speaks of one of its most successful entrepreneurs, twenty-seven-year-old Seth Warshavsky, as the "Bill Gates of smut."

The multinational corporations are also big into pornography. EchoStar Communications (later sold to Dish Network), the number two satellite provider, offers a hardcore sex channel and sells sex videos to nearly a million hotel rooms. AT&T offers a sex channel and owns a company that sells sex videos. Liberty Media, Marriott

International, Hilton, LodgeNet, Time-Warner, Comcast, and other corporate giants are all into the megabuck profitable business of pornography. They justify their involvement by looking upon it as good business. The remarks of Bruce Biddick, of Centrex Securities, are typical. When asked about the moral qualms of porn on Wall Street, he replied, "I'm not a weirdo or a pervert, it's not my deal. I've got kids and a family. But if I can see as an underwriter going out and making bucks on people being weird, hey, dollars are dollars. I'm not selling drugs. It's Wall Street."[5] That says it all. Dollars are dollars.

Third, we have become so jaded that we no longer realize that the marketplace is everywhere in the form of advertising; there is absolutely no place on the globe where advertising is not present. In schools, over eight million students watch Channel One, which not only gives them world news but exposes them to brand name products, along with ads for junk food and violent entertainment. Product logos are on their book covers, soda machines, underwear, caps, and T-shirts. Much to the dismay of the ultra-Orthodox leaders, there are kids' skullcaps (*yarmulke* in Yiddish, *kipa* in Hebrew) dotted with logos for Nike and sports teams.

Our videotapes have ten minutes of advertising before the main feature. We can't get to the Sunday comics until we tear off the advertising foldover. There are ads on the receipts for ATM transactions, on the handles of gasoline pumps, on dry cleaning plastic bags, and on the ubiquitous TV monitors that play as we stand in line at the supermarket, bank, and almost everywhere else where we are captive. There are no longer just stadiums and arenas named for sports teams, but places known as the Pepsi Center, CNN/SI Arena, USA Today Arena, American Airlines Arena, Blue Cross Arena, Coors Field, Compaq Center, RCA Dome, Molson Stadium, Continental Arena, First Union Center, Delta Center, MCI Center, General Motors Place, and so on. There are no longer theaters solely named after legendary stars and moguls, but after corporations: New York's venerable Selwyn Theatre becomes the American Airlines Theatre, and the Winter Garden becomes the Cadillac Theater. As someone said, "If you market your culture too much, marketing becomes your culture."

Every bus, taxi, billboard, and TV show is covered with advertising—the world is saturated with it. Advertising determines and creates our needs; it models our looks and behavior. It creates disposable celebrities and provides the identities, icons, and images that fill our minds. Who in this world does not know about Mickey Mouse, the Spice Girls, Donald Trump, Coca-Cola, McDonald's, and the free-wheeling figurines from the latest movies that fast food chains rotate before a yearning populace?

Sixth: Secularism targets the young

Our youth are especially vulnerable to the secular marketplace and its hedonistic values; after all, they have been raised on television. TV delivers audiences to advertisers, who were quite aware, for example, that teenagers would spend $160 billion in the year 2000, and they wanted their share of this money. Most teens know of no other world than the one they find through advertising. That is why no other market group is so sought after.

It is not without reason that a recent *New York Times Magazine* cover story (September 5, 1999) announced the latest remaking of Hollywood as "Teenseltown," referring to Hollywood's conviction that the teenage audience must be the target for their movies and TV shows. Advertisers spend $2 billion a year to reach this market. Indeed, they have now introduced a new category called "tweens"— children between the ages of eight and twelve—who are being promoted as the new spenders, who will hopefully spend the same number of dollars annually as their older brothers and sisters. In fact, all mass media, says Michael Wolff, is directed to teens:

> If you can't appeal to teens, you don't have a mass media business model. You need teen obsessiveness, the market power of

teen compulsion. To get at it, you have to offer something forbidden; some taboo has to get broken. It's evident in the lovely, sensuous, compelling voyeurism of films or the crossing of racial lines with rock or the sloth of television, or porn on home video. Now the Internet comes along, letting you circumvent one of the strictest taboos of all: it lets you talk to strangers.... These are strangers who share your darkest secrets, your most nagging itches, your most violent inclinations.[6]

All this input, all this highly appealing and sophisticated secular molding, is every concerned parent's nightmare. As one mother puts it:

Rachel's children today live in a world in which the selling of shares in one's life earnings is a growing trend, where $2 billion a year (roughly twenty times the amount spent ten years ago) is spent on advertising to children—advertising that often appeals to the worst human instincts, where many young children know the word cybersex (even if they do not know exactly what it is), and where a small mistake in entering the website address for Jack and Jill, a reputable African-American mothers' and children's organization of which my children and I are members, will lead straight to an unrelated pornography site.

These are a few of the little minefields that dot the landscape of mothering and fathering nowadays. These minefields represent frightening aspects of our children's culture: it is hedonistic, it is technology-driven, and it promotes an evermore pernicious brand of consumerism. Now comes the digital age. More threatening than the Trojan horse of television advertising, the technologies of the digital age unabashedly seek to deepen our culture's commitment to self-centeredness, and they are especially suited for—and targeted to—children who often understand the technology better than their parents do.

At the center of the digital worldview is the idea that for little or no effort everybody should have access to whatever they want when they want it—without intermediaries, without screening, without editing. Nowhere is this notion better embodied than on the Internet. What makes the technology appealing, in the words of one observer, is its ability to put individuals in charge. But there is another side to this technology. The Internet permits advertisers to target millions of people, not all at once as in the case of broadcasting, but one at a time. According to Marc Rotenberg, head of the Electronic Privacy Information Center, "now you're targeting a particular boy, one who has a particular program, who lives in a house, whose parents have a certain income...the opportunity for manipulation becomes much greater, really, almost overwhelming for parents trying to control the upbringing of their kids." The Federal Trade Commission has found that many of the children's sites on the Internet are aggressively collecting "personally identifiable information about children" including names, e-mail addresses, postal addresses, and telephone numbers, without notice and without parental authorization.[7]

This unbridled conditioning, this celebration of the here and now, this manipulation of everything from human genes to rainforests, this worship of transitory celebrities, the corporation control of public images as well as national and global stories, this huge maw of consumerism as the defining element of identity and success is soft secularism. It is the prevailing philosophy of a world shrunken and homogenized by mass communication and global corporations.

Secularism and faith

Secularism—hard and soft, high-tech, fast, alluring—is the air we breathe, the fabric of modern life. It keeps us chronically enamored with consumption and impatient with permanency of any kind. It substitutes for reflection, distracts from meaning, and dulls the religious impulse. One might readily say that by definition, secularism is hostile to faith, to the interior life (there's no "room" left in the mind and heart saturated by secular images) and to religion, which speaks of an Other who confronts and demands altruism, justice, self-denial, and the cross. As Ronald Rolheiser states in his book, *The Holy Longing*:

29

More than one observer has commented that our age constitutes a virtual conspiracy against the interior life. What they mean is not that there is somewhere a conscious conspiracy against proper values, the churches, and true spirituality, as paranoid conservatism likes to believe. What they mean is that, today, a number of historical circumstances are blindly flowing together and accidentally conspiring to produce a climate within which it is difficult not just to think about God or to pray, but simply to have any interior depth whatsoever. The air we breathe today is generally not conducive to interiority and depth.[8]

And secularism raises faith questions. As Joan Chittister ponders:

In an area of spaceships and microprocessors, of laser beams and satellites...we talk without end about technical and cultural changes....Russian cosmonauts reported that they saw no heaven in the cosmos, no God on a cloud. We groped to reconcile ancient spiritual images with raw science. We struggled to adjust to a concept of space that was, it seemed, only space after all. When the Hubble Telescope showed the world a universe of galaxies, the notion that the earth whirled unique in an empty void of rock-hard stars died once and for all....

Chicago physicist Richard Seed announced to the public that he intends to clone a human being within the next 18 months... the whole definition of life will be in question. We find ourselves on the brink of a world full of designer people where once we saw only the hand of a creating God.[9]

In such a climate it is not surprising that there has been a rupture between Catholicism and the technically sophisticated American popular culture. Today's society, with its unique, rampant materialism, its scientific mentality, and its consumerist and hedonistic lifestyles, is simply at odds with traditional Catholic teaching and beliefs. The traditional Christian answers to the questions "What is good?" are no longer viable. The Catholic community has been shattered and its practices and beliefs made to seem irrelevant. As Scott Appleby says:

Let us consider the world which the upcoming generation of Catholics is poised to inherit. For theists—for believers—living at the end of the twentieth century, the secularization process has reached an alarming stage. The operative agnosticism of the majority of professional, corporate, artistic, and intellectual elites in the United States has decisively penetrated mainstream media, political, educational, and cultural institutions, and shaped popular sensibilities to such a degree that American culture, while not systematically or comprehensively hostile to religious faith, nevertheless undermines its plausibility structures, erodes its ethical foundations, and debases its public manifestations.

Contemporary popular American culture, driven by the secular media and Madison Avenue, trivializes religion, commodifies the spiritual, confuses accidents for substance, absorbs and flattens potentially subversive ideologies, promotes a consumerist approach to traditions of wisdom, glamorizes artifice, scorns self-denial, creates need and exploits desire, celebrates superficiality, and courts violence.[10]

A mother's lament, which gives a human face to secularization, is a fitting closing for this chapter:

Christian mothers and fathers are in a battle for the minds and souls of their children. We live in a culture that long ago stopped watching what it says and what it does in front of children. It is a culture that sadly has stopped watching out for children. It has abandoned high moral aspirations. The voices of vice are much louder, more ubiquitous, and much more seductive than the voices of virtue. Such an environment especially needs virtuous people—people with the moral judgment, resources, and courage to discern right from wrong and to act on it; but it is harder and harder to raise up such people. There is no question that mothers and fathers who wish to raise children of virtue must stand against the culture in the United States.[11]

Her words are a challenge to the Church today.

2

The Suspicion of Institutions

We had to spend some time on the secular spirit because it defines so much of what we will subsequently say in this book. Now we move to some of the practical fallouts of secularism that affect the Church today. For one thing, secularism's teaching necessarily involves suspicion of all institutions, those entities which pass on tradition and meaning, for secularism's creed is that there is no meaning. The saying from the 1960s, "Trust no one over thirty," has been inflated to cast doubt on all authority. Authority of any kind is seen as limiting, an enemy of personal liberty, and is to be resisted. Social or moral constraints suffocate freedom.

Advertising constantly pushes the envelope of personal freedom by offering the compelling, infantile fantasy of a world without adults and rules: "The world has boundaries. Ignore them" (Isuzu); "No Limits" (Foster Grant); "Life without Limits" (Prince Matcha-belli); "No Rules. Just Right" (Outback Steakhouse); "No refs. No rules. No mercy" (an NFL video game); "Rules? What Rules?" (IBM); "The rules are for breaking" (The Spice Girls); "When I'm in uniform I know no limits" (an ad for the US Army—pretty scary if you remember Lt. William Calley in Vietnam). Rebellion, of course, has become a huge source of profit. As an article in *The Nation* pointed out, corporations, once scared of hippie trends, have found ways to market them:

The touchstones of the [1960s] counterculture—from the Volkswagen Beetle to bell-bottoms—have long been adopted by Madison Avenue. Mercedes-Benz has appropriated the peace symbol for its advertising campaign. The Jimi Hendrix hit "Purple Haze" can now be heard on Muzak. The newest blue jeans from the Gap? They're called "1969." And there is still a call for "revolution"—by Nike.

Because plenty of former campus radicals grew up to become the studio chiefs, movie producers, CEOs, magazine editors, and ad executives of today the cultural predilections of the baby boom generation have become the reference points for the rest of the country "They're in their prime. They're in power, and one of those places they're in power is in the media, so their self-obsessions tend to be-come everyone's self-obsessions," says cultural critic Todd Gitlin, the former president of Students for a Democratic Society (SDS), the leading national New Left organization of the time. "The '60s have this aura of being not just about their own youth, but about the youth of the twenty-first century. About the collective youth." This is cause for consternation to those who see the decade as a destabilizing social upheaval whose destructive effects have yet to be fully measured.

"You have to separate the good side of the '60s and the whirlwind we're reaping today because of it," former vice-president Dan Quayle said in an interview. "Look at the social problems we have today, the cultural challenges. These go back to the idea of trashing responsibility, authority, law enforcement."[1]

So all institutions, the seats of authority, whose main task is to define and pass on meaning, are mocked or have come under a cloud of suspicion—and often deservedly so. Case in point: the presidency and government are viewed with suspicion ever since the lies of Vietnam and the various "gate" cover ups, not to mention the personal conduct of some who have inhabited the Oval Office. Cynics point out that there is really no two-party system in the United States, just two branches owned by the large corporations, which pour billions of dollars of "soft" money into the coffers of presidential and congressional candidates. For example, I am looking at a report on the front page of the *New York Times* that talks about trial lawyers pouring money into the presidential campaign:

> Moreover, with lawyers' fees in the tobacco settlement running into the hundreds of millions, even billions, many of those trial lawyers have had a lot more to donate this election cycle. More than a half-dozen law firms involved in the tobacco settlement have each given the Democratic party more than $100,000 in the unlimited, unregulated donations known as soft money, some writing checks as large as $400,000.[2]

Campaign finance reform, talked about for the past dozen years, has yet to happen.[3] Congress has been so corrupted by corporate money that it can't pass laws it should—think of the tobacco and gun industries. This has forced the dubious and problematic ploy of using the legal system to overtake the legislative process as a way of bringing redress. Politics has a bad name. A review of Joe Klein's bestseller, *The Running Mate*, states:

> The betrayals, the mendacity, the exploitation of friends and family, the careless destruction of reputations and even lives, all these don't merely occur on a regular basis in contemporary politics, they are demanded by contemporary politics. An unwillingness to engage in them is sufficient to brand one as amateurish and weak....Loyalty, decency, compassion, love— these are, in Klein's fictional universe (and, presumably, not only in his fictional universe), irremediable, crippling flaws in a professional politician. Klein is a man who clearly loves politics, but in *The Running Mate* he has written the most damning indictment imaginable of its contemporary praxis and its contemporary practitioners.[4]

The military has fallen from grace with the reported incidences of hazing, racism, and sexual abuse. The police are routinely vilified for practices such as racial profiling, along with well-publicized cases of corruption and brutality. Since its actions against the Branch

Davidians in Waco, Texas, the FBI has lost its glamour and aura. The IRS, known for its bullying and harassment, has been humbled. Its budget has been cut by 30%, so it no longer audits big corporations and it has drastically cut back on efforts to detect tax fraud.

The criminal justice system has been scorned since the O.J. Simpson and Amadou Diallo cases. (In the latter case, a young west African immigrant was mistaken for a rape suspect and shot forty-one times by four white New York City police officers, who were eventually found not guilty of murder charges. The case un-leashed national demonstrations that raised charges of racism, prejudice against minorities, and police misconduct.) Organized sports makes up one large, money-driven enterprise. Universities are seen for what they are: servants of the marketplace, devoted to the utilitarian task of preparing students to participate in jobs, not life. As the universities increasingly turn to corporations for money, they surrender control over the creation and commercialization of knowledge.[5] Both cynicism and a distrust of all institutions have never been as prevalent as they are today.

Marriage, family and the Church

One significant social institution under suspicion and the object of radical change is marriage and family life. Starting in the 1960s, many people saw promiscuous sexual behavior as a sign of emancipation from the more rigid social constraints of previous decades. This, along with cultural conditions such as the development of radical feminism, the widespread availability of the Pill in the 1960s, and the Supreme Court decision on Roe v. Wade in 1973, dealt blows to the institution of marriage. "Paternity certainty" (as biologists call it) was lost, and many men walked away from their familial responsibilities.

Today, single, teenage mothers have become so much a norm that many high schools have programs specifically designed for them. Many of the young women who fill our colleges realize that eventually, they may not only support themselves but their children, as well. The marketplace has taken over marriage. It is being recast as another budget item, a property arrangement with prenuptial economic agreements routinely advised:

> [The] benefit of having a prenuptial marriage contract before getting married is enormous....As I said in the past, divorce or separation is as inevitable as death. It is bound to come....In my opinion, every couple should and must have a prenuptial agreement or marriage contract. Without this prenuptial marriage contract one's life will be ruined.[6]

"Divorce or separation is as inevitable as death. It is bound to come...." This thought plays in the subconscious minds of every bride and groom, especially those from broken families. There is a political cartoon that hits the mark on this point. It shows a Census 2000 poll-taker writing down a kid's answer. The kid is standing at the front doorstep, in his turned-around baseball cap, with a soda in his hand, responding: "Well, let's see...My mom's the head of the household, but she works three jobs so she's never home. Her boyfriend sometimes lives here with his two kids, but he's in rehab right now. My half-sister and I are moving in with my grandma tomorrow, so I don't really live here anymore anyway and...."[7]

Nontraditional families are a worldwide phenomenon. The Netherlands, for example, passed a law which forbids any mention of the terms "man and woman" or "husband and wife." The official term for cohabiting couples of any sexual orientation is "partners." Traditional marriage—described by the Jubilee of the Family document issued by Rome in October, 2000, as a contract between a man and a woman that is open to children, engages in sex only within the marriage, and holds up a lifetime commitment—is no longer the norm.

For example, some 54.4% of children were born to unmarried women in Sweden; corresponding figures are 50.3% in Denmark, 55.8% in France, and 66.9% in Iceland. (About 40% of children are born to unmarried mothers in the United States.) Birthrates in Europe are so low—especially in Spain, Portugal, and Italy, countries that traditionally have been Catholic—that they are now below replacement level. And the vast majority of women in Europe report that they use birth control. Divorce rates continue to climb (one out of every three marriages in Europe fails, compared to one out of every two in the United States), and so far, twenty five European countries have adopted laws providing for civil registration of homosexual partners. Marriage is increasingly an option that many Europeans are not choosing.[8]

As for the United States, the percentage of American households made up of married couples with children dropped to 26% in 1998, from 45% in the early 1970s. Just 50% of all children live in families where both biological parents are present. The percentage of households made up of unmarried people with no children is 31.2%, more than double the figure in 1972. The percentage of children living with single parents rose to over 31% in 2000, compared with less than 5% in 1972. One in four American children is exposed to family alcoholism or alcohol abuse while growing up, and more than one out of every three children is born out of wedlock. On average, children between the ages of twelve and fourteen stay home alone seven hours a week, usually after school, a time from 2:00 pm to 8:00 pm called "crime time" by the police, when half of all violent juvenile crimes in the United States are committed.

A poll by Roper Starch Worldwide (conducted May 10-17, 1997) reveals that between 1996 and 1997, family closeness lessened. For example, in 1996, 38% of all families attended religious services together. By the next year, this figure had dropped to 29%. The amount of time spent sitting and talking together as a family has dropped from 53% to 42% in this one-year period; eating the main meal together on a weekday has dropped from 72% to 58% of the time; and taking a vacation together, from 53% to 38%.[9] Family fragmentation, entertainment segregated by age and sex, sports, and busy schedules undermine family cohesion and influence. The trivializing of marriage on shows such as "Who Wants to Marry a Multimillionaire?" the social acceptance of casual sex, live-in arrangements, and having babies out of wedlock—think of celebrity single moms such as Rosie O'Donnell and Jodie Foster—the fight for gay marriage and, most of all, the relegation of marriage to just one lifestyle option among many others, have all dealt a severe blow to both society and to the Church.

In a chapter called "Types of Family," one college textbook notes: "There are numerous types of families that we discuss later in the text....We might choose the view that there is nothing inherently wrong with an array of alternate family forms (child-free, single-parent families, stepfamilies, cohabiting couples)."[10] Of course, the whole point for the students is choice. Since they are taught that the pursuit of personal freedom is the defining feature of any civilized society, they should be completely free to choose the way they lead their lives, and no form of social arrangement is deemed superior to any other. Those, for example, who opt for single motherhood should be supported in their choice.

All of this affects society because the one out of four children who are raised without fathers are statistically prone to future violence and crime; because each taxpayer in America annually pays $300.00 to support the babies of teenage mothers; and because of the grossly unfair burdens on grandmothers who have to raise the offspring of their unwed or divorced children. (There are so many grandparents raising their grandchildren that in some parts of the country there are grandparents' support groups.) The national social cost is also high. In Spain and Italy, two Catholic countries, the birthrate has been below replacement level for some time, and so the government must import foreign labor to fill open jobs. Along with this trend, these countries are alarmed that their national identity is being lost.

Target: Youth

In the last chapter we mentioned that youth are being targeted as very desirable consumers. Here we note that their immaturity is also a target:

Thirty years ago, adults controlled access to society's primary decision-making, education, and earning power, and they functioned as gatekeepers for information necessary to participate fully in the institutions of the American middle class. In short, it served young people's best interest eventually to identify themselves as grown-ups.

Today, the adult-youth relationship critical to identity formation is threatened by adult invisibility as much as absence. Participation in consumer capitalism requires purchasing power, not maturity—and American adolescents have purchasing power to spare, with or without identity achievement. Postmodern society views adolescence less as a life stage than a lifestyle, a choice available to adults as well as youth. Advertisers blur the lines between generations by pitching adult toys and child make-up. Adults strive to prolong their adolescence, while teenagers face daily decisions that potentially short-circuit theirs. Four months before President Clinton acknowledged his affair with twenty-two-year-old Monica Lewinsky, a Bennington College senior told *Rolling Stone*: "Adults no longer behave like adults. We have no role models; they're talking about sex and therapy and substance abuse, just like us."

The unmitigated relativism of postmodernity, coupled with the constant and overwhelming necessity of moment-by-moment choice, compromises identity formation's requirement that the adolescent invest in a central, governing life-view (what Erikson called an "ideology"). Facile, piecemeal role-taking, along with the hapless compartmentalization of life into distinct, even contradictory, categories, encourage a "self" cobbled together through bricolage, not integration. Instead of directing youth toward a center that holds, postmodern culture encourages adolescents to reinvent themselves for each of their proliferating social roles.

If youth ministry is to address fragmented, overwhelmed teenagers as human beings, and not as objects to be won and counted for the Church, then we must orient twenty-first-century youth ministry unapologetically toward the cross. God's fidelity in Jesus Christ, demonstrated by the cross, is a sign of love that suffers because it is true. As developmental theorist and ethicist James Fowler argues, the cross of Christ is crucial to adolescents precisely because it shows the extent to which God goes in order to win them.[11]

We might mention here that one of the devices used in appealing to the youth market is sex. This, sadly, is evidenced in the constantly lowering age at which children have sex, often as early as the middle grades (fifth through eighth). In an article from the April 2, 2000 issue of the *New York Times*, a psychiatrist from New York notes, "I can't tell you how many girls come in who are bereft about having had sex too soon." A psychiatrist from Minnesota states, "There are significant numbers of youngsters who are engaging in sexual activities at earlier ages." Another psychiatrist reports on groups of seventh and eighth graders who rent limousines to take them to clubs in Manhattan, then wind up having sex. "I see no reason not to believe that soon a substantial number of youths will be having intercourse in the middle-school years," says another.

The reasons given by the experts for children having sex at an early age range from the easy availability of condoms and the earlier onset of puberty to, in particular, a rising divorce rate and the emotional abandonment by parents. One thirteen-year-old boy, who has been engaging in oral sex since the age of twelve, says he does it between the hours of four and seven, before his parents come home from work.

Our highly secular culture constantly sends seductive marketing messages. "Sex is everywhere, and it's absolutely explicit. There's hardly a film that doesn't show a man and a woman having sex. There's MTV, lurid rap lyrics, and now we've got technosex on the Internet," says another psychiatrist. What is most troubling to these psychiatrists is the casual, indifferent attitude of the kids toward sex. One says, "I call it body-part sex. The kids don't even look at each other. It's mechanical, dehumanizing. The fallout is that later in life they have trouble forming relationships. They're jaded."[12]

The other area of dangerous youthful consumption is, of course, drugs. The "of course" testifies to the popularity and mainstreaming of drug use and to the alarming fact that the average age of first-time heroin use is dropping. Once thought to be an urban problem, fifteen- and sixteen-year-old suburban youths are also trying heroin; the number of high school seniors who say they have tried it reaches levels not seen since the 1970s. Most of these teens, in a familiar refrain, report that they come from broken or troubled homes, and use heroin to help cope with stress.[13]

No doubt, the authority of institutions—including marriage, the family, government, and churches—has been undermined. It is in-deed this subversion that concerns and challenges the Church as it ponders the attitudes underlying the changes we have mentioned. Yet we must keep in mind that it is harder to offer the benefits of organized religion and its deep traditions to those who are suspicious of and cynical about all institutions. It is harder to sing the praises of a faith community and a faithful God to children who commonly experience family breakup. It is harder to overcome negativity with the concept of a loving and caring Father in heaven if children have known only an absent father, or one who is brutal when present. It is harder to teach fidelity to children whose parents are divorced and who witness a parade of boyfriends or girlfriends. It is harder to offer commitment to those who have had easy sex since grammar school. It is harder to get across a steadfast love of the Good Shepherd to those who have never known steadfastness.

The bottom line is that so many people who are not from intact families or who have been abandoned emotionally or who are devoid of role models are not as disposed psychologically or spiritually to trust the Church, be open to its wisdom, or hear the Good News. Or, perhaps, for these very reasons, they are. In any case, it is a challenge—for us and for them.

The Bobos

Perhaps a good summary of these first two chapters is to end with the ironic wisdom of David Brooks's delightful bestseller, *Bobos in*

Paradise. Brooks uses the term "bobos" to describe the new-class rich, who he says are the blend of two opposites: the middle-class, reserved, merchant bourgeois and the free-wheeling, anti-establishment bohemians. The marriage of Wall Street and the Left Bank, if you will. What has brought these two groups together is the same thing that dominates the entire globe; that is, the marketplace, which turns ideas and emotions into products.

And so we have CEOs who earn six-figure incomes and wear faded jeans (which sell at an outrageous price), while half-naked, long-haired rock stars embrace their portfolios. The Bobos have found a way to be affluent successes and free-spirited rebels at the same time. They have found a way to be both hippies and corporate fat cats, artists and stockholders, high consumers and environmental sentimentalists. But above all, true to the spirit of individualism, they devote their lives to their physical and emotional health, and seek to expand their inner selves. These people are not just after a job. They must find interior "space" in their place of employment and the mechanisms to work toward their full potential. To appeal to the Bobos, whose mystical quest is self-development and whose cathedrals are health clubs and museums, companies must cater to the supreme "I." One company ad asks of prospective employees, "What do you want?" The ad answers in the voice of a young woman:

> I want to write my own ticket. High tech is a wide-open field. I'm helping to create public relations programs for companies that are on the leading edge of software development. What I'm learning is making one fabulous career. I want to hit the beach. I grew up on the West Coast. The ocean has always been my second home. Whenever I need to think things through, this is where I come. I want to keep climbing. Each year, my role gets bigger. My managers support my growth with professional development and mentoring programs. It's like being back in college. I want to go to Africa. Next year, I hope. (Incidentally, our health insurance plan is great.) I want to be my best. If there's a limit to what I'm capable of achieving, I'm not sure where it is or when I'll reach it. Never, I hope.[14]

It is quite inconceivable that your grandfather ever thought in such terms. Anyway, Brooks remarks, "This is Bobo capitalism in a nutshell. College, learning, growth, travel, climbing, self-discovery. It's all there. And it's all punctuated with that little word 'I,' which appears in that short paragraph fifteen times." Everything is measured in terms of the self. Befitting this, Brooks describes the spiritual quest of Bobos as "Flexidoxy," the desire to live autonomously while at the same time having a need to be grounded in something firmer. Brooks perceptively asks:

> And isn't this desire to balance freedom with rootedness the essence of the educated class's spiritual quest? This is a class that came of age rebelling against the authority of the preceding elite. Starting in the 1950s, the books and movies that most influenced the educated class have railed against conformism, authoritarianism, and blind obedience. Championing freedom and equality, members of the educated class cultivated a code of expressive individualism. They succeeded in smashing old hierarchies. They cultivated an ethos that celebrates, actually demands, endless innovation, self-expansion, and personal growth.
>
> Because of the reforms initiated largely by the educated class, people have more choices. Women have more choices: where to work or how to lead their lives. Different ethnic groups have more choices about where they can go to school or which clubs they can join. Freedom and choice are everywhere triumphant, right down to the gourmet whole-grain loaf you select at the farmer's market, or the kind of partner you prefer in the bedroom. But if you look around at the educated class today, you see a recognition that freedom and choice aren't everything. Free spirituality can lead to lazy spirituality, religiosity masquerading as religion, and finally to the narcissism of the New Age movement. The toppling of old authorities has not led to a glorious new dawn, but instead to an alarming loss of faith in institutions and to spiritual confusion and social breakdown.
>
> So if you look around the Bobo world, you see people trying to rebuild connections. You see it in Wayne, Pennsylvania, where

upscale consumers shop for farmyard furniture that evokes traditional rituals and simple styles. You see it in Burlington, Vermont, where educated upscalers have moved in search of the connections that are possible in small towns. You see it in the vacation preferences of the educated class, the way they flock to pre-meritocratic enclaves where the local peasantry live stable, traditional lives. And you see it in places like Montana, where the cosmopolitan class comes looking for a place to call home.

So progressive in many of their attitudes, the Bobos are spiritual reactionaries. They spend much of their time pining for simpler ways of living, looking backward for the wisdom that people with settled lives seem to possess but which the peripatetic, opportunity-grasping Bobos seem to lack. The question for the educated class is, can you have your cake and eat it too? Can you have freedom as well as roots? Because the members of the educated class show little evidence of renouncing freedom and personal choice. They are not returning to the world of deference and obedience. They are not about to roll back the cultural and political revolutions of the past decades, which have done so much to enhance individual freedom. They are going to try to find new reconciliations.

The challenges they face are these: Can you still worship God even if you take it upon yourself to decide that many of the Bible's teachings are wrong? Can you still feel at home in your community even if you know that you'll probably move if a better job opportunity comes along? Can you establish ritual and order in your life if you are driven by an inner imperative to experiment constantly with new things? I've talked about the mighty reconciliations the Bobos make. But these spiritual reconciliations are the most problematic. The Bobos are trying to build a house of obligation on a foundation of choice.[15]

This is what the Church must appreciate. Bobos struggle with the tension between being committed and being free, and we struggle with how to offer a gospel freedom that demands commitment. "If any want to become my followers, let them deny themselves and take up their Cross and follow me" (Mk 8:34). "Whoever loves father or mother more than me is not worthy of me" (Mt 10:37). It is easy to think of Bobos as being very much like Augustine before his conversion, someone who was troubled in mind and body, disgusted with his profession and with his craft, reduced to being what he termed a "phrase salesman" (what we would call today a public relations guru). It is harder to think of Bobos doing what Augustine did next: upon hearing a child's chant which sounded like "take and read," he picked up a Bible, opened it at random to the passage which read, "Be clothed in Jesus Christ," and then gave himself totally over to Christ. In pre-Bobo times you could have stories like the following:

> Tom Phillips was the president of the large company in the state of Massachusetts. He had a Mercedes, a beautiful home, a lovely family. He was a man of influence and moved in high circles. But Tom was not happy. In fact, he was downright unhappy. Something was missing from his life, but he didn't know what it was. Then one night, during a business trip to New York, something happened to him. Tom Phillips had a religious experience that changed him forever. Speaking of that experience, he said: "I saw what was missing from my life." It was Jesus Christ. "I hadn't ever...turned my life over to him." And that night Tom did just that. And that night Tom's life changed in a way that brought him a happiness he never dreamed existed.
>
> He had an acquaintance. Another powerful man, so high up in the government that he was the number two man. His name is Charles Colson. He too was a successful man. In his own words, he had "an office next to the President of the United States, a six-figure income, a yacht, a limousine, and a chauffeur." But he too was an unhappy man. In his own words, he had a "growing hollowness" deep inside him. Something was missing from his life, but he didn't know what it was.
>
> One August night in 1973, Tom Phillips had Charles Colson over to dinner and, in the course of the evening, told him about

his conversion. And the more Colson listened, the more he became convinced that Tom Phillips had put his finger on what was causing the "gnawing hollowness" deep inside him. He too was hungering for something. And now, for the first time in his life, he had an insight into what it was.

Charles Colson left the Phillips home that night knowing exactly what he must do. He hadn't driven 100 yards from the house when he pulled up alongside the road and began to cry so loudly that he was afraid the Phillips family might hear him. Describing what happened next, Colson said: "I prayed my first real prayer." It went like this: "God, I don't know how to find you, but I'm going to try! I'm not much the way I am now but somehow I want to give myself to you." He then added: "I didn't know how to say more, so I repeated over and over the words, 'Take me, take me, take me.'"

It is hard to envisage the self-actualized Harvard professional living in Silicon Valley, where there are more millionaires than people (figuratively speaking), who is conspicuously defined by her means of consumption, who mouths equality but practices privilege (she believes in the public school but, after all, the private school seems better for the kids), who sits in a gourmet coffee shop wearing her T-shirt that reads "Days of Rage," eating apricot almond feta loaf while her oversized, four-wheel drive Hummer, which never negotiates anything more treacherous than a slippery driveway, sits outside as a mark of status, is finding it very difficult to submit to any outside commandment because she values autonomy too much. Yet—and here is the tension—she feels the need to submit to something more than her circumscribed self. Still, she finds it hard to bring herself to say "Take me, take me, take me."

3

THE THIRD CHALLENGE

Religious Illiteracy

The triumph of the secular spirit is found in statistics which reveal that attachment to organized religion is down all over the globe. In Catholic France, only 14% of the population goes to church; in Catholic Quebec, it is only 4%. Among the young, the figures show that, in Catholic Ireland, 34% go to church; 40% in the United States; and twenty-nine percent in Germany. The Catholic churches in Australia are losing parishioners at more than five times the rate of loss of the Protestant churches.[1] And so it goes.

All of Europe, as we shall have occasion to mention again, is in the rapid process of de-Christianization. The Church in Latin America is hemorrhaging. To move from the global to the particular, it is safe to say that no one reading these words right now doesn't have a child, grandchild, or relative who is no longer a practicing Catholic, or who has not divorced or joined another religion. Add to this mix the agnosticism, skepticism, and religious hostility of the intelligentsia, which have become the mainstream philosophy, and you have a secular interpretation of life. Further add to this mix the fact that Americans in general are quite historically illiterate—and that is the subject matter of this chapter.

We seldom appreciate just how huge the gap is between the historical experiences, memories, and traditions of each generation. For example, colleges have to remind their faculties that, concerning the incoming students who were born after 1995,

- They have no recollection of the Reagan era.

- They were not born when the Soviet Union broke apart and do not remember the Cold War.

- They have never feared a nuclear war.

- They are too young to remember the space shuttle blowing up.

- Tiananmen Square means nothing to them.

- Their lifetime has always included AIDS.

- As far as they know, stamps have always cost about forty cents.

- They have never seen a TV set with only thirteen channels, and do not even know what UHF or VHF means.

- They cannot fathom having a TV set without remote control.

- Jay Leno has always been on the "Tonight" show.

- The Vietnam War is as ancient history to them as World War I, World War II, and the Civil War.

- They have no idea that Americans were ever held hostage in Iran.

- There has always been MTV.[2]

To these social and political episodes of history, Father Richard McBrien adds these religious categories:

- The Second Vatican Council is as much ancient history to them as the Council of Trent.

- They have no memory of the Latin Mass, or of the distinction between a low Mass and a high Mass.

- Women have always been readers and Eucharistic ministers at Mass.

- Nuns have always worn ordinary clothes.

- Communion has always been distributed in the hand.

- They have never seen a Communion rail.

- They have no idea what a biretta is.

- They have never kissed a bishop's ring.

- They never made the Nine First Fridays.

- They never tipped their hats or crossed their foreheads when passing a church.

- They never marched in a May procession.

- They never pinned a handkerchief to their hair if they forgot to wear a hat to church.

- They have no memory of the original debate over contraception in the Church, and have no idea how anyone could possibly be opposed to birth control.

- They have always lived in a society which allows abortion.

- They have at least one Catholic relative or friend who has been divorced and remarried without Church approval and they see no problem with it.

- With rare exceptions, they do not know the name of their bishop.

- They have never worn a cassock and surplice to serve Mass.

- They have never had to ask permission to read a book not approved by the Church.

- They have never heard of the "Fighting 69th" and would be utterly amused to find out that it referred to a campaign to help Catholic teenagers keep the Sixth and Ninth Commandments.

- They have never been in a confessional box.

- They have no idea what scrupulosity means.

- They have never checked the Legion of Decency ratings in a diocesan newspaper to see if a movie was "condemned."

- Most of the films they see are R-rated.

- They never think of hell.

- They have never ransomed a pagan baby.

- They have never contributed to a spiritual bouquet.

- They never read their diocesan newspaper and have probably never seen a copy.[3]

They are, in a word, as disconnected from their religious past as from their political past. A poignant reminder of this disconnection comes from an African-American columnist who writes that one day, she overheard her eleven-year-old daughter and her friends hopping to a rap song by a rap singer named Sisqó and singing along with him lyrics which used the word "nigger." "It was as if they were singing a love song, instead of a word once tossed like grenades into the faces of black men and women by racists." She comments that they had no clue of the word's bitter roots. When challenged, her daughter was nonplussed, wondered what the fuss was all about, and remarked that the mother was carrying baggage from the past that didn't concern her.

> In her world the ugly N-word was simply an expression of bonding among young black people....[She is] a child never scarred by segregation or overt racism; one never denied entrance to a good public school. She didn't realize that I carried this baggage gladly, so she wouldn't have to do so.[4]

It is like that with post-Vatican II Catholics: the events, words, and meanings of their tradition are foreign to them in the land of Now.

It's like this joke, where one little kid says to another, "Look what I found on the veranda—a condom!" The other kid asks, "What's a veranda?"

Generations X and Y

The "Boomer Catholic" parents and grandparents of the young people born after 1982 were taught long ago by their professors to make up their own minds on political, economic, religious, and moral matters. They are now fully accepted mainstream Americans, captured by "choice" in everything, concocting their own spiritual identities by dabbling in all the novel, multitudinous self-help programs and New Age offerings. If they stick with religion at all, they declare that they place a higher value on being good Christians than on being good Catholics.

Regarding the offspring of these "Boomer Catholics", Michael Farrell, a former editor at the *National Catholic Reporter*, writes:

> Away from the practice of Christianity for a generation, [the youth] lack, and will lack even more as time passes, the community consciousness, the tribal memory of their religion that was never just a set of formulas and facts but bred in the bone, an allegiance alive under the skin.
>
> They don't and won't know the story. The New Testament story, for starters. The history of the Church: the controversies and break-throughs, the sinners and do-gooders, the big names and epochal events that made us. They won't know apostles, the popes, won't know the Council of Nicaea or even Vatican II.
>
> It may be argued that millions of their forebears didn't know these either. But it was different then. In the past the majority of Christians were uneducated. We often called them the simple faithful, and there's a load of significance in those two words. But now people are educated and not likely to buy a

whole religion, with all its temporal and eternal ramifications, which they do not understand....All that history, philosophy, science, theology, all the legends and anecdotes and doctrines—they're all fading into some Christian twilight.

If the young members continue to dwindle until only a skeleton of the old faith is left, only a vague cultural memory, then a new story will surely be born because even God abhors a vacuum.[5]

So, living in a society which has dropped off drastically from religious observance, and who therefore are far less religiously literate than their parents, the "Boomer Catholics" understandably did a poorer job of handing down the faith to their own children, those who are part of Generation X, the eighty million Americans born between 1962 and 1982. As a result, these Generation X-ers no longer have a recognizably Catholic moral or religious vocabulary. Scott Hahn, an Evangelical minister who converted to Catholicism, said that when he was a minister, he found Catholics to be "pushovers." He writes:

When it came to leading Bible studies for high school kids, I strategically aimed my teachings to reach Catholic young people, who I felt were lost and confused. I was especially alarmed at their ignorance—not only of the Bible but of their own church's teachings. For some reason they didn't even know the basics of the catechism.[6]

Walter Burghardt, SJ, adds his testimony as a Catholic teacher: "After sixteen years at two Catholic universities, I still marvel at a paradox: the number of Catholic students who live a modest or even profound spiritual life and are utterly ignorant of their rich tradition."[7] What adds to the ignorance is the tendency to introduce students to the controversial areas of contemporary theology before they are familiar with the tradition they are criticizing. Professors with an agenda are also a considerable problem. They often recommend to their students books of very controversial authors who are out of sync with the Church. One professor's recommended reading list for first-year students at a Catholic university included books by John Dominic Crossan, Robert Funk (both of the Jesus Seminar), Uta Ranke-Heinemann, and Bishop John Shelby Spong—none of whom could be considered even remotely sympathetic to the Church. What's more, no mainstream authors were recommended.

Add to all this a time of experimentation in the late 1960s and throughout the 1970s, when the curricula of parochial schools and religious education programs attempted to wed traditional Catholic doctrine with borrowings from pop psychology, secular values, and non-Catholic religious precepts. Now you have a recipe for what is one of our most bedeviling problems: religious illiteracy. The combination of less religious observance, parents who have "dropped out," a highly penetrating secular culture, and religious illiteracy has left Generation X adrift from the moorings of Catholicism. And now Generation Y, the teenage children of Generation X, are adrift as well. What they get, when they do get anything, is a kind of sentimental virtual Catholicism. As Scott Appleby puts it:

> This is religiosity marketed through popular songs, television, and movies, breezy bestsellers and the worldwide web. At its most spiritually deadening, Virtual Catholicism offers its practitioners a pose rather than a plunge into mystery, a passing encounter with the hard-won truths of the faith, and a brushing up against the symbols and stories of the Tradition as these are selectively recycled through MTV, cyberspace, and popular art.

> While a superficial approach to the gospel is nothing new—"Catholicism Lite," as every pastor knows, is one of our most abiding traditions—Virtual Catholicism is more formidable a rival to mature faith because it has arisen as an intentional response to the experience of dislocation and drift. Resembling a high-tech, cyberspace version of what Chicago's Joseph Cardinal Bernardin memorably criticized as "supermarket Catholicism," it is a disembodied, disembedded form of religion that has arisen in response to the historical fragmentation, scattering, and ideological hardening (into

camps of "left" and "right") of the Church's actual formative communities.[8]

Which is not to say that the present younger generation is godless; on the contrary. (We'll come back to that.) "Spirituality"—that slippery word—has never been more "in," as young people noisily proclaim that they are "spiritual but not religious," or they "believe in God but not the Church." As one German professor of theology writes:

> We live in the final phase of a culturally supported Christianity, yet by no means in a secular world. The Christian churches are losing their significance, but the demand for religion is strong. Cover stories of magazines such as *Newsweek*, *Time*, *Der Spiegel*, or *Psychology Today* confirm this trend. The nature of the trend is clear. Received doctrines and traditional forms of worship are rejected; at the same time, however, the "search for the sacred," the search for religious experience, and the "flight into spirituality," are growing. According to *Newsweek*, one third of adult Americans report religious or mystical experiences, one fifth have the feeling that God has been revealed to them in the past year, and one eighth sense the presence of angels. The situation in Germany is similar. Every seventh person believes in magic and witchcraft, every third person considers the future predictable, and if *Der Spiegel* is right, then there are more seers and fortunetellers offering their services than all Protestant and Catholic clergy put together. One thing is indisputable: Religion has not lost its fascination, but the church has lost its power of attraction.9

A recent poll shows that better than eight out of ten Americans believe that God performs miracles (84%, mostly Christians), 79% believe in the Biblical miracles, and almost half believe that they have experienced or witnessed one themselves.[10] The young, then, are sincere searchers but they have no guides in the search. It means that they have no way to appropriate a Catholic sensibility into their quest: the music, videos, and cyberspace they are devoted to draw almost exclusively on popular religious imagery which demands no theological knowledge and does not demand a spiritual life lived in communion and community with others. Nor does it raise the issue of the "Other," the belief that there really is something more than themselves, there really is Someone who makes demands on them; that there are imperatives beyond their own personal interpretations; that there are moral urgencies beyond their own feelings and desires, which summon them to the Cross.

With no formative Catholicism, armed with the pop catechesis they graduated with at Confirmation, the young people of today do not possess the critical tools needed to detect the fraudulent. For example, the fact that James Redfield's book, *The Celestine Prophecy*— rightly called by Yale scholar Harold Bloom the worst claptrap he's ever read—was on the bestseller list for over a hundred weeks and is testimony to the naïveté of the religiously illiterate public. Regarding Redfield's latest book, *The Secret of Shambhala*, one critic opens his review with these words, "James Redfield's latest guide to spiritual enlightenment is a complete shame, and the only thing that will be (en)lightened is your wallet. This is a torturous 235 pages of bunk, hokum, bilge, foolishness and schlock."[11] Yet these words will not prevent people with little or no knowledge of their own religious heritage but hungry for real spirituality from devouring the contents of this book.

A new agenda

Religious illiteracy is not confined to the young, of course. Most Catholics are relatively educated people, and through the media and Internet they are aware of the bewildering diversity of information that is available out there. But in general, they are woefully illiterate when it comes to their knowledge of Christianity. When and where do they learn to read the Scriptures? What do they know of Catholic heritage? If we went to a doctor or lawyer who had the same lack of knowledge that most Catholics have about their faith, we would either be dead or suing for malpractice.

We live in a culture that is ignorant of or hostile to Christianity. And so, as a Church we must marshal our resources and creative energies to educate our people. Some have even suggested a return to the old concise and pocket-sized "penny" catechisms. A year after her death, one such penny catechism was found in Princess Diana's apartment at Kensington Palace, causing worry that she was flirting with Rome, for such a catechism, as the London Times said, "is usually carried only by sincere believers."

I read somewhere of a university professor who warned his colleagues that the old format of a lecture given from yellow ledger paper notes is fast becoming passé. Why? Because of the Internet. Why should you drone on and on about fourteenth-century Paris when the students, with a few strokes of the computer keys, can call it up in authentic living color on their screens? They can do the same for Mars, Saudi Arabia, Julius Caesar, ancient Mexico, and Alexander the Great.

In fact, colleges are now offering classes and degrees on the Internet because whole courses can be downloaded and made available on ever-faster computers. And, what's more, these classes are available at a mere fraction of what it would cost if they were taken at a college or university. Cyberlibraries will soon be made available to everybody everywhere. Students will never have to leave their homes. So serious is this technology that a man named Michael J. Saylor has recently put up $100 million to launch an online university and library as a means of "free education for everyone on earth." Think of that.

I have despaired of convincing the bishops to put a Catholic spokesperson on commercial television (remember Bishop Fulton Sheen, who captured the largest TV audience of his time?). Will they be equally Luddite, if not indifferent, to the incredible opportunity to offer, via the Internet, the theological and spiritual formation I have mentioned above? Will they fund and encourage whole courses that might introduce a global network to the teachings and the glories of the Church? The possibilities are mind-boggling and endless. Do we have the vision to meet them?

One final thought. Religious illiteracy becomes even more of a problem today because we have been encouraged by the Church to explore the good in other religions. Along with this, we have been indoctrinated by a culture of choice to pick and choose our own lifestyle, religious or otherwise. Information on religions both old and new is very accessible today, and our bookstores are filled with writings about various religious ways of life. Crossover from one religion to another is a common occurrence. Therefore, it becomes more important than ever for Catholics to have an intelligent stance from which to assess these other religious traditions. As Tom Hart advises:

> It is one thing to stand within a religious tradition, and discerningly incorporate into it elements from other traditions. It is quite another to throw one's tradition away and stand nowhere, and then try to piece together a new spirituality out of a bit of this and a bit of that. In the first case, one already has a worldview and an approach to life, and is modifying and enriching them. One possesses something tried and true and is endeavoring to make it even better. In the second case, one is starting from scratch, without even a principle of discernment. One is vintage pioneer, charging into the forest without a map. But is that the best way to go?
>
> Those of us who were raised in the Christian tradition do best to stay within it despite its problems, to refurbish its own best possessions, and to incorporate into it whatever else of value we might find. University of Chicago's Martin Marty, renowned historian of religion, is fond of putting it this way: Keep one foot inside the tradition, and let the other foot wander.[12]

To keep one's foot inside one religious tradition in order to discern others presumes a certain amount of religious literacy. But the reality is that this is largely absent. Not surprisingly, this literacy is even absent in seminaries that train not only candidates for the priesthood but also lay ministers. A very important recent book called *Seminaries, Theologates and the Future of Church Ministry*, by Sr. Katarina Schuth, shows a common pattern—the seminary professors (like those in secular colleges) must engage in a great deal of remedial work because of a basic lack of intellectual and cultural formation. As Robert Imbelli summarizes in a review of Sr. Katarina's book:

> A lack of religious literacy makes the study of theology seem excessively abstract to students and can foster a defensive anti-intellectual posture. A growing absence of intact families can lead to unrealistic demands being placed on relations with faculty and peers...many younger students react against the impoverished religious education of their adolescence and sense the loss of a "thick" and nourishing Catholic culture.[13]

In his book *Education in the Forming of American Society*, Bernard Bailyn wrote that education is "the entire process by which a culture transmits itself across generations." If this classic definition still holds, then we have a large challenge ahead of us.

4

THE FOURTH CHALLENGE

The Loss of "Thick" Catholicism

Writing in England, Agatha Christie, the world's most popular mystery writer, could turn the denouement of many of her stories on the fact that Catholics could not divorce. Here in our own country, in 1949, Paul Blanchard could write an anti-Catholic book entitled *American Freedom and Catholic Power* and have it go through many reprints. Its theme? Catholics were different. According to Blanchard, Catholics always were and would be foreigners in a Protestant land, subject as they were to a foreign pope; they would, of course, vote as their priests, on orders from the pope and which directed them. They were basically disloyal, a threat to American freedom.

He need not have feared. After World War II, many Catholic Americans entered the mainstream quite readily and easily. (After all, wasn't Cardinal Spellman of New York going around blessing the rifles of the soldiers who were fighting communism?) This entrance into the mainstream was hastened during the years from 1945 to 1979, when the old Catholic ghettos broke apart.

In the past, the Church had survived largely because of its ethnic enclaves. The coherent subcultures of Irish, Germans, Italians, Poles, Lithuanians, and others were held together by a common religious center and a universal catechism—as well as by their ethnic religious festivities. The vast pockets of Catholic European immigrants sent their kids to parochial schools, jealously preserved their national customs, faithfully attended novenas and missions, held processions, ate ethnic foods blessed by the priest, wore crucifixes and medals, prayed to patron saints, and built shrines in their houses. There was a complex network of ethnic identity and neighborhood community mixed in with faith and Church. Nationality, customs, public rituals, and religious practices were one, and this created a fundamental cohesive force for the Church. To this degree, the Church lived in the culture but was not a part of it.

This marriage of religion, ritual, and ethnicity, this mutual interpenetration of social and religious life, this easily lived identity of culture and faith is what we call "thick" Catholicism, and it formed a cocoon of institutions, beliefs, and practice. The staples of the faith—the requirement of fasting from midnight, a strict Lent, the ember days, fish on Fridays, the cult of the saints, parish missions, the habits of the nuns, the cassocks of the priests, incense, miraculous medals, novenas, sodalities, weekly or monthly confession, the Latin Mass, the Angelus, first Fridays—all blended into the rhythm of the liturgical year. Someone described the old texture of Catholicism this way:

> The Catholic Church of yesterday had a texture to it, a feel: the smudge of ashes on your forehead on Ash Wednesday, the cool candle against your throat on St. Blaise's day, the wafer-like sensation on your tongue in Communion. It had a look: the oddly elegant sight of the silky vestments on the back of the priest as he went about his mysterious rites facing the sanctuary wall in the parish church; the monstrance with its solar radial brilliance surrounding the stark white [H]ost of the tabernacle; the indelible impression of the blue-and-white Virgin and the shocking red image of the Sacred Heart. It even had a smell, an odor: the pungent incense, the extinguished candles with their beeswax aroma floating ceilingward and filling your nostrils, the smell of olive oil and sacramental balm. It had the taste of fish on Fridays and unleavened bread and hot cross buns. It had the sound of unearthly Gregorian chant and *flectamua genua* and the mournful *Dies Irae*. The Church had a way of capturing all your senses, keeping your senses and your being enthralled.

Everybody knew who was a Catholic, including the Catholics themselves. Their language gave them away. Who else went around talking about "serving Mass," or using words like transubstantiation or contrition or occasion of sin? Who else crossed themselves when passing a church or didn't eat meat on Friday? Catholicism had a coherent philosophy and respected writers. Catholics even gained some measure of respect with their vocal anti-Communism, the appearance of popular public figures like Bishop Fulton Sheen and Thomas Merton, and the popularity of blockbuster movies like *Going My Way, Come to the Stable, On the Waterfront,* and others that gave a favorable face to the Church and clergy. The old mantra "Catholics can't be Americans" went underground.

Mainstreaming

Gradually, the ethnic neighborhoods, the "glue" that provided for a "thick" Catholicism, disappeared. After World War II, the GI Bill allowed Catholics, for the first time, to enter secular colleges and move into the professional mainstream. People escaped to the suburbs in the 1930s, '40s, and '50s, which, long before Vatican II, had a powerful effect on breaking down Catholic identity and community.

Through education and the media, the grandchildren of the European immigrants were homogenized into secular "Americans" who no longer spoke the language, kept the customs, or went to church—in fact, they were embarrassed by these things—and who wore designer labels and got divorced, like everyone else. In fact, Catholics fell all over themselves to be just like any other middle-class, affluent American. Thus corporate capitalism, education, upward mobility, the suburbs, and prosperity moved Catholics, who no longer clustered around their parish churches, into mainstream America. Then in 1962, along came Vatican II with its openness to other religions and to democracy. A few years later, in 1968, we saw the very negative fallout from Humanae Vitae, the encyclical against birth control, which further fractured the Catholic community.

The move of American Catholics from the identifiable margins to the non-identifiable center stage of American culture has had, to put it mildly, mixed results.

> Some American Catholics now remember the tribal cohesion of their Faith in the late 1940s and 1950s as constituting a happier and more desirable ecclesial identity (even granted its perhaps too effusive confidence)—an identity more durable and resistant to the acids of modernity than the current one, which they would describe as heading in the direction of a "culture religion" not much different from the Protestant one that unraveled earlier in the century. Other Catholics feel mostly relief that the walls of the Catholic ghetto came tumbling down in the decades after World War II and see in their less confident and more fractious community a faith truer to that of the early church "on pilgrimage" with their Master amid the vicissitudes of history.[1]

The net result is that today, as we have mentioned previously, Catholics are indistinguishable from their fellow citizens in terms of ethical values, social mores, and cultural tastes. The net result is a certain loss of identity, the loss of a specifically Catholic lore and ritual. We do get divorced like everyone else. We do eat meat on Fridays like everyone else. We do consume like everyone else. We do cherish the manufactured images, whether those of celebrities or the latest Disney character, like everyone else.

Further, we do not have crucifixes on our bedroom walls or little holy water fonts in our children's bedrooms. We do not recall the ember days or go to church with our missals. We do not wear religious medals or eat hot cross buns. We do not have our eyes fixed on heaven for, as Garry Wills has observed, such a view has given way to "the displacement of man's hopes from the hereafter" to the here and now. Ashes on Ash Wednesday, yes. Forty Hours, no. The fact is, there remains only a dwindling minority of Catholics who were formed by the "old Church," who remember its architecture as well as the pervasive catechetical and devotional bonds that gave meaning and magic to their lives. Catholics of that era believed that the common wisdom of the Church, and not the individual, was the moral judge in matters of personal and sexual morality.

But, of course, as we have seen, all that has changed. If, for example, six out of ten pre-Vatican II, old-time Catholics said that the Church is important, fewer than one-third of their children think so. That the older generation went to Mass twice as frequently as do their children is no surprise. That the older generation thought the Catholic Church was a privileged and exclusive means of salvation is to be expected, and that their children, as we have observed before, think of Catholicism as just one more denomination, no more false or true than any other, is also to be expected. Catholic colleges and universities have now long supplanted the old Thomism with narrative, feminist, and other theologies, and this has trickled down to the religion textbooks. Lost to most American Catholic kids has been any kind of unifying force or identity, or any kind of specific "Catholic" thing that sets them apart.

We shall take note of the growing Latino presence and its coming dominance in American Church life later on in Chapter 7, but here we want to consider its challenge to our liturgy and popular devotions. The truth is much of our liturgy, as well as our theological concerns, reflect the conceits of upper, white, middle-class intellectuals. Freed from most economic and political turmoils, armed with college degrees, medical plans, and portfolios, we can forge a parish and a liturgy to our own image and likeness.

But the Latino community, like Israel of old, comes from the experience of suffering, exile, suppression, and the need to survive. Consequently, they bring with them a supernatural worldview and a sense of family, along with motifs of life, suffering, death, redemption, and resurrection. These people are looking for something that they are not finding in the Catholic Church. One Hispanic lady who joined an evangelical church said, "I found that when I went to the Catholic Church, it was like they were reading a book. But at my church it is like I feel the Holy Spirit wrapping his arms around me." Anglos may smile patronizingly at their Via Crucis, their Guadalupe processions, their scapulars, perpetual adoration, and rosaries. But Latinos bring with them an incarnational and sacramental Christianity, a sense that God is real, here and now, and the conviction that the agonies and glories of living are passageways to the sacred, opportunities for potential encounters with God. The eventual encounter of Latinos with the rationalist Generation Y, who feel no need of redemption (from what? life is pretty good) and have little experience of such sacramental "earthiness," may be fruitful in resurrecting a richer Catholicism.

Where's my scapular?

There is a need to once again "thicken" our Catholicism because we have lost so many of the distinctive rituals and devotions that once "thickened" our faith—although there is no doubt that some are rightly retired. But we let go too soon and too much. Ironically, Protestantism, long resistant to ritual and itself now in deep decline, is considering what Catholics have abandoned. They are beginning to talk about "practices of the faith," by which they mean devotions that speak to the heart, and they are looking to old-style Catholicism for guidance.

After the Second Vatican Council, the liturgical pioneers of the Catholic Church disdained the Baroque devotions as signs of decadence, indications that the laity were indeed alienated from the liturgy and had turned to popular devotions in compensation. The reformers thought that once the liturgy was understood and the people engaged in "active participation," they would no longer need such distractions. Well, they were surely correct in that some of the popular devotions were only tenuously tied to Biblical realities, others were somewhat lurid to say the least, and some came close to outright magic. But, like all ivy-towered theorists, the liturgists were out of touch with the hearts and needs of the people and they overreacted, and the corrective they offered went to extremes. And so, since the Council, the devotional life of the Church has declined.

That has been a loss, because the simple truth is that the Mass is not enough. After all, it should be remembered that many of our favorite devotions, such as the rosary, the Stations of the Cross, and the various novenas celebrated both individually and communally, came about as a way of inviting the laity to participate in the prayer life of the religious communities. Surely in this age of active lay participation in the Church, we need devotions to sustain the laity. Moreover, devotions not only express people's faith, they reinforce it. As one author writes:

> If used in their proper context, devotions point us back to our Christian story, to the dying and rising of Jesus Christ. But they do so through imaginative ways: through literature, dance, art, music, symbols, gestures, and prayers. They engage our heart, body, mind, and soul in meditative reflection. And we need that today. When we allow ourselves to move past preconceived notions—that devotions are rigid rituals that have nothing to contribute to modern culture—we begin to learn their value, their relevance, and their wisdom.[2]

The irony is that the secular world is replete with ritual, symbols, and popular art. Look at any sports fan whose shirt and cap are decorated with the logo of his or her favorite team, singing the chants that drive the team on to victory. Look at the high "vestments" of the rock stars. Remember the funerals of Princess Diana, John F. Kennedy, Jr., and many other celebrities. These forcefully show that if the churches do not satisfy the deep hunger for rituals which express strong religious feelings, people will invent them.

We need to revive the Catholic imagination that compels and mystifies. I remember a story told by a Generation X-er whose grandmother had died in Ireland. She went over with her mother to attend the funeral and was absolutely fascinated with the rhythmic chant of the Litany of Loretto, which she never heard before. "Tower of Ivory," "House of Gold," "Gate of Heaven," "Mystic Rose"—all these lovely images were falling from the lips of devout people. She was captivated by it all.

Yet this type of interest is becoming commonplace with Generation X-ers, who are fascinated with the old devotions and religious artifacts of their grandparents: rosaries, scapulars, novenas, crucifixes, holy water, ashes, hot cross buns, benediction, Gregorian chant. They are so immersed in secularity that any sense of the grand, rumors of angels, or rites of ceremony and pageantry that give hint of Another hold great appeal for them. It would seem that parishes should excel not only at good liturgies but also at good paraliturgies and devotions that bespeak presence and mystery.

This writer's words are relevant as we close this chapter:

> Historians, to judge from the record of previous practitioners of the field, make lousy prognosticators of the future. And yet if I were a betting person, I would put my money on the rich category of "ethnicity" as described by Andrew Greeley and discerned by Theodore Hesburgh as providing the most promising identity for American Catholics navigating the treacherous rapids of a new century in an even more pluralistic land. "An ethnic group of ethnic groups," porous but distinct, is a good place to start in constructing studies of the North American Catholic community as it faces a new millennium.[3]

5

THE FIFTH CHALLENGE

Anti-Catholicism

Like peppery seasoning to a stew, a good sprinkling of anti-Catholicism—"America's oldest intellectual tradition," according to Arthur Schlesinger, Jr.—adds a feisty flavor to the mix of secularism, suspicion of authority, the loss of a Catholic ethnic culture, and religious illiteracy. Old-time rabid anti-Catholicism in this country goes back to the roots of the sixteenth-century Reformation polemics.

That old hatred is still very much alive in some parts of the country—think of the notorious Chick publications, anti-Catholic pamphlets that look like comic books and are distributed to the hundreds of thousands of Catholic youths who turn out for papal visits. Remember too the recent words of the president of the Southern Baptist Theological Seminary, who openly stated on television, "As an evangelical, I believe that the Roman Church is a false church and it teaches a false Gospel. And indeed, I believe that the pope himself holds a false and unbiblical office."[1] Bob Jones University, which popped into the news when a presidential candidate unwisely visited it, boasts of its founder, who, in 1928, fearing a Catholic (Al Smith) in the White House, said, "I'd rather see a nigger as President." His son continued the bigotry by calling the Catholic Church "the Mother of Harlots," and also stating that, "If there are those who wish to charge us with being anti-Catholic, we plead guilty"—unsurprising words from the head of an institution which classifies the pope as the "anti-Christ" and the Catholic Church as "satanic."[2]

Such direct biases have transmuted to the indirect, sophisticated, liberal attacks of the intelligentsia who view the Catholic Church, in the words of Peter Steinfels, religion editor for the *New York Times*, as an "authoritarian monolith; its doctrines are hopelessly premodern; its rites are colorful but mindless; its sexual standards are unnatural, repressive, and hypocritical; its congregations are anti-Semitic and racist; its priests are harsh and predatory; its grip on the minds of believers is numbing."[3] That is an accurate assessment of the anti-Catholic perspective.

Indeed, the prevailing concept, played out in the media, is that the Catholic Church is really out of touch; that it is based on discredited medieval beliefs (the word "medieval" is always used in a pejorative sense in our society); that it is clearly awash in superstition; that it sexually represses everyone, while all the time its clergy are libertines; and that the laity are kept in ignorance by the hierarchy and are saved only when exposed to the truth of more reasonable thought or when they have the "courage" to remain Catholic but do their own thinking.

Here's an incident that shows how this plays out in life. In the article cited above, Steinfels describes a Washington social event where a woman with an impressive track record in liberal, humanitarian causes was singing the praises of her daughter-in-law:

> "She's a Catholic, you know," the woman said, "but she's a thinking Catholic." Can one imagine that woman saying to someone, "She's an African-American, you know, but she's an educated African-American"? "Thinking," or an equivalent term like "independent," is usually a code word. It refers to a Catholic who disagrees with Church teachings on abortion, contraception, ordination of women, etc., regardless of how much or how little actual thinking or independence has gone into the disagreement.

The press

The press delights in highlighting disputes within the Church, a favorite theme being the intractable, moronic, out-of-touch, sex-obsessed hierarchy at odds with the noble, oppressed, democratic, freedom-waving Catholic clerics or laity. If the hierarchy is obsessed with anything, it is the theme of social justice, judging by the relentless tons of documents, directives, speeches, encyclicals and pastoral letters on this subject. But, of course, that doesn't sell as well as sex, and so the press consistently reduces all Catholic Church positions to that single issue.

The campaign for assisted suicide in Oregon aimed its ire at the Catholic Church for its opposition to their initiative. A *Don't Let 'Em Shove Their Religion Down Your Throat* committee was founded and Blanchard's old bromide, that the Church should not contribute to any campaign because it is a "foreign power," was raised. This was much like the movement by the so-called Catholics for a Free Choice, who campaigned to have the Vatican thrown out of the United Nations so that it could not influence votes on abortion. An article in *The Nation* (January 25, 1999) by Jennifer Baumgardner called for the use of anti-discrimination laws to force Catholic hospitals to perform abortions, and that same magazine called the pope "a homicidal liar" who "endorses murder." In San Diego, on Ash Wednesday, a woman went to work marked with ashes only to be ordered by her supervisor to remove them. When the woman refused, the supervisor took a rag and wiped them from her forehead.

In the current debates on school vouchers, anti-Catholicism is never far below the surface. David Boldt, an editorialist for the *Philadelphia Inquirer*, quoted the president of an Easton, Pennsylvania teacher's union who said, "If the Catholic Church were to disappear today, it would be better for all of us." Boldt continues:

> It has been said that anti-Catholicism is the anti-Semitism of the liberal intellectual. And, as anyone who has dealt with the

issues learns, anti-Catholicism runs like a river beneath the public debate on school choice, inside and outside legislatures. In my own discussion on school choice, I have often gotten responses like "I just don't want Catholics to get all that money" spoken without a hint of the implicit bigotry.[4]

The liberal *New York Times*, editorializing on Pope John Paul II's well-publicized March 2000 apology for the sins of the Roman Catholic Church over the centuries, was compelled to note that the pope also owed women an apology for not allowing abortions—the role of women always being a hot-button topic for commentators. In its March 27, 2000 issue, the *New Republic* called its readers' attention to the irony of two headlines from the *San Francisco Examiner* that appeared on the same day, from the same writer: "Priest's healing hands credited with miracles" and "Priest admits touching boys." Congress was under fire for blatantly passing over a Catholic to be its chaplain until finally, under pressure, they appointed the first Catholic chaplain in history on March 23, 2000.

On March 8, 2000, the Catholic Cathedral of Montreal was desecrated. A group of vandals burst into the cathedral, shouted anti-Catholic slogans, sprayed paint on the altar, littered the church with condoms and sanitary napkins, and tried to overturn the tabernacle. Several people were arrested, but shockingly—although not surprisingly—the police said that a hate crimes charge would not be lodged against them because they were voicing issues of public concern and expressing their opinion. Even the *Canadian National Post*, a secular paper, sensed the blatant double standard. It asked in an editorial, "Where is the outrage?" and said rightly that if similar attacks were made in a Jewish synagogue, or if the Ku Klux Klan burned a cross in front of an African-American church, "these hateful acts would dominate the national media for days and politicians would be denouncing the perpetrators." It should be noted that the Associated Press ran a story on March 8, 1999, about a synagogue which was vandalized in Siberia thousands of miles away, but nothing about the desecration of the Montreal Cathedral next door a year later.

This same kind of silence is found concerning the persecution of Christians. One thinks of the fine series of articles written by A.M. Rosenthal in the *New York Times* citing the terrible persecutions of Christians in China and pointing out the shame of the mainstream press's silence on the matter. One thinks of the horrible Christian persecutions going on right now in the Sudan. While celebrities, civil rights activists, and the Clinton administration were vigorously opposed to apartheid in one part of Africa, they were strangely silent about the persecution of a people, largely Catholic, in another part of Africa where millions were literally starved, driven from their homes, kidnapped, and sold into slavery.[5] The Islamic regime has unleashed a terrible persecution against non-Islamic people, many of them Catholic. But still, silence. A noted Christian author, Philip Yancey, did some research and came up with this conclusion: "I was startled to realize that the twentieth century has seen more Christians martyred for their faith than any other century. The average per year of those killed for their faith in the Christian family is 150,000." And author Nina Shea, in her book, *The Lion's Den*, writes, "Christians today are the most persecuted religious group in the world, and that persecution is intensifying." Meanwhile, the media trashes Catholicism with a regularity and impunity that it would never dare show to other groups.

The stage and TV

We also see themes of anti-Catholicism played over and over again in theater productions, television sitcoms, comedy shows, museums, and movies. The artistic community especially seems virulently hateful of the Catholic Church. Since writers and producers are extremely clever and prominent, media from magazines to movies are powerful purveyors not only of the secularist creed but of insidious anti-Catholicism.

Television, for example, is full of cheap shots at Catholic beliefs and practices. During Holy Week in 1998, a show on ABC called *That's*

Life opened up with the usual anti-Catholic diatribe about how "the Church treated women, and their views on abortion, homosexuality, censorship." Of course there were the required jabs at priests: "Father Doyle said he needs an altar boy today." "Yeah, well, he does go through them," and snide remarks such as "Church is dying because everybody our age with a reasonable amount of intelligence has left." The confessional, is referred to as a "spiritual toilet." (Again, imagine similar things being said of any other religion.)

On the "Early Show," co-host Jane Clayson was joined by Mark McEwen in taking cheap shots at nuns, prayers, and Catholic traditions. "Everybody Loves Raymond" trivialized Catholicism, making offensive jabs at the consecration of the Mass. NBC has paid author Glenn Kleier one million dollars for the rights to his book *The Last Day* for a miniseries. Rich Horgan, who worked with Kleier on the book said, "This is a book that's going to be a sort of kidney punch to organized religion and to the Catholic Church specifically."[6] And a top British comedy team is readying a cartoon series titled "Popeman," which portrays the pope as a retarded man with an emotional age of seven who plays practical jokes.

On ABC's *Politically Incorrect*, host Bill Maher parodied Pope John Paul II's new CD, and another time, Maher remarked, "Catholics practice what they want to practice. They go to see the pope because he's a big celebrity, but they go home and they masturbate, they practice birth control...." Fox's *MAD-TV* ran a skit depicting Mother Teresa as a voluptuous woman who strips off her clothes to warm a dying man and then performs an exotic dance clad only in red bikini underwear. A post-Super Bowl episode of *The Simpsons* included a scene in which a scantily-clad woman was shown wearing a huge cross as she gyrated to rock music, while a voiceover said, "The Catholic Church—we've made a few changes." Appearing on *60 Minutes*, Madonna made her usual denigrating remarks about the Catholic Church—yet, interestingly enough, she had her out-of-wedlock baby daughter baptized Catholic. And an episode of *Ally McBeal* featured a sexually active nun.

Movies like *Blessed Art Thou* (the title should give a clue) is about a monk thought to be a homosexual who turns out to be a pregnant woman. The movie *Julien Donkey Boy* features masturbating nuns. The popular movie *All About My Mother* features a character who is a pregnant, HIV-infected nun. *Jeffrey* shows a vulgar-talking priest sexually propositioning a man in the sacristy, and when the man is taken aback, the priest exclaims, "Maybe you didn't hear me. I'm a Catholic priest!"

Movies have a tremendous impact on people and, of course, they reflect the secular philosophies of those who make them. While straight, married folk are often depicted as sex-driven, hypocritical, foolish, or adulterous, all gay characters are always wonderfully balanced and faithful (recall the gay couple in the movie *American Beauty*), not running the human gamut of nobility or failures as we all do. In the same manner, all American Indians are noble while all white men are despicable (for example, *Dances with Wolves*).

Any character in uniform is expected to commit some terrible felony (e.g., *The General's Daughter*), while low-ranking whistle-blowers are pure; all the good politicians are liberal Democrats (e.g., *The American President*) while all bad ones are conservative Republicans; all talk show hosts are honest and searching while all the ministers they interview are finally revealed as anti-Semitic, anti-abortion bigots. Abortionists, in fact, are noble (e.g., *The Cider House Rules*) while those who oppose abortion are narrow-minded religious fanatics. In fact, at the Academy Awards presentation, John Irving, who adapted his novel *The Cider House Rules* for this movie, thanked the Academy for honoring a film that deals with abortion, and ended his acceptance speech by thanking "everyone at Planned Parenthood" and the National Abortion Rights Action League. (It should be no surprise that Planned Parenthood is showing the film wherever it can.)[7]

Anti-Catholicism continues in the theater. The off-off-Broadway play *The Most Fabulous Story Ever Told* is a retelling of the Bible with male frontal nudity, filthy language, and a damnation of God for AIDS. The play *Sister Mary Ignatius Explains It All for You*, which is vehemently anti-Catholic and was even denounced by the Jewish Anti-Defamation League, plays well in New York and on tour around the country. The title of the play *The Pope and the Witch* tells it all, and the play *To Hell and Back* has the Virgin Mary pictured as the "Great Harlot." *Corpus Christi* depicts Christ as having sex with his apostles, while *Late Nite Catechism* features a sadistic nun in a classroom.

Planned Parenthood handed out green condoms at a St. Patrick's Day parade. The Sisters of Perpetual Indulgence, a gay group in San Francisco, dressed up in nuns' habits and held a "condom Savior Mass," where condoms were given out as Holy Communion. This group also held a public exorcism of the Pope when he visited this country in 1987. A new bestselling book about the sexual longings of Jesus has provoked ire in Greece. The list of anti-Catholic biases in the arts just goes on and on.

The intelligentsia

It is among the intelligentsia, the university people and the trend-setting sophisticates, that anti-Catholicism takes on its most subtle and damaging form. In a brief biographical sketch, Paul Mariani, poetry editor of *America*, writes of the attitudes of his time (and our time, too) in college:

> I took a job teaching 20th-century poetry at UMass, Amherst, and settled in for the long haul. Teaching at a public university taught me early on to check my ardor for things religious at the threshold to the classroom....One sensed a sort of quiescent, genteel form of anti-Catholicism. Many of my colleagues considered themselves former Catholics or, worse, recovering Catholics. Once I listened as an older colleague—a man in his 50s with a national reputation—talked of the wafer good Catholics believed in. Weirdly, the comment had not been uttered with animosity, but merely as if that were the way things must seem to any straight-thinking intellectual this far along in

the post-Christian 20th century. Divorces were prevalent, free love the new drug of choice. Drugs were everywhere. I saw— as Allen Ginsberg had said—the best minds of my generation destroyed, including the young carried off to hospitals in the middle of the night, screaming and suffering from hallucinations.[8]

The reason for such hostility is basic: the Catholic Church teaches values that are viewed as hostile to a libertine culture that celebrates abortion, euthanasia, assisted suicide, condoms, uncommitted sex, free love with multiple partners (Rutgers University professor Helen Fisher is a leader in contending that men and women aren't programmed for monogamy but are biologically "poly"), and relativism. The Church's teachings on the sanctity of human life, on monogamous, permanent marriage, and on social justice are irritating signs of contradiction. The way the Church runs is dubbed as undemocratic and almost anti-American. Its traditional emphasis on community is seen as a threat to the individualism that reigns in our society, and its talk of transcendence seems superstitious to a "scientific" world. It is too much "other" to sit well with a secular culture. Also, in contrast to most Protestant denominations, the Catholic Church is exceedingly visual and colorful in its rituals and sacramentals, and these provide natural fodder for ridicule.

The point here is that this steady, unrelenting stream of ridicule and hatred of all things Catholic affects the TV-addicted youth of today. It creates an undertone of cynicism and embarrassment, and shapes an image of the Catholic Church as an institution to which no thinking person would admit they belong. The constant trafficking of anti-Catholic stereotypes, the obligatory sneers on television and in the movies, the intellectual disdain for Catholicism in the universities—all are likely to make it harder for impressionable adolescents or young adults to claim their beliefs or to maintain them.

6

THE SIXTH CHALLENGE

Catholic Culture Wars

After the 1960s, America experienced a cultural divide when the counterculture of the time not only challenged traditional moral norms but eventually overturned them. The counterculture's intent was to liberate everyone from "bourgeois values" that were stultifying. In some instances, this movement was right on target—think of the Civil Rights movement it spawned—but it also wound up liberating people from values that had a stabilizing and moralizing effect on society. This movement gave rise to two cultures in America: the dominant one, which is dedicated to protecting and extending individual freedom in all directions, with its secular, relativistic, and nonjudgmental outlook; and the weaker culture, the one whose outlook is rooted in religious faith, moral conviction, concern for the traditional family, civility, and respect for authority. The two cultures are at war in our society today.[1]

The same two cultures are at war in the religious world, as well. Sides have been taken on the hot-button issues of the role of women, homosexuality, abortion, the death penalty, the nature of the family, authority, identity, and competing ecclesiologies. In the Jewish community, for example, you have books like *Jew vs. Jew: The Struggle for the Soul of American Jews* by Samuel G. Freedman, which addresses the fact that fierce divisions among its various factions, along with both our highly secular culture and intermarriage, have undermined and absorbed the Jewish faith. The conservative and moderate

Baptists have been at odds over whether to rebuke former President Clinton for declaring June as National Gay and Lesbian Pride month, as well as for his appointment of an openly gay man as ambassador to Luxembourg. They also clashed over purging seminaries and calling on wives "to submit graciously" to their husbands. The Methodists are divided over same-sex unions and gambling. And so it goes.

The Catholic Church is no exception to the culture wars; indeed, there the divisions seem most pronounced. At least they certainly seem to generate the most publicity. There are reasons for this. The social thinning of American Catholicism—the breakdown of ethnic cohesion and the adoption of the same values as everyone else—has been accompanied by sharp and acrimonious polarization and fragmentation among Catholics. Perhaps as symbolic as anything else of the Catholic culture wars was that fateful day, the first Sunday of Advent in 1964, when the altars were turned around and Mass was said in English for the first time:

> Centuries-old styles of worship and piety were changed on that Sunday morning for excellent theological reasons, changes that almost all American Catholics now agree were beneficial to the liturgical life of the community. But that Sunday also unleashed deeply divisive "battles for the Masses" and "relevant" songs. Next to sexuality, the battles over liturgical style and substance that began that Sunday morning divided American Catholics into categories largely unknown up to that date: "conservative" and "liberal" now became designations that Catholics used of each other, posing new and unprecedented questions for an identity that had hitherto been largely undivided and shared.[2]

So the lines were drawn: shall we kneel or stand? Organ or guitar? Communion in the hand or on the tongue? Sign of Peace or not? Gregorian chant or the St. Louis Jesuits? Ironically, the Eucharist, our summit of unity, now divides us. In August of 2000, for example, during a Jubilee year, thousands of arch-conservative Catholics from Europe, England, Ireland, the Philippines, North America, and elsewhere poured into Rome and conducted their own three-day, Holy Year pilgrimage, defiantly celebrating Mass in Latin on a dusty hilltop across the River Tiber, urging the Church to return to the Latin Mass and other traditions it abandoned after the Second Vatican Council.

In the days following Vatican II, and especially after the encyclical on birth control in 1968, when the pope went against the advice and recommendations of his own committee, camps were quickly formed: Call to Action, Woman-Church, FutureChurch, Catholics for Choice, Pax Christi, and the newspaper *National Catholic Reporter* were positioned on the left; Cursillo, Catholics United for the Faith, Opus Dei, *The Wanderer*, and *First Things* were on the right. Now it is liberal versus conservative Catholics all up and down the line, from priests, nuns, and religious education directors to the average parishioner. Issues divide and divide again: divorce and remarriage, the pope and papal authority—is he a defender of the faith or a curial dictator?—patriarchy, gender equality, contraception, abortion, and gay marriage, each camp adamantly insisting, "We are the Church; you are not."

A community fractured

Boomer Catholics are divided over the interpretation of the teachings of Vatican II, not realizing how irrelevant these concerns have become to their children, who find it all boring and meaningless. Ultra-conservative Catholics tend to find their own orthodox churches, while basic conservative Catholics stay within the parish or join support groups, while liberal Catholics strive to extend the reforms of Vatican II. The polarizations brought on by the Catholic culture wars have not been pretty to behold. They offer consolation to the Church's enemies, scandal to its friends, and cynicism to its youth.

I remember reading about some nuns who refused to go to Mass because the celebrant was male. One can surely sympathize with these nuns in their zeal for women's rights and full acceptance into the Church, even encourage and applaud their efforts. But in refusing to celebrate the Eucharist, the symbol of unity and the summit of worship, they are, theoretically, neither religious, since community is the charism of religious life, nor Catholic, since they refuse to break bread with those with whom they disagree.

In short, these nuns have let their ideology become an idol, greater than community and greater than the central act of worship—that is, breaking bread "in memory of me." This is a far cry from my own experience of parish life, where people I knew from opposite sides of the liberal/conservative spectrum would never dream of not celebrating the Eucharist with one another or sincerely offering the Sign of Peace. To their credit, they knew that the unity Jesus prayed for was far greater than their personal agendas. Sadly, these nuns sow division not by their opinions but by their actions. By publicly separating themselves from the Church's communal worship, they keep the culture wars going, while ordinary people who live with conflict and diversity all the time are scandalized.

This type of situation is in sharp contrast to the early Church. Lord knows there were heresies, sects, and schisms all over the place—read Paul's epistles to the Galatians or Corinthians, for example—but these were never allowed to rupture the Church's one-ness. These and subsequent disagreements were local, isolated, rarely out of control. As patristic scholar Walter Burghardt expresses it:

> There were different theological currents, schools, tendencies; but all coexisted within the one Church. There were geographical and cultural mentalities, but not to the destruction of the one body. Despite divergences in race and culture, in language and mentality, in exegesis and theology, Basil of Caesarea could write: "The faith we profess is not one thing in Seleucia, another in Constantinople, another in Zela, another in Damascus, and still another at Rome. The faith that circulates today is no different from the faith of yesterday; it is always one and the same." Hyperbole? Perhaps, but a rich basis in reality.

This oneness was not an abstract unity parroted by bishops in council. It was a life, and its foci were the local Church and the Eucharist. Five decades of research keep me from misrepresenting the early Church as a heavenly Jerusalem, where the saints of God without wrinkle or spot danced to a single tune in undisturbed harmony. But I have come away time and again from the Church of the Fathers mightily moved by its stress on the We. This was to be expected in the persecuted Church, from Nero to Diocletian, if only because the blood of martyrs is indeed the seed of Christians, and because fire and sword seem specially suited to separate the wheat from the chaff.

The We was imperiled in an established Church torn internally, where "Christian" emperors like Constantine could control ecclesiastical policy, a Cyril of Alexandria could call a Nestorius "the new Judas," and venerable sees like Rome and Constantinople could challenge one another with unchristian coldness. And yet, somehow, the We of Christians characterized the patristic era; the magic word was not authority but community; and the Eucharist was still capable of linking hostile hands in love, still the most powerful force for building up the Body of Christ.[3]

The real tragedy with the Catholic culture wars—and it is a profound tragedy at this point in history—is that not only have we fought over authority at the expense of community, making even the Eucharist divisive, but that the public squabbling itself has deflected energies, preventing cooperation. For we Catholics, liberal and conservative, need to meet on common ground in order to confront a dangerous common enemy: the secular culture and, more importantly, its offspring—that is, the crisis of belief and meaning.

There is a crisis of belief in a skeptical society where everything is challenged; where the Bible is debunked; where Jesus, who many scholars claim is not historically attested to outside the Bible,[4] is reduced to a nice moral figure like Socrates; where the sins of Christianity in general and Catholicism in particular are paraded across the pages of newspapers and television screens; where science seems to be triumphant in its claims to satisfy all human needs; where traditions have been abandoned and ancient wisdom ridiculed; where the Church has been discredited; where self-centered pop psychology has replaced religion, celebrities have replaced saints and talk show hosts have replaced priests; where people are left only to themselves. This crisis of belief is indeed a core challenge to the Catholic Church.

The younger generation of Catholic Americans, severed from their Catholic tradition, religiously illiterate, living in unprecedented economic boom times, having more choices in everything than ever before, affluent yet nevertheless sensing a deep hollowness beneath it all—as depicted in the movie *American Beauty*—this generation is desperately searching for meaning. And we? We are fighting the culture wars among ourselves, mining the documents of Vatican II, not for the wisdom they can offer both the young and us, but for ammunition.

A Parable

A wise old story captures the problem with culture wars: Once upon a time, a flock of quail lived near a marsh. Every day they would fly to the nearby fields to feed. But there was a Bird Hunter who lived nearby, and of late he had snared many quail in his net so that he could take them to a nearby market to be sold. He had grown very successful in catching the quail because he had learned to imitate perfectly the call of the Leader. The Bird Hunter gave the call, and the quail, thinking it was the Leader, flew to his area where he tossed his net over them and captured them.

One day the Leader called all the quail together for a conference. He said, "We are becoming decimated! Soon there will be none of us left. The Bird Hunter is catching us all. I have found out how he does it. He learned my call and deceives you. But I have a plan. The next time you hear what you think is my call and fly to the area, and the Bird Hunter throws his net on top of you, here is what you are to do: all together you stick your heads through the openings in the net, and in one motion fly up with the net and land on the thornbush. The net will stick there, you can extricate yourselves, and the Bird Hunter will have to spend all day freeing his net." And this is what they did.

The next day the Bird Hunter came, gave the imitation call, and the quail came. When the net was thrown over them, as one body they stuck their heads through the openings and flew away to the thornbush. They left a frustrated Hunter trying all day to get his net loose. This went on for some time until the Hunter's wife bitterly complained that her husband was bringing home no quail to bring to market. They were becoming poor. The Bird Hunter listened to his wife, told her of the actions of the quail, and with his hand on his chin, added, "But be patient, dear wife. Just wait till they quarrel. Then we shall catch them again."

Well, it so happened that one day when the Bird Hunter made his call, all the quail rose up and flew to the area where he was. But as they were landing, one quail accidentally brushed against another. "Will you watch where you're going, you clumsy ox!" cried the one quail. The other said hastily, "Oh, I'm sorry. I really am. I didn't mean to do it. It was an accident." "An accident, was it," cried the first quail. "If you'd watch where you're going instead of peering all about, you wouldn't be so clumsy." "Well," said the second quail, "I don't know why you take that attitude. I said I was sorry, and if you can't accept that...." And they got to quarreling. Soon the others, perceiving the argument, gathered around and took sides, one for the first quail and the other for the second.

Meanwhile, the Bird Hunter had his net ready and threw it over the birds. They began to cry to one another, "Come, let us stop arguing and hurry or else we'll be caught. Let's fly over that way!" But the other quail responded, "No, we're always flying over that way. We're always doing what you people want. Come, let us fly this way!" And while they were arguing which way to go, the Bird Hunter, with a smile on his face, gathered them up in the net, brought them to market, and that day made a fine penny.

This is a perfect parable for what has happened and is happening in the Church today. There is Catholic infighting while the whole issue of faith and belief and the yearning of a generation goes begging. That is why we should pay attention to the late Cardinal Bernardin's Common Ground Initiative (if you're not familiar with it, you should be), which calls us to Christic conversion and commitment. Issued in 1996, its inaugural statement, "Called to Be Catholic," unambiguously confesses: "Jesus Christ, present in Scripture and Sacrament, is central to all that we do; he must always be the measure and not what is measured." The intent of Common Ground is to draw Catholics into new ways, other than invective and ridicule, of confronting controversial issues. The Initiative is a good start; even so, four U.S. cardinals expressed reservations about starting something without the approval of the Vatican or the leadership of the National Conference of Catholic Bishops, and some notable theologians were wary of a secular approach to dialogue rather than dialogue within the context of Christian reconciliation and the Eucharistic community. These concerns are basically irrelevant, I think. The Common Ground Initiative simply wants to open discussion.[5]

You may sense the deep and tragic irony in all of this. Nothing has been more profitable over the past decades than the painstaking but largely successful ecumenical dialogues of Catholics with Protestants and Jews. Opponents have met on equal footing. The result has been a growth in mutual respect and even agreement. Who does not recall the recent joint Catholic-Lutheran statement on justification? Who does not remember (as we shall note again) the vast chasm between Catholics and Jews, which shrank during John Paul II's historic visit to the Holy Land, where he spoke a heartfelt apology? Catholics, it seems, can sit down and talk with centuries-old enemies but they cannot do the same with other Catholics. As John Dominic Crossan parodied in another context, "See how those Christians hate one another."[6]

Scott Appleby summarizes the problem nicely when he writes:

> The besetting preoccupation of American Catholics as the new
> century dawns will not be the clash of postconciliar visions of
> authority, lay involvement, or women's rights in the [C]hurch.
> Rather, the [C]hurch will be engaged by a far more profound
> and disturbing crisis of belief and meaning. In light of the ex-
> tent and depth of this crisis, the attention given to the Catholic
> culture wars will come to be seen as an unaffordable luxury.[7]

Talking with one another is a challenge. Yet perhaps we might follow,
as a guide, the traditional attitude of the Church in its great theological disputes throughout history, when it tried to avoid an either/or
position while holding divergent views in tension. Richard McBrien
sums it up well:

> Catholicism is a comprehensive, all-embracing, [C]atholic tra-
> dition, characterized by a both/and rather than an either/or
> approach. It is not nature or grace, but graced nature; not
> reason or faith, but reason illuminated by faith; not law or
> Gospel, but law inspired by the Gospel; not Scripture or
> tradition, but normative tradition within Scripture; not faith
> or works, but faith issuing in works and works as an expres-
> sion of faith; not authority or freedom, but authority in the
> service of freedom.[8]

7

THE SEVENTH CHALLENGE

Pluralism

There is a great divide between pre- and post-Vatican II Catholics. The pre-Vatican II generation was taught mostly by priests and nuns (in cassocks and habits), raised in the "one true Church," instructed to see the importance of the Church and to obey its teachings, and registered in the local parish. They went to Mass weekly and married other Catholics. The post-Vatican II generations, on the contrary, are more apt to have been taught by laypeople, raised in an ecumenical atmosphere—which they interpret to mean that one religion is as good as another—feel that a personal relationship with God is far more important than any relationship with the Church, are not registered in the parish, make up their own minds about what they believe, dissent from Church teaching (especially in the area of sexual morality), may go to Mass occasionally, and marry outside their faith. To put it mildly, there is pluralism right within the Catholic family, and this challenge is high on the list of concerns of seminarians and lay ministers preparing for future ministry.[1]

Further, there is pluralism and diversity in the growing mix of Catholics from other lands and other cultures. In some large urban areas, it is not uncommon for a parish to house some dozen languages and nationalities, each with its own customs, folklore, lifestyle, and ways of worship. Sometimes each ethnic group insists on its own Mass in its own language. In fact, 30% of U.S. Catholic parishes celebrate Mass in a language other than English.

In the next few decades, both our country and our Church will be peopled with "minorities." New waves of immigration are not coming from Europe, but principally from Latin America, Asia, and the Pacific region. Census Bureau figures released in August of 2000 show that in the ten years between 1990 and 1999, the Asian population in the United States grew 43% to 10.8 million people, and the Hispanic population grew over 57.9%, to 35.3 million. (California has the largest Hispanic and Asian populations.) By the year 2020, the so-called "new ethnics" will comprise the majority of Catholics, and by the year 2056 the "average" U.S. resident will have origins different from the European ones we have known in the past. Imagine the challenge of ministering to such a diverse congregation. In the Archdiocese of Los Angeles alone, for example, Mass is celebrated in more than fifty languages.

So large is the immigration from Latin America and the Caribbean that the United States is now the fifth-largest Spanish-speaking country in the world. 71% of the growth in the Catholic Church over the last forty years has been due to Hispanic Catholics. Here are the facts: some seventy to 80% of the thirty million Latinos living in the U.S., the fastest growing segment of the U.S. population, are Catholic; of 150 dioceses surveyed recently, forty-four have already updated their ministry to the Hispanic community, with budgets increasing over 80% in the last nine years; the staffs assigned to Hispanic ministry have nearly doubled since 1990; dioceses that require seminarians to study Spanish have increased 67% since 1990; and there has been an increasing level of Hispanic participation in diocesan offices.[2]

The move to increase ministry resources for Latinos is wise, for two reasons. First, there is severe leakage among Hispanic Catholics. Andrew Greeley says that one out of seven Hispanics has left Catholicism, and he estimates that about 600,000 of them are lost to the Church each year. He adds that if the trend continues for the next twenty-five years, half of all American Hispanics will not be Catholic. By the way, the Hispanics are mainly going to the evangelical religions because, as we saw in Chapter 4, they find Catholicism too head-orientated. There are other reasons, as well. Catholics tend to "read a book at you," in contrast to the Evangelicals, who are warmer and inspirited; Catholicism is too fuzzy, whereas Hispanics delight in the clarity that Evangelical beliefs bring to their lives; and finally, Hispanics find Catholicism morally undemanding. As one former Catholic put it, "The Catholics, they drink and they dance. When you accept Jesus, you don't do any of those things."

Second, it is an educated estimate that Latino Catholics represent the future of Roman Catholicism in the United States. As we have already noted, they will bring a significantly different worldview to the Church from the one held by most Anglo Catholics. They do not now, and will not, offer the top-down, hierarchical, doctrinal model of being Catholic that Anglos seem to favor, but a model that operates from the bottom up, that is, from the religious experiences and practices of ordinary folk, freed from clerical control (due mostly to the lack of native clergy), defined by popular religion along with its liturgical and devotional traditions. Which is why, perhaps, small faith-sharing communities take root in their culture.

Still, for all these projections, it is acknowledged that more often than not, many parishes ignore the Hispanic presence. In a study released in March of 2000, the United States bishops concluded that Hispanics are twice as likely as other Catholics to worship in "separate and unequal settings," and that relatively few Latinos are entering the priesthood or religious life. This is considered a great loss, since Hispanics tend to focus on family and community, a focus that is much needed in the Church today. A Protestant seminary professor, speaking at a University of San Diego symposium, put it well:

> North America, driven by a market economy, is caught in an insidious individualism that undermines the practices of the values of care, compassion, and the will to sacrifice that are necessary to form and sustain communities. Hispanics, in contrast, hold onto relational patterns, such as family, friendship, hospitality to strangers....The life of the group is tremendously important.[3]

In other words, Hispanics are more prepared to show us the way out of pathological individualism and self-centered measurements. This must be given due attention as we embrace a diversity of Catholics.

Diversity

In the summer of 2000, the U.S. bishops organized a large gathering, called Encuentro 2000, to celebrate and better understand the multicultural makeup of the Church in the United States. Under the theme "Many Faces in God's House," some 5000 people, from Latinos to Asians to African-Americans to Native Americans, came together to call attention to and redress past and present injustices, as well as to build a more equitable future. During the gathering, a service of reconciliation was held for the pain caused by the offenses and discriminations against minorities.

In past times, the Church typically met the immigrant presence by segregation, that is, by establishing separate, national parishes. When the country was more stable and ghettoed, this was a workable solution—but not now, in an era of upscale mobility and a global economy. Nowadays, we have a single parish trying to blend various ethnic groups into one sense of Church, and it is a formidable challenge to form relationships that transcend cultural differences. The parish must be able to recognize that the dominant "white" culture, which is apt to be seen as central and normative, is operative in most parishes and, therefore, in need of adjustment. The parish must also avoid separate, parallel communities; learn intercultural communication; incorporate the language, music, food, and celebrations of the various ethnic groups into the fiber of the parish; provide hospitality as "they" understand it, not we ("have a nice day" doesn't cut it); and value the differences between the different cultures. All of these are enormous challenges that must be met.

On a wider scale, there is a diversity of religions which did not exist in past times in this country. Here is a sobering fact: of the approximately

1,600 religions and denominations in the U.S. today, half were founded in our lifetime. Furthermore, there are some 800,000 Hindus in this country (compared with a mere 70,000 twenty years ago); there are as many Muslims as there are Presbyterians; and there are 750,000 Buddhists, the fastest growing Eastern religion in the U.S.[4] We live and will continue to live in a world that is more and more secular, religiously pluralistic, and economically monolithic. We are but one tiny voice in the midst of many churches, temples, mosques, Home Depots, Price Clubs, Disney Worlds, chat rooms, McDonald's, Tommy Hilfiger outlets, and MTV shows. Diversity is our landscape.

There is such a diversity of religions, outlooks, philosophies, and lifestyles that only tolerance can make living together bearable. Unfortunately, tolerance has translated into relativism. The result is not only a rigidly enforced tolerance of all views (political correctness) by liberal fundamentalists (to use Roger Rosenblatt's term), but also a seismic displacement of one's own certainties, of one's confidence to make value judgments. In this regard, I always like to quote Jesuit Joseph Leinhard's words: "A generation of college students has been so anesthetized by relativism that they cannot say that Shakespeare was the greatest master of the English language for fear of offending someone who thinks Danielle Steele is." Then he continues with these words of wisdom: "But if they can never say 'You are wrong,' they can never say 'I am right,' either." And they can't. It would be politically incorrect.

Which is why, as we have seen, the post-Vatican II generations, X and Y, have a very loose connection to the institutional Church and a very cavalier outlook toward it, considering Catholicism one among many valid denominations to be embraced or discarded as the spirit moves them. In a culture of disbelief (to use Stephen Carter's words) and relativism, diversity presents a challenge to a Church that claims eternal truths and objective norms. Once again, learning to be united but distinct, building a Pentecostal church from many tongues, is another challenge for American Catholics.

8

THE EIGHTH CHALLENGE

Contending with Scandal

Among the chronic scandals of the Catholic Church, we can list hard-nosed clerics, authoritarian bishops, sadistic nuns (yes, someone has merchandised the fire-breathing nun caricature "Nunzilla," and "I survived Catholic School" T-shirts), stupid rules that crush the Spirit, or the larger issues that Pope John Paul II recently apologized for—the Crusades, the Inquisition, the treatment of women and minorities, the silence of Catholics during the Holocaust, and so on. But for most people today, when you talk of scandal in the Catholic Church, they immediately think of only two well-publicized situations: financial mismanagement and the sexual predation of the young. It is hard to overestimate the damage these types of scandal have done.

As the reader knows, it is not uncommon to see headlines of mismanagement. Bishop Thomas Daily of Brooklyn, for example, had to announce that two million dollars was missing from a particular parish, diverted from parish funds by a former pastor. A priest in Denver has been removed after being accused of embezzling church money, to the tune of one million dollars. More examples could be given, but the reality is that financial scandals are always accidents waiting to happen in a top-down organization such as the Church, where usually only one person has total control of the money and where secrecy is the norm. It is the pastor, after all, who normally draws up the end-of-the-year financial statement, not the canonically mandated parish financial board. In most cases, the public is not made aware of any savings accounts or portfolios belonging to the parish, or told where the parish or diocesan monies are invested.

When you think of it, only the Church, with its rigid, hierarchical structure, hands over the financial reins to just about anyone who is ordained. Pastors who are in complete control of parish money have been caught in quick-buck schemes that backfired, sometimes costing the parish hundreds of thousands of dollars. If there is not someone who oversees their work, even lay parish workers, as the news media has revealed, can embezzle huge sums from naïve or un-suspecting pastors. At times there have been outright thefts by laity and clergy, or great sums of parish money left to the housekeeper upon the pastor's death. Usually these incidents are covered up, but more and more they are becoming public. As financial abuses mul-tiply and are made public, the cry will continue for less secret and more open accountability, along with a system of checks and bal-ances by the laity.

But it is the second issue, sexual scandal, that bothers us all, whether clergy or lay, and it is this issue which has received the most publicity.

If I were to ask you what you thought was the world's most Catholic country, you would most likely say Ireland. And you would be right. Or, you would have been at one time. As we have seen, churchgoing in that country has dropped sharply under the pressures of the Celtic Tiger (as the unprecedented economic boom in Ireland is called) and secularism. But most of all, the fall from grace of the Catholic Church in Ireland is due to the revelations of child sexual abuse. An Irish journalist, John Horgan, writes:

> The allegation, made in a new biography of John Charles McQuaid, archbishop of Dublin from 1940 to 1972, that this most powerful prelate in twentieth-century Ireland was a pe-dophile, has poured salt into an open wound in the Catholic church in Ireland. That wound was opened only in the past couple of years, but as yet it shows no sign of healing. The allegation is not well-documented, but it is a measure of the

controversy that swirled around McQuaid during his life that even an anonymous accusation (which, in effect, this is) has introduced a wide new seam of debate.

Many well-known liberals, who engaged in fierce critiques of McQuaid while he was alive, have attacked the biographer's use of anonymous sources. The fuss about the accuracy of the allegations continues apace, as the biography has been widely serialized. But many of the faithful, concluding that there is no smoke without fire, are simply averting their gaze in mute despair. Underlying this despair—mixed, on occasion, with anger—is a series of scandals involving physical and sexual abuse in Church-run institutions which add up to a crisis of credibility in the institutional Church.

Public and media interest in this hitherto unexplored area of Irish Church life was given a major boost with the publication before Christmas of *Suffer the Little Children* (New Island Books), by two researchers—also the subject of a TV documentary—enumerating incidents of sexual and physical abuse in Church-run institutions. Added to the growing material prosperity and secularization which are already undermining traditional religious loyalties and practices in Ireland, these revelations have contributed to a general air of impending, if not actual, crisis in the Church.

The crisis of confidence among many priests and religious is palpable. They now feel deeply troubled by the continuing stream of revelations, and are all but terrified of showing friendship or affection in any physical manner to young people with whom their work brings them into contact.

The bishops have been stung by repeated allegations that they failed to fulfill their pastoral responsibilities adequately. In the light of allegations that complaints about some abusing priests had merely resulted in their being moved to pastoral duties elsewhere, the bishops, like their American counterparts before them, have now drawn up detailed guidelines designed to prevent a repetition of such occurrences, and have strengthened reporting systems and procedures.[1]

There you are. And other countries have similar stories. In the United States, sex scandals began surfacing back in 1985 when, from Cajun country in rural Louisiana, the startling story broke of Fr. Gilbert Gauthe, who had molested scores of boys. The world was shocked, and the Catholic Church was stunned. Then, in 1992, came a watershed story about Fr. James Porter of Massachusetts, which broke the dam. Ninety-nine people each accused him of molesting them during the ten years between 1950 and 1960. In 1993, Porter pleaded guilty to molesting twenty-eight children, and he was sentenced to some twenty years in prison.

In no time, sexual victims of priests appeared from all over the country and their stories made headlines. Quickly it became apparent that the scandal was not confined to the terrible deeds of these men, but included the fact that the official Church had acted in a duplicitous manner regarding the abuse. Indeed, the hierarchy had denied, covered up, stonewalled, and ignored the victims while they tried to protect the perpetrators—some of whom were sent away for a while to rehabilitation places, like the Servants of the Paraclete Treatment Center in New Mexico, then assigned to parishes where they found new victims. To add to this sordid story came the revelations of seminarians who had been molested by their professors, a story yet to be fully examined.

Recent revelations

Sadly, the revelations continue. Recently, after a six-month investigation by the San Jose police department, the Academic Dean of St. Patrick's Seminary in San Francisco was arrested on suspicion of solicitation of sex with minors via the Internet and suspicion of child sex abuse.

Another recent case occurred in Santa Rosa, California. There, Bishop G. Patrick Zeimann was sued by one of his priests, Fr. Hume Salas, a shadowy figure apparently ordained without completing

seminary training, who was accused of molesting boys. Salas also admitted stealing from the Church, and he was subsequently dismissed
by the bishop. So why was Salas suing the bishop? Because he said
the bishop blackmailed him, agreeing to keep silent over his stealing
in exchange for sexual favors. The bishop admitted he did have sex
with the priest and resigned (he is currently in a treatment center),
and a new bishop was sent in to clean up the mess. But no sooner
had this scandal been seemingly resolved than the new bishop and
the people learned of grave financial abuse that had occurred within
the diocese: a $30 million dollar financial crisis that involved secret
overseas bank accounts. And this on top of the millions of dollars the
diocese was already paying out because of the sex scandals.[2]

Perhaps nothing has changed the way priests are perceived in recent
years, by both Catholics and non-Catholics alike, as much as these
revelations and others like them. No diocese in the United States
has been without at least one pedophilia case. Hardly a day goes by
without some newspaper blaring a headline like "Church Settles with
Alleged Victim," citing a usually large amount of money paid out of
court. The latest example I've read tells of the Franciscan Friars of
California, who paid $1.7 million to an alleged victim.

The suffering of the victims and their families, the initial cover-ups,
the guilt, the shame, the money paid out to victims, have all taken
their toll on how Catholicism in general, and the priesthood in particular, is perceived. As we have indicated, Ireland, Canada, and
other countries have been rocked with revelations of the sexual
abuse of minors by priests. And let me add a sensitive and shocking
note—namely, that abuses by Catholic priests are significantly more
frequent than by clergy of other religions. In addition, roughly 90%
of priest abusers target teenage boys as their victims—this reflecting,
as we shall see shortly, the presence of a disproportionate number of
gay priests.

A 1995 survey of 19,000 counseling professionals, funded by the
National Center on Child Abuse and Neglect, found that in the
United States "94% of abuses by religious authorities were sexual in

nature and over half of these cases (54%) were Catholic, even though Catholics comprise only 25% of the United States population." Also, "the minor victims of priest abuse are overwhelmingly boys," a percentage which is contrary to the pattern of abuse in the general population.[3] In any case, by the mid-1990s, it was estimated that some six hundred priests had been named in abuse cases and more than a half a billion dollars had been paid out in injury awards, settlements, and legal fees.[4]

The widespread prevalence of sexual abuse and financial misman-agement in the Church calls for new forms of management and better accountability. Meanwhile, the damage to the Church has been enormous, and a deep suspicion—experienced by Catholics and non-Catholics alike—hangs over the Church, and certainly over its priests. Great patience and sensitivity are needed to heal these scandals, to move from turmoil to trust. This is indeed a challenge.

9

THE NINTH CHALLENGE

The Priest Shortage

Few people, I think, realize the severity of the priest shortage and its impact on the Church. Priests themselves are facing a number of losses: respect (gone forever is Bing Crosby's Fr. O'Malley); identity, as they move unsteadily from a cultic to a servant role; and numbers—so many of their peers have left the priesthood (some 20,000 of them), and so few young men want to follow in their footsteps. Such realities have been known for years but they seldom have been openly discussed.

But the crisis has reached such proportions that in June of 2000, at their annual summer meeting in Milwaukee, the American bishops went public with their wrenching anxiety over the present and their alarm over the future. No longer did they express "pastoral concern over the declining number of priests." The priest shortage, they declared, is their most practical, pressing problem, as indicated by a two-year study presented to the bishops. That study said, "It is true that the best-kept secret is the shortage of priests. We have kept it from the laity. We have covered it up in every way imaginable and pretended it does not exist." But now is the moment of truth. As one bishop said, "The problems are enormous."

The Center of Applied Research in the Apostolate (CARA) provides the statistics. It tells us that in 1965, there were almost 36,000 priests in the United States. In 1998, that number had dropped to some

31,000, of whom 7800, says the official Catholic Directory for that year, are "retired, sick, or absent." The number of priests in religious orders went from some 22,000 in 1965 to a little over 15,000 in 1999. The current number of married, permanent deacons is 12,000. Of the 19,000-plus parishes in the United States, some 2500 do not have a resident pastor. (This is true mostly in the far and Midwestern dioceses of the U.S.). In this country, the total number of ordinations to the priesthood in 1965 was 994. By 1997 the number had dropped to 521. By April of 1998, there were only 346.

What all these statistics mean—and they have gotten more dire in subsequent years—is that, on the front lines, things are desperate. The Archdiocese of Dubuque, for example, which had 286 priests in 1985, is projected to have only 117 priests in 2005. The Archdiocese of Boston has announced that it ordained nine men in May of 1998. Such a number can't come near to replacing the twenty-five to thirty who retired or died in that same year. If you want to put it more dramatically, consider it this way: in the Archdioceses of Boston and New York combined, with four million Catholics and 800 parishes, only fourteen men were ordained in 1999. How about this: in the four years from 1997 to 2000, seven dioceses with a combined Catholic population of more than one million had no ordinations at all.

In the Pittsburgh Diocese, the number of active priests today is 350; only a decade ago it was 467, almost a hundred more. Directly citing the shortage of priests, the Diocese of Evansville, Indiana is planning to close or merge parishes, admitting that many people will have to travel fifteen to thirty minutes to find a Mass. The Archdiocese of Milwaukee, which ordained only one man in 1997 and one in 1998, lost thirty-four priests through retirement and resignation in the year 2000, and it will have lost 185 more by the year 2016. This diocese has already closed about forty parishes with more to come. The Diocese of Toledo, Ohio serves 325,000 Catholics in its 127 parishes with 105 active priests, far short of adequately meeting the needs of the people. The diocese expects to have fifty fewer priests in just six years. Thirty parishes are already served by visiting priests and six others have full-time, non-ordained leaders.

The Archdiocese of Newark expects to have only 192 priests twenty years from now, compared to the 439 it has today. Major archdioceses like Boston, New York, Chicago, and Los Angeles all ordained fewer than eleven new priests in the year 2013. There is hardly a diocese in the country, then, that has not or is not planning parish closings or mergers. In a recent study projecting to the year 2015, Lawrence Young says that the priest population will have declined 45% from its 1966 levels.[1] By 2005, four years from this writing, only one in eight priests will be under age thirty-five, with the average age of priests close to sixty. Many people are unaware of the small number of priests under forty right now.

In terms of sustaining a viable and vital Catholic life, then, the priest shortage is a catastrophe that shows no signs of abating. It should be noted here that the shortage is not confined to the United States; other countries are far worse-off. In Latin America, for example, as many as one in every four priests leaves the priesthood, mostly to get married. A recent visit of the Pope to Mexico highlighted the fact that in Latin America, there is one priest for every 13,000 Catholics— leaving the field wide open, incidentally, for the highly successful recruitment efforts of the Protestant Evangelicals.

In the Diocese of Melbourne, Australia, there were some eighty parishes without a priest in 2000, one-third of all its parishes. The laity-priest ratio in the backlands of Brazil is 40,000 Catholics per active priest. In Dublin, Ireland's largest diocese, personnel officials are predicting one-priest parishes within the decade. They also note that fewer than 20% of its clergy are under thirty, while over 60% of their priests are over fifty. Godfried Cardinal Danneels, of Malines-Brussels, is on record as saying that Catholics will be starved of the sacraments without an influx of new priests. In fact, the lack of priests could wipe out the Church's sacramental tradition in the Western countries, as Catholics are forced to rely more and more on the Bible—thus inevitably forcing them to become more and more like Protestants.

Seminarians

While the number of seminarians has leveled off in recent years, there are many fewer than in the 1960's and 70's. For every 100 men enrolled in Catholic seminaries in 1965, there are only forty today. And, it seems, those who do enter the seminary are of a decidedly conservative bent.

Before those from the liberal side rush to too negative a judgment about this conservativeness, several things must be remembered. First, these young men were raised in the 1970s and 1980s, during the upheaval following Vatican II and the cultural revolution. Thus, they have never experienced the religious and communal reliability and cohesion experienced by their parents or grandparents. They have known only division and fragmentation and so, like some of their secular counterparts, they are searching for some religious and moral stability, along with community.

Second, note that nearly half of these young seminarians have converted from another religion or returned to Catholicism after leaving the faith, so they have felt the attraction and the comfort of tradition. Finally, they have found that many of the older priests, still engaged in the social activism of the 1960s, lack spiritual foundation and are indistinguishable from do-gooders. This has left many people actively engaged yet spiritually hungry. A veteran of the activist '60s, Msgr. Phil Murnion of the National Pastoral Life Center, asks, "In our desire to extend the meaning of the sacred, did we end up with a situation in which nothing is sacred?" So the seminarians feel they must lead the way back.

In her study of seminarians, Sr. Katarina Schuth concludes, "the majority of seminarians see their role as very much spiritual, celebrating the Eucharist, praying with people, administering the sacraments." Well, whatever their history and ideological bent, their numbers are down drastically. Why? Why are young men not attracted to the priesthood anymore? I suggest four main reasons.

The first reason is secularism. Celibacy is often cited as a barrier to priestly vocations, and perhaps for some it is a factor. But it pales beside the pervasive secular attitudes of today. We know this because of the measurable fact that all clergy of all denominations are in a shortfall. In the Episcopal church, which allows married clergy, "the situation is grave," according to the Rev. Hugh Magers, a member of the congregational ministries cluster in Manhattan. In Reform Judaism there is a critical shortage of rabbis, and about 200 out of 895 congregations are without a full-time rabbi. Reform rabbinical ordination classes have dropped from having sixty candidates twenty years ago to only twenty today. Orthodox Judaism is experiencing the same shortage.

So it is not primarily the celibacy issue. Rather, those concerned blame a robust economy, which is attracting people to other, more lucrative fields. Former Jesuit Peter Awn, who has taught at Columbia University for twenty-one years, says he has seen only four students who majored in religion pursue careers in the clergy. In his view, however, the declining appeal of a life in ministry is more a result of the rejection of authority than of the lure of more lucrative jobs. "A profound suspicion of political and religious institutions has taken hold," he says.[2] The problem of the priest shortage, then, is the larger issue of cultural secularism.

It is interesting to note that a good number of seminarians today are of non-Western European ancestry, and come from Latin America, Eastern Europe, and the Orient. In fact, statistics show that one-fourth of the new priests in the U.S. ordained in the year 2000 came from racial or ethnic minorities. (The men who were ordained, by the way, had a median age of thirty-six, reflecting the second-career syndrome).

Case in point: the majority of Vietnamese immigrants are Buddhists. But about a third of them are Catholic, and their presence is growing in the United States, with Vietnamese parishes opening everywhere. Relatively fresh to this country, they are producing a disproportionately high number of young men and women studying to become priests and nuns. In New Orleans's Notre Dame Seminary, for example, Vietnamese students make up one-fifth of the student body. Across the country, they make up 3% of the entire seminary population. The Vietnamese students are very religious, usually come from large families, and are socially conservative. But cracks are beginning to show. As they become rooted in this country, the secular culture is beginning to grab them as it grabbed those immigrants before them. Their religious leaders are already noticing the strong attraction of Vietnamese adolescents to the secular culture. As one nun put it, "Money and fashion often preoccupy them. Most of the teenagers, they've got peer pressure. It's very hard to listen to the inner voice, to listen to the heart."[3] The secular culture is a hard thing to resist.

But those who target affluence as a deterrent to a vocation to the priesthood are right, as well. A booming economy, the enticement of extreme sports, endless entertainment and distraction, and, more to our point, an array of exciting and challenging professions are more attractive to young people than the options offered by the priesthood. There are so many paths that lie open to the young man of today, paths he can follow with an expectation of social and financial success. We read all the time how computer-savvy kids are creating websites and racking up money working their stock options. A *New York Times* front-page story comments:

> A new sort of American childhood is being forged in the land where each day brings the dawn of an estimated 60 new millionaires. It is one in which the CEOs are the superheroes, family banter is often likely to include talk of multiples and IPOs, and where a recent collision between two students in a high school parking lot involved a Toyota SUV Forerunner and a Mercedes 500SL.[4]

Kids are contending with the "sudden wealth" and "affluenza" syndromes, and not a call to the priesthood. At one time, in a poor economy, the priesthood and religious life was a way out of poverty. But not now. Any stirrings the MTV-watching, Lexus-driving, bungee-jumping, high-spending young man may have toward the priesthood may simply go unheeded.

The second reason for the declining number of men entering the priesthood is this: when looking at the shortage of seminarians, we must also consider the falling Catholic birthrate. Traditionally, vocations to the priesthood have come from large families. But today there are two children or fewer in the average Catholic household, with most families having but one son. So families are not going to "squander" that son on a celibate life that will produce no grandchildren. Factor in the high divorce rate, approaching 50% of all marriages, and the number of traditional Catholic families with more than two children is significantly reduced.

The third reason brings us to a whole cluster of new social issues: women's consciousness of their own growing power in both society and church, the devaluation of celibacy, the pedophile crisis, and gay priests, to name a few. Who would want to join a group facing these issues? Here is a powerful quote from Donald Cozzens's book, *The Changing Face of the Priesthood*, which puts the problem in a nutshell:

> A former Kansas City-St. Joseph vicar general, Fr. Norman Rotert, a priest for forty-two years, spoke with considerable candor at a 1995 luncheon talk to the Catholic Press Association:
>
> "The shortage of priests is not going to be solved by gritting our teeth and praying for more vocations. Women are the ones who identify and nurture vocations, and they are not doing it anymore, and they are not going to do it. If you don't believe me, talk to them. I've interviewed them. They say, 'A Church that won't accept my daughters isn't going to get my son.' 'I know my son has a vocation to the priesthood but he won't accept celibacy.' 'I don't want my sons to go through what you and other priests have had to go through since the pedophilia issue surfaced.'"

Rotert's candid remarks reminded me of a conversation with a priest colleague who, like most of us on the seminary faculty, did supply work on weekends. After Mass one Sunday morning, a young man approached him and said he might be interested in the priesthood. Apparently prepared for just such a moment, the priest handed him some vocation materials. Suddenly his mother stood between them and grabbed the pamphlet from her son's hand. Throwing it down, she said with a voice of steel, "No son of mine is going to be a damn priest!" Perhaps surprised at her own vehemence, she added, "Nothing against you, Father. It's just that no son of mine is going to be a priest."

This kind of anger isn't often evident to priests greeting people after Eucharist on Sunday mornings, but it is there nonetheless. It matters little whether priests feel it is unfair and unwarranted, whether it's displaced or disproportionate. This mother's angry response falls into context, however, when viewed in the light of a recent CARA report sponsored by the National Conference of Catholic Bishops. When asked to react to the statement "You would encourage your child to pursue a career as priest or nun," parents' response fell into the following four categories: agree, twenty-five percent; strongly agree, eight percent; disagree, forty-eight percent; and strongly disagree, nineteen percent. A staggering sixty-seven percent disagreed or strongly disagreed with the statement. Only thirty-three percent agreed or strongly agreed. The angry mother in question apparently has a good deal of company.

In light of this report, one in five Catholic parents would strongly resist a child pursuing a vocation to the priesthood or religious life. Evidence that two-thirds would withhold encouragement to a son or daughter considering a vocation underscores the challenge facing vocation directors and seminary recruiters. It also reveals an important factor in the vocation crisis that is regularly overlooked. Catholics, in stark contrast to parents of previous generations, are no longer likely to see priesthood and religious life as a healthy way of life for their children.

Near the end of Rotert's Catholic Press Association talk, he summarized the forces alienating Catholic parents and Catholics in general:

> "The paternalistic attitudes, the increasing consciousness of women, the lack of appreciation for the value of celibacy, the large percentage of gay priests, the pedophilia crisis, all have so impacted our vocation recruitment efforts that I see no possibility of salvaging the priesthood as we know it today. We must talk about the issue if we are going to find a creative solution. Non-ordained lay pastors, closing parishes, twinning parishes are all temporary, stopgap measures. We are a sacramental Church. We must celebrate the Eucharist or we will die."[5]

Reluctant recruiters

The fourth and final reason why young men are not attracted to the priesthood is that priests themselves do not encourage vocations. Roger Cardinal Mahony of Los Angeles remarks in a pastoral letter, "A further tension remains: while most priests claim to be happy and fulfilled in their ministry, they give little evidence of enthusiasm for promoting priestly vocations."[6] Indeed, surveys show that while more than 80% of priests are pleased to be priests and would choose that vocation again, they are reluctant to invite young men to follow in their footsteps. One survey shows that only 33% of priests have actually encouraged boys to enter the seminary.

Why is this? If morale is as high as is sometimes claimed, why don't priests proclaim their satisfaction with their lifestyle to the young? Again, surveys show that three-fourths of current priests spoke of the influence of other priests' active witness on their own lives. The priest as "inviter" is still a powerful force. Why doesn't he invite? What's wrong with this picture?

In searching for an answer, I think Andrew Greeley is on to something. He says that, yes, the polls are right, consistently so: as a group, priests are happy and find satisfaction in their work. But two things are happening that may keep them quiet about it. One is what we might call a kind of circular propaganda that operates this way: while the individual priest is happy, he doesn't think others are. While the individual priest does not find celibacy a burden (although statistically, he personally favors optional celibacy), he thinks—especially under the pressures of strong anti-celibacy groups, both clerical and lay—that other priests are burdened by it. While an individual priest's morale is high, he thinks the morale of other priests is not. So you get one of those self-defeating, "Gift of the Magi"-type scripts, which would be comic except for the tragic outcome: less recruitment and fewer priests.

The other thing that makes priests reluctant recruiters is the celibacy issue. Donald Cozzens in his book, *Freeing Celibacy*, indicated that mothers say their sons might be interested in the priesthood except for the celibacy requirement. Poet and author Kathleen Norris, while extolling celibacy, feels compelled to note that "we need only to look at newspaper accounts of sex abuse by priests to see evidence of celibacy that isn't working." Later on in this book, we will look at celibacy in a positive light, but also with the caution that it should not be made an idol which subverts a prior need for the Eucharist and the care of souls.

At this point, several things need to be said concerning celibacy, since it does impact the topic of this chapter—that is, the priest shortage. One is to repeat that the polls consistently show priests as happy and satisfied, and that for them, celibacy is not an insupportable burden. Yes, maybe a quarter of them have left the priesthood—a significant number—but three-fourths have not. As Greeley argues, those who have left did so not primarily because of celibacy, but because they were unhappy. They just did not like being priests or the work the priesthood entailed. The situation is similar to what happened when women left unhappy marriages because they now had the opportunity to work and gain financial independence and they now had the ability to control fertility. Those who stay in marriages these days, when it is so easy and so socially acceptable to get a divorce, do so because they want to. Likewise, the majority of priests who stay do so because they want to. They find satisfaction and happiness in their work, and celibacy, while an issue for some, is, for most, simply not the determining factor in leaving or staying. So it comes down to this: the real cause of the vocation shortage, it might be argued, is the reticence of those priests who are happy but who, taken in by circular propaganda and the loud complaints of the anti-celibacy group, do not recruit others to their ranks.

The second thing to mention, as Kathleen Norris did, is the idea that celibacy just doesn't work: look at all those cases of pedophilia we mentioned in the last chapter. The fact is, however, that pedophile activity has nothing to do with celibacy. To argue that enforced celibacy causes deviant behavior is like arguing that marriage causes spousal abuse. It is well-known that pedophilia is a syndrome acquired quite early in life and has nothing to do with celibacy, as evidenced by the fact that most pedophiles are married men. Further, pedophilia cuts across all professions, from lawyers to dentists to factory workers. It affects other religious denominations, including those with married clergy. It is simply not true that frustrated celibate males become pedophiles, and if only they were married, pedophilia would go away. It is the other way around. Pedophiles become celibate clergy and their condition will not go away whether they are married or single. These people are in need of help, no matter what their state.[7]

In later chapters, I will argue for a married clergy to exist alongside a celibate clergy for serious pastoral reasons (for example, the priest shortage we have been discussing). But none of that is to be construed as a lessening of the appreciation of the gift of celibacy. Meanwhile, if the priesthood is perceived as an unhealthy way of life, then only happy priests who give evidence of their fulfilled lives can dispel that perception. The unhappy and aggrieved minority, making the rounds of talk shows eager to hear their thoughts, should not undermine the happy warriors on the front lines. Perhaps, then, these words, from the introduction to a book aptly titled *Extraordinary Lives*, in which thirty-four priests tell their stories, are a good ending to this chapter.

During the recent barrage of negative reporting about priests, who could have foreseen the outcomes of two national surveys conducted in 1994—one by the *Los Angeles Times* and the other by the National Federation of Priests' Councils? These surveys present a picture of the priesthood quite at variance with books and articles which portray priests as disagreeing with the pope, disliking their bishops, wanting to marry, and inclined not to choose the priesthood if they had it do to over again. In July and September of 1994, Fr. Andrew Greeley, a priest of the Archdiocese of Chicago and a professor at the University of Chicago and the University of Arizona, wrote two articles for *America* drawing conclusions from the surveys mentioned above ("A Sea of Paradoxes," July 16, 1994, p. 6, and "In Defense of Celibacy?" September 10, 1994, p. 10). Greeley found results which run counter to the image too often portrayed of the American Catholic priesthood. His conclusions were:

1. The much-discussed morale crisis in the priesthood does not exist.
   70% say they would definitely choose to be a priest again; 20% say they would probably do so.

2. Celibacy does not seem to be the problem that it is often alleged to be.
   Only 40% say they would definitely marry if the Church approved.

3. Priests are generally satisfied with the quality of their work performance.

4. Most priests give Church leadership moderately high marks.
   83% approve the job performance of Pope John Paul II; 72% approve the job performance of their own bishops.

We, the authors of this book, one a cleric and one a layman, believe that it would be worthwhile to explore in greater detail what happy priests think about their vocation.[8]

A good idea. As the crisis of the priest shortage grows dramatically, bishops are being forced to go public. Bishop James Griffin

of Columbus, Ohio, has issued diocesan guidelines for "Sunday Celebrations in the Absence of a Priest." According to these guidelines, these are the people who are to preside over celebrations when there is no priest available, listed in descending order:

1. the deacon

2. a religious/lay pastoral associate

3. a seminarian or permanent deacon candidate

4. another parish minister

5. a reliable, trustworthy parishioner.

Moreover, the guidelines contain statements concerning the people's expectations of the overworked, overextended priest, for example, that he should have at least one day off, work no more than fifty hours a week, and so on.

Bishop Thomas Daily of Brooklyn has issued a pastoral letter to his people telling them that the shortage of priests has officially entered the "crisis" stage, and he called the situation both "sobering" and "urgent." Well he might. Ordinations in his diocese are down 92% from twenty years ago, and there are 39% fewer priests than in 1980, leaving some 416 active priests to serve the two million Catholics in 223 parishes and chapels. (It should be noted that in the next ten years half of those active priests will be eligible for retirement.) So the bishop has asked every parish to review its schedule of Masses and number of parishioners in preparation for cutting back on the number of services, as well as for the clustering of parishes.

We will see more and more such pastoral letters that inform people of the shortage and offer systematic plans for reducing the sacramental life of the Church. You have to shake your head in disbelief. Rather than look to the obvious solution of a married clergy, bishops are now offering creative ways to subtract the Eucharist from the people, even on the Lord's Day. The Eucharist, the center of Catholic liturgical life, will have to be curtailed even on Sundays because of the priest shortage. If Catholics will continue to get only a "celebration" instead of Mass, why shouldn't they go to the local Protestant church, which may have better music and better preaching?

What is dismaying in all this is the lack of courage on the part of the bishops. All they would have to do would be to tell Rome that the Mass is increasingly being denied to their people, and that their clergy are overworked and aging. Therefore, out of pastoral compassion and need, the bishops should demand that the people who have a right to the sacraments be given them by widening the requirements for ordination, as was done in the ancient Church. That the bishops would rather issue pastoral letters, deny the Eucharist to their people, blend beloved parishes, and overwork their aging priests (the median age of priests in this county in 2013 is 64, compared to 45 in 1970) with each succeeding year, than face Rome or publicly raise the taboo subject of a married clergy bespeaks a submissiveness, betrayal, and pastoral cowardice that would have puzzled their predecessors.

10

THE TENTH CHALLENGE

Gay Clergy

We have mentioned that there are a large number of gay priests in the United States today—and we must now add gay seminarians. That this topic should be mentioned at all is a surprise and scandal to some people. Yet the reality has been there for a long time.

As early as 1987, writing in a national Catholic magazine, Richard McBrien publicly brought up the issue of homosexual priests. Two years later, in a national Catholic newspaper, Andrew Greeley wrote about "lavender rectories." More recently, in 2000, Donald Cozzens, a respected seminary rector, professor of pastoral studies, and vicar for priests, wrote *The Changing Face of the Priesthood*, a careful, balanced book that openly revealed the extent of the problem. This book, widely publicized and reviewed, sent shockwaves throughout the Church and gleaned considerable public attention; much of this chapter is indebted to Cozzens's revelations. Finally, in that same year, Marco Politi, an Italian author who had co-written, with Carl Bernstein of Watergate fame, the book *His Holiness*, a biography of Pope John Paul II, published a book entitled *La Confessione*. This book presents the testimony of an unnamed priest who not only reveals his struggle with homosexuality but also reveals a whole network of homosexual priests who are active in the Italian Church and its seminaries.

The biggest revelation, it seems, is that there is a significantly higher percentage of homosexual priests and seminarians than there are in society at large. This may be why 90% of all the cases of clergy sexual abuse of minors involve high school boys—not girls. Which is not to say that all gay priests are predators, only to say that the abuse runs proportionately in accordance with the number of gay priests. We don't know exact numbers, but those in seminaries and those who have been around a while all speak of the disproportionate number of gay men in the priesthood and seminaries. One report shows that:

> Catholic seminarians score highest on the femininity scale of the MMPI...these seminarians felt insecure and inferior. This insecurity seemed to be partly due to the anxiety of trying to live out these "feminine" traits in a masculinized and patriarchal culture....Frank Kobler, who investigated screening tests for applicants to the religious life, found that his sample of 323 minor seminarians "had profiles that resembled those for females in the general population." Solid psychological evidence now supports an old suspicion: boys and young men with a feminine perception of themselves tended to be attracted to a vocation....One survey of priests in 1984 revealed that only two out of every ten priests actually saw themselves as masculine, while four out of ten admitted to a strong feminine identification.[1]

An NBC report on celibacy found that "anywhere from twenty-three to fifty-eight percent" of the Catholic clergy have a homosexual orientation. Other studies indicate that half of the clergy population has a homosexual orientation; the percentage of gay priests in religious congregations appears to be even higher.

As expected, not far from the question of the number of gay priests is the issue of AIDS. In spite of recent publicity on the issue, it remains, for the official Church, a secret and closed topic. On the contrary, the secular press has long lifted the veil on priests who have died of AIDS, particularly the *Village Voice*, the *New York Post*, the *St. Paul Pioneer Press*, and the *National Catholic Reporter*. But the topic really hit the public eye with a survey published in January 2000 in the *Kansas City Star*, which said that the incidence of AIDS among

Catholic priests was almost four times higher than that of the general male population. That statistic, as well as the series itself, was in fact quite seriously flawed, and the figures in it were roundly criticized by pollsters, sociologists, and journalists.[2] Nevertheless, the fact that many priests have died from this disease can be documented. (Not all cases came from sexual contact, but also from blood transfusions, not to mention those who may have become infected before entering the seminary.)

Contributing to the disproportionate number of gay priests is the exodus of heterosexual priests, those approximately 20,000 men who left to get married. This has altered considerably the gay/straight ratio so that the homosexual proportion of the whole number went way up, while their absolute numbers stayed the same. These numbers result in a distinctly identifiable subculture. As Donald Cozzens says, "the need gay priests have for friendship with other gay men, and their shaping of a social life largely composed of other homosexually orientated men, has created a gay subculture in most of the larger U.S. dioceses. A similar subculture has developed in many of our seminaries."[3]

The imbalance between the number of homosexual priests and heterosexual priests is at the heart of the anxiety about gay clergy. Whether motivated indeed by homophobic sentiments or merely desiring a more representative balance, many people are worried about the shift in numbers. And many worry about the polls that show that many gay priests do not observe celibacy, but have lovers—often, like their gay counterparts in the secular community, many lovers. Some even had sex in the seminary. Garry Wills is hard on non-celibate gay priests:

> What is wrong about gays and lesbians as priests or ministers? Nothing is—as other denominations are realizing when they ordain them. But that does not make the presence of gay "celibates" in the current Catholic priesthood a healthy thing. They may claim that they are "celibate" by their own private definition of that word. But they took a public vow of celibacy,

117

and the aim of any oath is communicative, is a contractual commitment. Both sides of the contract must agree on its terms. Gay priests are living a lie. It may be imposed on them by a senseless rule. Yet they uphold the resulting structure of deceit. People are fooled by them. One reason pedophiles have been given access to children is that Catholic parents were under the misunderstanding that priests refrain from all sex. In the surveys made of them, the gay priests say they must be careful to keep others from learning their secret.[4]

I think we can say that most laypeople are largely sympathetic and respectful to a priest who might be gay as long as he is a good and hardworking priest, keeps his vows, and does not become a part of any gay subculture. They would have a hard time, perhaps, if he hung out in gay singles bars. On the other hand, the heterosexual seminarian has a different problem. He is understandably put off in a seminary that has a strong gay subculture—not to mention that the faculties of the seminaries also include a disproportionate number of gay teachers. In a survey, 101 gay priests ordained after 1981 said that their seminaries were 70% gay. A heterosexual seminarian has to feel out of sync in such a place, sense that he doesn't fit in, and maybe even conclude that he doesn't have a vocation.

Perceptions

If our seminaries become or are perceived as predominantly gay then the priesthood of the future will likely be perceived as a gay profession. That imbalance will not do the Church any good, and vocations to the priesthood will decline even more. This perception is attested to in Garry Wills' book *Papal Sin* when he writes, "In fact, the admission of married men and women to the priesthood—which is bound to come anyway—may well come for the wrong reason, not because women and the community deserve this, but because of panic at the perception that the priesthood is becoming predominately gay."[5] Perhaps the columnist who calls himself Pastor Ignotus in Britain's Catholic periodical, *The Tablet*, says it best:

Equally disturbing is the tendency of bishops to overlook the fact that a disproportionate number of homosexuals are being recruited into our seminaries. I know of one seminary where, two years ago, 60 percent of the students identified themselves as "gay," 20 percent were confused about their sexual identity, and only 20 percent considered themselves heterosexual. I have no objections whatsoever to welcoming homosexuals into the priesthood. I know some excellent priests who are homosexual and that has never been a problem in their ministry. But there would be cause for concern if, in order to maintain the status quo, the Catholic priesthood were allowed to become primarily a "gay" option.[6]

Throughout the Church's history, of course, there have been homosexual popes, bishops, and saints. Seminaries accept homosexual candidates who vow to be celibate, and no one denies the giftedness and holiness of many gay clergy throughout the ages. Historian John Boswell, author of the prize-winning book *Christianity, Social Tolerance, and Homosexuality*, offers this perspective:

Celibate religious life offered women escape from the consequences of marriage—for example, having to sleep with a husband and bear children—which might not only be unwanted but even life-threatening. It afforded both genders a means of avoiding stereotypical gender roles. Women could exercise power in religious communities, among other women, without being subordinated to the male of a household. Men could become a part of a community of equals, all male, without the responsibilities of fatherhood or ruling a household; or they could exercise through the priesthood skills of nurturing and serving otherwise associated with women and considered shameful for men. Men could avoid obligations of warfare, and devote themselves to study; women could become literate and learned, an opportunity rare for their sex outside religious communities after the decline of Rome.

It is reasonable, under these circumstances, to believe that the priesthood and religious communities would have exercised a particular appeal for gay people....Indeed, lesbian and gay

> people would hardly have needed a spiritual motivation to desire to live in a same-sex community of equals.[7]

And so, historically, homosexual men and women naturally have found the priesthood and religious life attractive. Once you enter the seminary, there is no need to explain why you are not dating or getting married. So by not having to worry about the issue of marriage, along with a sincere desire to be of service to others and a natural "feminine" aptitude for ritual and liturgy, the way is open for an appealing vocation and lifestyle. The gay man in religious life can love God in the context of community and noble celibate service.

Ironically, the ecclesiastical law mandating celibacy has unwittingly helped create an environment that is quite hospitable to the emotional needs of gay priests, rather than those of straight priests. After all, a priest can go on vacations with other male priests, and take his days off with another male, and go out to dinner with a man, and none of this raises any eyebrows. In fact, people are glad Father is relaxing. But let a priest have lunch with a woman and it is entirely another matter.

The contributions of gay men in the priesthood and religious life have been profound and many. In a way, the Church has offered a magnificent opportunity, along with comfort and refuge, to gay people throughout its history—a point often overlooked by militant gays who hate the Church. Yet the question remains: if the priesthood is perceived as a gay profession, how does this affect vocations? Will they decline even more now that gay men are out of the closet, are openly accepted in society, and therefore have other options for a "safe" lifestyle?

Priests and mothers have always been the two groups who do the most to recruit men to the priesthood. But gay priests tend to seek out gay young men and vice versa, and that will increase their numbers. Mothers who intuitively sense the gay subculture will naturally be hesitant to send their heterosexual sons to the seminary. Fathers will have the same apprehensions, even more so. Straight seminarians will continue to experience dislocation in a predominant gay subculture and may drop out.

The disproportionate number of homosexually orientated priests and seminarians, not to mention the presence of homosexuals on the faculty, simply must have had some causal effect on the drastic reduction of the number of candidates for our seminaries. Furthermore, if indeed almost half our priests and seminarians are homosexual, then that also means that half of our priests and seminarians are being recruited from roughly 5–8% of the general population of American Catholic men.

Given the current context of a large number of gay priests, plus a critical need for clergy and the disproportionate number of women in ecclesial ministries, it would seem to be wise to open up the priesthood to married men and to offer the gift of celibacy along the lines Jesus himself suggested: "Not everyone can accept this teaching, but only those to whom it is given" (Mt 19:11). It would seem further that, in the current context of an all-male clergy, when the clerical culture takes on a gay coloring, it no longer represents the Church at large. And so the challenge here is to achieve a balance that does.

The official Church keeps silent about sexuality in general, and homosexuality in particular, among its clergy. The normal, human needs of priests for intimacy; the numbers living clandestine, active sexual lives; the emotional burden of gay priests—none of these topics are ever openly addressed. Jon Fuller, SJ, a medical doctor and assistant director of the Adult AIDS Program at Boston Medical Center, describes the anxieties gay priests face:

> Central to many workshops on AIDS for religious and diocesan leaders have been panels of priests and religious living with HIV infection. During the first such conference (organized by Damien Ministries in 1988), participating priests felt so stigmatized and fearful of negative repercussions as they shared their experiences that they wore paper bags over their heads. Panelists have spoken of never being able to talk

about their sexuality, and of living in fear that they would be rejected or ostracized if their homosexuality were discovered.[8]

Ironically, the Church defines homosexuality as "intrinsically disordered." Yet it relies on gay men to celebrate the sacraments and carry out the work of the Church, while at the same time withholding support and keeping their experiences and needs forbidden subjects. On the whole issue of gay clergy, dialogue, not suppression, is needed.

11

THE ELEVENTH CHALLENGE

Women and Men

A language instructor was explaining to her class that French nouns, unlike their English counterparts, are grammatically designated as masculine or feminine. She told them that things like "chalk" or "pencil" have a gender association, although in English these words are neutral. Puzzled, one student raised his hand and asked, "What gender is a computer?" The teacher wasn't certain which it was, and divided the class into two groups, one group all male, the other all female. They were to decide which gender should be applied to "computer" and give four reasons for their decision.

The group of women concluded computers should be referred to in the masculine gender because:

1. In order to get their attention they have to be turned on.

2. They have a lot of data but are still clueless.

3. They are supposed to help you solve your problems, but half the time they are the problem.

4. As soon as you commit to one, you realize that if you had waited a little longer, you could have had a better model.

The group of men decided computers should definitely be referred to in the feminine gender because:

1. No one but their creator understands their internal logic.

2. The native language they use to communicate with other computers is incomprehensible to everyone else.

3. Even your smallest mistakes are stored in long-term memory banks for later retrieval.

4. As soon as you make a commitment to one, you find yourself spending half your paycheck on accessories for it.

This humorous introduction, plus the length of this chapter, provide sufficient evidence of the caution with which I, or any author, approach the gender debates. But look we must at women and men in society and Church if we are to work together for a common goal.

Gains of women

No one denies that during the past forty or fifty years the gains of women in the first-world countries have been a little short of amazing. True, much remains to be done, but no one can help being in awe at the enormous strides women have taken to be free of the home and dependency on a spouse, in control of their reproductive lives, and able to enter the marketplace. And the future is most promising for women. Consider these facts:

- In society at large, women already make up the majority of voters.

- Women are about to become the majority of the workforce.

- Women have made gains in politics, and have headed up some of the most important and largest nations on earth. Here in the United States, a woman ran for vice-president, another was Surgeon General, another was Secretary of State. Women also govern states. In 1992, a banner year, women won four seats in the Senate and twenty-four in the House of

Representatives. In the year 2000, there were about a dozen women running for the Senate and about 140 for the House.

- There are women on the Supreme Court.

- Women play ice hockey in the Olympics, and the U.S. women's soccer team won the World Cup in 1999.

- Women are a large influence on the marketplace. They buy half of the new cars and a quarter of the new trucks. 75% of purchasing decisions for families are made by women or influenced by them.

- Women are now the primary target of both daytime and prime time television—always a key measurement of power and influence in a consumerist society.[1]

- A recent report (2000) released by the Department of Education shows that girls. in fact, do fare better than boys (see pages that follow), and have since the 1980s.

- Over half of the country's college students are female, and it is reasonable to assume that in the next generation or two women will make up the majority of college and university professors, teachers, professionals, and corporate leaders.

- Nearly half the medical students in this country are female.

- Although only three women head Fortune 500 corporations, they have started their own companies at twice the national average and currently own 38% of all U.S. firms. Since 1987, the number of female-owned ventures has doubled from 4.5 million to 9.1 million.

- In spite of more than thirty years of assumptions that there is a pay disparity between men and women—namely, that women are routinely paid less for doing the same work as men—latest studies indicate that the adjusted gap has narrowed to about 5%.

Women, then, are in almost every conceivable job. They are in board-rooms as well as classrooms. It is hard to think of any secular position from which they are absent, whether it be astronaut, construction worker, police officer, or combat pilot. As might be expected, there are downsides to all these remarkable achievements. First, although they are indeed in high places in the corporate world, women still lag behind considerably as leading inventors or manufacturers. Not many of them are found among the new dot-com billionaires.

Second, while women do have enormous buying power and are therefore targeted by manufacturers, this targeting is also hugely adept at commodifying them and, consequently, trivializing them. So slick is the beguiling advertising, so pervasive the secular spirit, that all this is done with the willing consent of women. As Patricia McGuire, president of Trinity College in Washington, D.C., says:

> In a remarkable article in the February 13, 2000 *New York Times Magazine*, Francine Prose skewers the new "women's culture" in which the Internet only extends the mindless, infantile trash that has largely been the fate of women in the infotainment complex for years. Web sites designed "for women, about women" have all of the intellectual charm of the Cosmo girl—I checked it out myself. On Sunday, March 19, the much-vaunted iVillage Web site for women headlined "Learn About Aphrodisiacs" and "21st-Century Solutions: No. 79—How to Make Lipstick Last." I was kind of hoping that a "21st-century solution" might at least have something to say about attaining equal pay for equal work, at long last. Ms. Prose writes that, aside from treating women as "stupid and narcis-sistic and desiring childish, mindless entertainment," the Web sites and other media practice "the ultimate deception: the marketing, research-driven con, the appalling bait-and-switch practiced on the woman who is being promised relationship, being sold on community, and who is in fact buying into a pro-gressively deeper isolation and seclusion."[2]

Third, although girls do better in the classroom, they are twice as likely to suffer from depression after the age of fifteen than boys. They attempt suicide more often than boys (although, it should be noted, more boys succeed at it). Girls are also at far greater risk for eating disorders.

Fourth, women are always in danger of being co-opted by radical feminists who, as we shall see shortly, belittle men, marriage, and family life and who have, for the most part, left unsolved the most needful and compelling issue of all: who will raise the children?

Fifth, in other countries, especially third and fourth world countries, women are routinely exploited sexually, physically, and economically. They have few rights and are far behind the gains of first world countries. These women need constant, ongoing support. It is estimated, for example, that 50,000 children and women are sold each year to the United States by unscrupulous people to be used as cheap labor, servants, and prostitutes.

Sixth, even here in the United States, minority women are still largely in the underclass of poverty and indenture. Many feminists themselves have noted that a good amount of female liberation rests on the backs of other women: servants, housekeepers, nannies, female daycare center staff, and countless grandmothers who are raising the children of their single or divorced daughters. And these caretaker women are mostly women of color. Feminist Barbara Ehrenreich notes:

> Among my middle-class, professional women friends and acquaintances, including some who made important contributions to the early feminist analysis of housework, the employment of a maid is now nearly universal....One thing you can say with certainty about the population of household workers is that they are disproportionately women of color; "lower" kinds of people for a "lower" kind of work.[3]

Men

The downside to the gains made by women in the long-overdue revolution is that men have become devalued and have lost in many areas.

- Technology has replaced the need for the equipment evolution has dealt men. Larger in body weight than females, stronger in frame, more developed in muscle, hyped with testosterone (the average women has 40 to 60 nanograms in a deciliter of blood plasma, while the average man has 300 to 1000 nanograms)—which correlates with energy, competitiveness, confidence, strength, and sex drives—the male has no place to put his strength and drive except into extreme sports and aggressive or boorish behavior. After all, any seven-year-old kid can press a button which will engage the hydraulic machine which in turn will lift the heavy lumber. Today's information, computer, online world, which requires brainpower and mental dexterity, is open to all, from the frail to the brawny. In this sense, the male body is becoming more and more obsolete.

- The sexual revolution and its technology have rendered men socially passé. Women today are completely and solely in charge of reproduction. For example, a man cannot prevent an abortion even though it is his child, too. The law is heavily weighted against men in custody cases; often, they are forbidden to see their children. Women don't need a man to support them financially, and they don't even need a man to have children. And so radical feminists have pronounced man obsolete. He used to be the breadwinner, and that gave him some identity and purpose. But the term "breadwinner," like the role, is now passé, as working women with equal pay are becoming more and more a reality.

Sperm comes in a catalogue, and single motherhood is acceptable. The male's traditional roles of father and provider have vanished. (Some males, of course, revel in this institutionalized irresponsibility. A man can have as much free sex as possible with no need to have a shotgun wedding if he gets the girl pregnant, and no need to make any payments if she decides to keep the child—nor does he have to pay for the abortion.)

- A endless stream of propaganda has deprived boys of help and status by declaring that "schools shortchange girls." This theme was loudly proposed by the American Association of University Women (AAUW) in their well-publicized 1991 report entitled "Shortchanging Girls, Shortchanging America," based on the research of such books as the wildly popular and widely quoted *A Different Voice*, by Carol Gilligan of Harvard (*Ms. Magazine*'s Woman of the Year in 1984), and Mary Pipher's *Reviving Ophelia*, and promoted by feminists such as Anna Quindlen. And so not only did the notion of educational unfairness pass into common lore, but, on the strength of the AAUW report, Congress passed the Gender Equity in Education Act in 1994, designating millions of dollars to study the plight of girls and how to counter the educational bias against them. The almost universal message disseminated from this report was that redress must be done to girls so they can catch up with the boys.

The problem is that none of these claims are true; they have been proven to be false. It is a classic case of personal agendas being politicized with the cooperation of a gullible and conspiring media. The stark fact is that, in spite of the pervasive mythology to the contrary, girls are thriving in school by virtually every measure. It is the boys who are in danger. The research that purported an education bias against girls gradually has been shown to be riddled with errors and duplicity. (Interestingly, none of the research was ever published in peer journals for critique, only in popular magazines.) No real evidence exists to support the claims made.

On the contrary, more accurate research has shown what every teacher knows: girls outshine boys in almost every department.

Diane Ravitch, former U.S. Assistant Secretary of Education, said in retrospect, "That [1992] AAUW report was just completely wrong. What was so bizarre is that it came out right at the time that girls had just overtaken boys in almost every area....There were all these special programs put in place for girls, and no one paid any attention to boys."

In fact, a 1997 MetLife study contradicted most of the findings of the AAUW study. It said, "Contrary to the commonly held view that boys are at an advantage over girls in school, girls appear to have an advantage over boys in terms of their future plans, teachers' expectations, everyday experiences at school, and interactions in the classroom." In 1998, sociologist Judith Kleinfield proposed that the AAUW and other so-called studies were simply "politics dressed up as science."

Educationally unequal

Consider this: the typical girl is a year and a half ahead of the typical boy in reading and writing, is more committed to school and, as we have seen, more likely to go to college. Girls get better grades and participate in advanced-placement classes at higher rates. As the Department of Education study mentioned before points out, girls now outnumber boys in student government, honor societies, school newspapers, and debating clubs, and they do better on the SATs. They read more books and outperform boys on tests for artistic and musical abilities.

Girls consistently do more homework than boys. More girls than boys study abroad. More join the Peace Corps. In 1997, full-time college enrollments were 45% male and 55% female, and the imbalance continues to swing in favor of the females. Girls are faring better in almost every area. The only area where boys are dominant is sports, and women's groups are targeting them with a vengeance.

On the other hand, consider this: more boys are suspended from school than girls, more are held back, and more drop out. Boys generally have poor literacy skills and will have more difficulty finding employment in an information era. Boys are three times as likely to be pegged with attention deficit disorder (ADD). Even little boys acting like little boys are drugged early on to "modify" their normal testosterone behavior. More boys are involved in crime and more succeed at suicide. And boys, more than girls, are affected by absent fathers.

Research indicates that very often, aggressive and violent boys, as well as those most at risk for juvenile delinquency, are the ones who are physically separated from their fathers. This is an ominous finding, since the U.S. Census Bureau found that in 1960 children living with their mother but not their father numbered 5.1 million; by 1996 the number was more than 16 million. Along with the increase of these numbers, there has been an increase of male violence. In response to this, some feminist theorists say the answer is "to raise boys like girls" (Gloria Steinem), which, of course, is to deny biology and testosterone—as if boys needed rescue from their masculinity. True, boys are aggressive and competitive, but they are also capable of loyalty, compassion, and heroism and are quite susceptible to the call of honor. In any case, it is the boys who are at risk in our society today. It is the boys who are lagging behind the girls.[4]

But that is not all. When these boys grow up, they come under attack. Radical feminists regularly berate men and dub them all "potential rapists." Men are routinely denied due process in sexual accusations at most colleges, and they are often put down, even at Catholic gatherings. The media, blinded by political correctness, falls into line. Movies and television, for example, which commonly show all adults—and particularly parents—as incompetent and marginal, are especially hard on males. Movies present men as solitary heroes, crude and vulgar people who sit and drink beer, or as womanizing, larger versions of little boys. As male prototype, television gives us Homer Simpson sitting on his sofa, beer in hand, a blank stare on his face.

The title character in *King of Queens* dreams of turning his basement into a private hideaway for watching sports on a big-screen television.

The father of the title character in *Everybody Loves Raymond* sits hypnotized in front of a television football game, responding only with grunts. The upwardly mobile bachelors on *Friends* pig out on sports telecasts. The men on *Ally McBeal* are as insensitive and insecure as the women on that show. And so it goes. Critic Anita Gates writes:

> But television sports mania is not these characters' only fault. Men in a growing number of comedies are depicted as rude, crude, sex-crazed, sexist, childish, and blindly egotistical....In their desperate attempt to lure male viewers (and all the dollars advertisers believe they are ready to spend), the powers that be in television seem to have decided to appeal to the lowest common denominator. And it's remarkably low.[5]

And because political correctness does not allow anyone to offend women, blacks, gays, or animals, the only category left to ridicule (besides Catholics as a class) is men, who up to this point in history have been in power. The ridicule often has to show them as out-smarted, out-maneuvered, and outwitted by women who, after all, are superior. (Agent Mulder on *X-Files* is portrayed as smarter than everyone else—except his female partner, Scully.) In one classic episode of *The Simpsons*, Lisa, the bright, intelligent daughter of Homer and Marge Simpson, goes into a depression when she realizes that she has Homer's undesirable, idiocy-prone genes. Her parents try to reassure her by gathering as many of the Simpson relatives together as possible who, naturally, turn out to be jerks and failures. That is, until she meets the female Simpsons, who are all brain surgeons, rocket scientists, and professors.

According to Children Now, a media advocacy group, the top television role models for boys between ten and seventeen are Tim Allen, Kramer, who is the bumbling, lunatic sidekick on *Seinfeld*, and Homer Simpson, along with his son Bart and his admonition to "Eat my shorts."

The feminization of society has robbed men of role models and outlets. In her book, *Stiffed: The Betrayal of the American Male*, Susan Faludi says that at the turn of the twenty-first century, men are searching for a way to recapture the masculine camaraderie and purpose of World War II, their fathers' proving ground.

Hard to be a man

In short, modern times have simply taken their toll on the male psyche. At the same time, radical feminism, which extols the independent woman, straight or lesbian, who can be a mother and a breadwinner without a husband, has declared men obsolete. Males are suffering a crisis of identity. As Patrick Arnold writes:

> As women have long told us, the far-reaching changes that feminism creates necessarily demand corresponding spiritual work by men to free themselves from their own oppressiveness, numbness, and unconsciousness. Until recently, however, this men's consciousness-raising about gender and sexuality primarily meant reading feminist literature and adopting the feminist agenda—an invaluable method of entering empathetically into women's experience and listening to their pain, but an impossible way to understand masculinity.

> Feminism must speak for women—it cannot speak for men. Since women can't directly experience what it means to be a man, and since most men are too numb to tell them their experiences, feminist literature can't articulate much more than women's experience of men, which is so often the product not of men's souls but of their numbness, of their domination, insensitivity, and even brutality. Feminist literature, as a result, sometimes concentrates on the worst side of men, and is unable or unwilling to probe beneath this cultural wreckage to find anything valuable or graced. Most contemporary conversation about the male gender, therefore, is clearly one-sided and tainted with prejudice, which is why men themselves must correct the imbalance and speak forcefully from their own experience.

Much of this strongly negative current literature and rhetoric about men is influential in academia, the media, the arts, and liberal religion, where it has achieved "politically correct" status. Moreover, there is presently little information or discussion that would give a correspondingly positive treatment about the male spirit: few men's classes in college gender studies programs, few empathetic programs on television about men, and no courses on men's spirituality in any theology school of my acquaintance. One measure of the distance men have to go in articulating their unique experience is available in any serious bookstore; volumes on women's spirituality sometimes occupy entire walls while books about men (many of them strongly negative) often conveniently fit on one shelf.

What is at stake here is not numerical competition or sexual debating points, but the entire public intellectual, affective, and spiritual atmosphere in which men live and young men grow up. The growing cultural inability to fathom men, however, creates an opportunity: the challenge for men to understand and speak for themselves. Men must therefore do their own intellectual work, define their own terms, set out their own agenda, confront negative projections and stereotypes, and engage in constructive self-criticism—all in the context of calm and reasonable self-affirmation.[6]

Brother Joseph Kilikevice, OP, who specializes in retreat work with men, says all men are wounded:

Many of us have been reared by women, with strong mothers in the home, and absent fathers who work themselves into an early grave. [Robert] Bly talks about the industrial revolution changing how men work together and live together. We no longer go out into the fields to plant crops with our fathers, or out to the barn. Many of us never knew where our fathers worked or never saw their work place. We are strongly influenced by women. There are few male teachers in grade school. Those are very formative years.

There is, of course, nothing wrong with being reared by women, but it's out of balance. A woman cannot provide a man with what is needed for the deep masculine journey, any more than a man can provide it for a woman. It's the way God made the world. We certainly need women. Many men will say that all their emotional support and their entire emotional lives are tied up with women. Men recognize this out-of-balance state.[7]

There is a need today for male challenges and struggle and separation. Note the success of the Knights of Columbus in the past and the success of current Catholic groups such as Opus Dei and the Polish Solidarity Movement, and the Protestant group known as Promise Keepers (founded by a former Catholic). One writer defends such movements:

> Some observers have dismissed the Men's Movement, which emerged in the 1990s in the work of such writers as Robert Bly (*Iron John*), and Michael Thompson (*Raising Cain*), as false pathos of masculine self-regard and victimization, as yet another manifestation of our culture's deep-seated sexual narcissism. Other have mocked its claims that men have been victimized somehow by feminism and its alleged excesses, pointing to continued male dominance in nearly all areas of our civilization. But surely these critics miss the real point of this crucial social and philosophical revolution....
>
> It's so very hard to become a man....Everything threatens to beat us down, to strip us of our biological birthright, to destroy us simply for asserting our essential, metaphysical manliness. And it is this...that concerns true adherents of the Men's Movement, which has so little to do with actual male dominance in the material world.[8]

So, what is new in our culture, we repeat, is the devaluation of men. The rise of contraception, abortion virtually on demand, and radical feminism have, as we have seen, enabled men to walk away from relationships, as well as personal and family responsibilities.

What is new in our culture is the glorification of those male athletes, rock stars, and celebrities who continually make the headlines for committing crimes, for sexual abuse, for infidelity, for religious mockery, and for marathon sexual escapades. What is new—truly new—is the current male search for the ideal, steroid-boosted body that actors and models display, because in an age when women fly combat missions, the question becomes: what can a modern boy or man do to distinguish himself as being masculine? Such an ideal body quest is indeed tied in with the ascendency of women. As the authors of *The Adonis Complex: The Secret Crisis of Male Body Obsession*, write:

> As women have advanced, men have gradually lost their traditional identities as breadwinners, fighters, and protectors. Women are no longer so dependent upon men for these services. Accordingly, as the importance of these other identities has declined, the relative importance of the male body appears to have increased, although men may not be consciously aware of these motivating forces.

> Muscularity in particular has become increasingly important, because it symbolizes masculinity.... Mishkind, Rodin, and other authors, like ourselves, have similarly noted a connection between the recent rise of women and society's increasing focus on the male body. For example, authors James Gillett and Philip White have suggested that "the hypermasculine body symbolizes an attempt by men to restore feelings of masculine self-control and worth." They further hypothesize that the desirability of a "hypermasculine" body and the recent explosion of bodybuilding may be rooted in the growing "threat to male privilege" caused by the ascendancy of women. Aaron Randall and his colleagues, similarly, have written about "the dilemma posed by democratic relationships emphasizing equality between the sexes, leaving men with few sure bases for acting as providers and protectors." Becoming strong and muscular is a clear way for men to radiate power and manliness. As Barry Glassner writes, "Muscles are the sign of masculinity."

> These authors argue that in bodybuilding—the surest way to achieve muscularity—the male body symbolically represents power and strength, and represents men's attempts to reclaim

feelings of masculinity. Randall and his colleagues argue that "bodybuilders embody the traditional message that muscles are the sign of masculinity."

Gillett and White, similarly, discuss "the erosion of conventional notions of masculine identity." They write that "one way in which men can attempt to reclaim and reassert this conventional patriarchal version of masculinity is through the cultivation of their bodies according to some hypermasculine body image."

Sociologist Michael Kimmel, similarly, has chronicled the ascent of women into traditionally masculine arenas, particularly the workplace. Men are no longer defined by their role as "breadwinners"—a term used since the early 1800s, but now fading from our vocabulary. Kimmel believes the current interest in the male body is a result of "the collapse of the workplace as an arena in which to test and prove masculinity." In another recent book, *Stiffed: The Betrayal of the American Male*, feminist author Susan Faludi has argued, through the use of rich case examples, that masculinity is in crisis as gender lines have blurred in contemporary society. Journalist Michelle Cottle, in an influential recent article, has noted that "with women growing ever more financially independent, aspiring suitors are discovering that they must bring more to the table than a well-endowed wallet if they expect to win (and keep) the fair maiden."[9]

What is new in our culture is the huge rise in single motherhood and the absent father (whose absence, it has been noted over and over again, has wreaked havoc on the black community). This is a deadly combination not only from a social perspective (fatherless boys commit far more crimes, use more drugs, and are more engaged in anti-social behavior) but also from a religious perspective, in that the numbers of men who live out their responsibilities motivated by religious commitments and practice have declined.

Women in the Church

We now turn to the Church and the role of women in it. Let us take note: as in society at large, there is no doubt that women in the Church have made long-overdue advances in a relatively short time. These advances are the result of a steady, uninhibited look at the past and at the crises of the present, such as the priest shortage.

Mary, the mother of Jesus; Mary Magdalene, dubbed an apostle and the first witness to the risen Christ; the Samaritan woman at the well, who announces the Messiah to her townsfolk; the woman caught in adultery; the woman who anointed Jesus' feet; the impressive list of women in the Acts of the Apostles and in the epistles—Priscilla, Trophosa, Julia, Dorcas, and so on: all of these women speak of vital discipleship and shared ministry in the early Church. A recovery and appreciation of that tradition has been celebrated in the present time. For example, in his 1963 encyclical, Pacem in Terris, Pope John XXIII wrote that one characteristic of modern times is:

> Women are gaining an increasing awareness of their natural dignity. Far from being content with a purely passive role or allowing themselves to be regarded as a kind of instrument, they are demanding both in domestic and in public life the rights and duties which belong to them as human persons. (41)

The Second Vatican Council boldly talked about "the new social relationships between men and women," proclaiming that there is "in Christ and in the Church no inequality on the basis of race or nationality, social condition or sex." A continuous stream of documents, from the writings of Pope John Paul II to the statements of the U.S. bishops, have propelled this trajectory right up to the point of declaring as worthy for Sainthood such diverse modern women as Mother Katharine Drexel, Sister Benedicta (Edith Stein), and Dorothy Day.

As a result, there is hardly a position, short of ordination, women do not fill today in the Church. They serve as Eucharistic ministers, lectors, DREs, principals, diocesan chancellors, marriage tribunal advocates, canon lawyers, pastoral associates, parish administrators, chaplains in hospitals and prisons, spiritual directors, campus ministers, liturgists—actually, in all areas of lay ministry. The Study on Parish Ministry points out that of the 30,000 lay ecclesial ministers currently in the Church, some 85% are female. Nor should we fail to note that from 1970 on, an increasing number of women are studying theology. Recent research estimates that by 2010, in the English-speaking world, 60% of all theologians in the Catholic Church will be laypeople and three-quarters of those will be women. (What is often forgotten, by the way, is that in the early Church a sizable number of theologians were laypeople or wrote some of their works before taking on the clerical or religious state, for example, Justin Martyr, Origen, Prosper of Aquitaine, and Egeria, the lady who gave us the fascinating journal of her journeys. It was only later, in medieval times, that theology got clericalized, too.)

The prominent role of women in today's Church is the result of solid Christian feminism, which has rightly confronted a tradition that, for almost two thousand years, marginalized women. Christian feminism has challenged the female experience of being devalued accessories to men, which led to a denial of basic political, economic, educational, and legal rights. Thus Christian feminism defines itself as:

> A worldview or stance that affirms the equal human dignity of women, criticizes patriarchy for violating this dignity, and advocates change to bring about more just and mutual relationships between women and men and human beings with the earth—and does so based on the deepest truths of the [G]ospel itself. Its assumptions, criticisms, and goals are drawn from the message and spirit of Jesus the Christ encountered from the perspective of women's experience.[10]

As we have noted before, there is a loud—since they have the media's ear and teach at the universities—radical, "pagan" style of feminism that denigrates men, family life, motherhood, and children, sees women as victims rather than morally responsible persons, and uses inflated rhetoric and statistics to bring division rather than unity.[11] But Christian feminism takes a different stance. It looks for equity between men and women, not the dominance of one sex over the other. Its model is Jesus' community of equals rather than a community modeled after ancient Rome. It seeks partnership in the Church, not subservience. Thus, lecturers in spirituality at St. Mary's College in Notre Dame, Indiana, issued "The Madeleva Manifesto" (named after a pioneering woman, Madeleva Wolff, CSC) in April of 2000, which declared, "We deplore, and hold ourselves morally bound to protest and resist, in [C]hurch and society, all actions, customs, laws and structures that treat women or men as less than fully human."

Yet even as you read this, such treatment is still an uphill struggle because, as Margaret O'Brien Steinfels writes:

> The institutional, hierarchical [C]hurch remains a male pre-serve. It is difficult for a tight-knit, self-perpetuating group of priests and bishops—not so much as individuals but as a group and institutionally placed—to comprehend and imagine the earth shaking, world-changing revolution going on in women's lives: by education, by fewer children, by longer life expec-tancy and by the expansion of women's roles into every nook and cranny of the world.[12]

This is a large challenge: to provide the laity—men in general and women in particular—with a legitimate forum to offer their dis-cernment, since the world belongs "principally to them." Yes, lay folk can offer opinions on Church matters, but such opinions are still under the authority of the clergy. There is no equal partner-ship between the laity and the clergy, and women, traditionally marginalized, rightly feel this most strongly. Above all, they are excluded from power and, as we said, have no voice in influencing the Church's teaching. Their gifts are not being used to shape a brave new Church, and that is both tragedy and loss. The common good will never be common until all are included.

The fact is, the Church in the post-Christian era can never function rightly until women are given equal voice, equal input, and an equal forum. When that comes, it is hoped that, as they come to the roundtable, women will avoid the institutional concerns that so preoccupy the male hierarchy and instead focus more on personal and global issues.

A red flag

If we put all that we have written so far about the gains and losses of men and women in the larger social context into the context of the Church, then there are certain cautions concerning the presence of women in the Church. Let's begin with words I wrote in the book *The Parish of the Next Millennium*:

> [The] in-place phenomenon of feminized male clergy is heightened now by the predominance of women in ministry and ministerial positions. In fact, more than once it has been observed that the Catholic Church has a masculine structure and a feminine soul—but now even the structure is turning feminine. The result is that if some women are alienated from the Church because of its masculine structure, some men are alienated from the Church because of its feminine soul and growing feminine structure. We have a growing imbalance. Men (in comparatively small numbers) may attend Church, but they do not pray, have no or little interest in spirituality, and less in ecclesial concerns. They do not relate to the feminine Church-soul. They sense this feminine dominance in the songs that are sung, the liturgy and paraliturgies, the architecture, the decorations, the liturgical dance. Go to any workshop or first penance for children or a communal confession or conference and you'll be present at a lovely service attuned more to women than to men. All these things that so often reflect the sensibilities of the female and psychologically "femininized" priests do not attract men.

In point of fact, men are seen in church less and less. Franklin Graham, Billy's son and successor, is quoted in *Time* as saying, "We're losing in this country to Islam." By that he means that in the future, if things keep up, churches will be filled with all female worshippers and mosques with all male worshippers. My guess is that the growing popularity of such movements as Promise Keepers is a subconscious need to reclaim identity and affirmation vis à vis a highly aggressive feminine agenda. If you put the absence of men in church and church positions into the social context of today, you sense a wider picture of alienation.[13]

These words were given new emphasis in a recent book entitled *The Church Impotent: The Feminization of Christianity*, by Leon J. Podles.[14] In it he points out the fact that, with the exception of Eastern Orthodoxy, Christianity is the only one of the world's religions to have a higher proportion of women than men in its membership. In some parishes, he reports, the ratio is as high as 7:1, whereas Islam and Judaism and the Eastern religions have a predominantly male membership with almost two males for every female.

He traces this decline in males within Christianity—they used to be predominant in Christianity until the thirteenth century—to the affective spiritual movements and mysticism of that century, along with the very feminine popular devotions that followed, devotions that held up Mary as the model of passive obedience. Even men were to be "brides of Christ." It is noteworthy, Podles says, that in the fourteenth century, the rate of canonized female saints rose from 50% to 71%, and "the remaining male saints were not laymen, but monks and clerics." Podles is concerned that as the number of men in the Church continues to decline and the number of women in it continues to grow, then indeed we will have completed the feminization of Christianity. As one commentator on this book said, "Perhaps the Church's message needs to be gender adjusted. We can try changing the sign in front of the church from 'We Care about You' to 'Faith Demands Things of You.'"

I think we need to go back and reread the plight of men, along with their struggle for identity, in order to appreciate the context for the following remarks. It comes down to this. Already denigrated by social stigma, taught for most of their lives by women in school, soon to be tutored by Catholic theologians who will be predominantly female, what do the men and boys who do go to church see? If they see the dominance of a female congregation, female acolytes, female Eucharistic ministers, female lectors, and now female preachers—Bishop Milone of Great Falls-Billings, Montana has recently commissioned eighty laypeople to preach at Sunday communion services—if the iconography and hymns are feminine; if the liturgies are feminine, executed by those priests who bring feminine sensitivities to the service; if the Gospel message of sweet consolation is not matched by a "masculine" call to strive like an athlete and lay aside sin; if the call is to be like "sweet Jesus" and not to honor and valor; if the number of priests who serve as role models actually continues to decline (especially if we do have female priests); finally, if once more we take into account the current sociological context—namely, that they may be among the one out of every four babies born without a father or part of the large cadre of households led by females only or victims of the nearly 50% divorce rate—then common sense tells us that the Church has really nothing to offer to men but more of the same. Why should they go to Mass? Why shouldn't they drop out?

Does this mean that as a corrective I would advocate diminishing the ministry of women? Hardly. I have no desire to subtract the role of women but rather, on the contrary, to add to the role of men. In the interest of true collaboration, of genuine diversity, I am advocating a balance of male and female. The absence of men is not well-served by filling the vacuum with women. More male role models, both in lay ministry and as clergy, will do more for the Church than substituting an overabundance of females to take over the tasks of absent priests.

When all is said and done, matriarchy is a poor substitute for patriarchy. We have to offer better pay for ecclesial ministries in order to attract men who want to raise a family. We have to offer liturgies that appeal to both sexes. Just as when the clerical culture takes on a gay tilt it no longer represents the Church at large, so too, when the Church culture takes on an unbalanced, feminine tilt, it no longer represents the Church at large. Little boys who are invited to kneel quietly at the shrine of Mother Faustina yet are not allowed to wield the ax of St. Boniface will not feel compelled to grow into the Catholic men we need.

Perhaps Andrew Sullivan's intriguing words in a provocative piece he wrote for the *New York Times Magazine* sum it up:

> As our economy becomes less physical and more cerebral, as women slowly supplant men in many industries, as income inequalities grow and more highly testosteroned blue-collar men find themselves shunted to one side, we will have to find new ways of channeling what nature has bequeathed us. I don't think it's an accident that in the last decade there has been a growing focus on a muscular male physique in our popular culture, a boom in crass men's magazines, an explosion in violent computer games or a professional wrestler who has become governor. These are indications of a cultural displacement, of a world in which the power of testosterone is ignored or attacked, with the result that it reemerges in cruder and less social forms. Our main task in the gender wars of the new century may not be how to bring women fully into our society, but how to keep men from seceding from it, how to reroute testosterone for constructive ends, rather than ignore it for political point-making.[15]

Thus, the main task in the gender wars of the new century may not be how to bring women fully into our Church, but how to keep men from seceding from it.

12

THE TWELFTH CHALLENGE

The Crises of Authority and Identity

Authority there must be. Hierarchy there always was and will be. The issue for both is use, not abuse. As for hierarchy, it exists in the mineral, vegetable, and animal kingdoms. It is not surprising that it is part and parcel of human society—or even of a religious society where we not only loudly proclaim that "Jesus Christ is Lord," but also a Lord who told his leaders that they would rule over the twelve tribes of Israel (not very egalitarian!).

At its worst, the word "hierarchy" connotes oppressive control. It is often associated with authoritarianism, domination, patriarchy, and rigidity. And too often, the association has been accurate. Yet, because every sizable society needs hierarchy to function, the word should not always have a negative association. What matters is whether we are talking about a top-down type of hierarchy, or one that is more participatory. The former is exclusive and unilateral; the latter is inclusive and shared. The latter honors subsidiarity, does not interfere with autonomy, and is open to dialogue and consensus. Participatory hierarchy is much like that of the first council of Jerusalem, where the issue of circumcision was discussed, then the decision made and delivered by James, not Peter. People really do not mind hierarchy—they live with it all the time and know that someone has to be in charge—as long as they have input into the process. It is the lack of such input that has been the problem with the hierarchy of the Church. No doubt, reform is needed in the Church today in order to make the hierarchy more open to the people and representative of them.

It's hard to avoid comment about the famous or infamous Vatican bureaucracy. Let's say that it's liable to all the faults of any bureaucracy. (Think of our government.) Lobbyists buy influence, factions undermine each other and the papacy, The Roman Curia is a hotbed of intrigue. There is a lack of coordination among the many departments. Status is very important, with titles sought and position indicated by red shoes, ornate brocades, *cappa magnas* (those long billowing trains like brides wear). Finances are shady. For instance, in June of 2013, the Italian police arrested a bishop, Nunzio Scarano, a senior Vatican bank official, and two other men on suspicion of financial fraud connected with the Vatican's Institute of Religious Works.

Authority issues

Church authority—at least its current form of operation—also is in need of reform. And this stricture goes all the way to the top. First, John Paul II, sensing that something is out of whack, himself called for a reform of the papacy. In an important encyclical entitled *Ut Unum Sint* ("That All May Be One"), he addressed the changes that need to be made in the exercise of the papal authority, which could make the papacy a source of unity rather than division. He invited Church leaders and theologians to dialogue with him so that together they could "find a way of exercising the primacy, which, while in no way renouncing what is essential to its mission, is nonetheless open to a new situation" (#95, 96). John R. Quinn, the former archbishop of San Francisco and former president of the National Conference of Catholic Bishops, was one person who picked up on the invitation and wrote a book provocatively entitled *The Reform of the Papacy*.

Actually, the call for reform of the papacy goes back centuries, from the cries from the Augustinian monk, Martin Luther, to those of the Catholic Bishop St. John Fisher. These days, however, the reform being called for is not personal, as indeed it was in the heyday of the "bad popes." To wit: Stephen VI was imprisoned and strangled, John VIII was hammered to death, and John X was murdered. Sergius

III had a son by one of the daughters of the infamous Theophylact's family, and this son eventually became John XI, who in turn witnessed the marriage of his mother to her brother-in-law. John XIII was not yet twenty when he became pope and died while visiting his mistress. Benedict VI was strangled. John XIX was a layman who in one day received all the ecclesiastical orders in order to ascend the papal throne. Sylvester III sold his papal title to Gregory VI. Alexander VI had mistresses. And so it went, like a modern-day soap opera. The good news is that for almost the last two centuries, the occupants of the papal throne have been honorable and even saintly men, a refreshing change. Thus, the call is for reform of the papal office itself and of the corporate extension of its will, the Curia.

The papacy

Few people outside of historians realize how unimportant the papacy was in the early days of the Church. There was, of course, never a debate that the bishop of Rome indeed had a primacy of position and respect conferred by Christ, ruling as he did in the hallowed place where the pillars of the Church, Peter and Paul, were martyred. The pope could claim some special prerogatives, but his actual influence was quite limited and well within the prerogatives circumscribed by his fellow bishops elsewhere.

As Cardinal Ratzinger wrote, it was only after the Council of Nicaea in the fourth century that the question of the relationship between primacy and episcopacy could be posed as one might pose it today. Even the word "pope" (father) was for several hundred years a title commonly given to any bishop. For the first thousand years or so of the Church, the pope was a marginal figure, presiding over only one spot in a disconnected, far-flung world. He did not "run the Church," issued no encyclicals—they are a relatively modern invention—defined no dogmas, had no bishops pay him an official visit, and did not call or preside at the ecumenical councils, which were convened, like the very first one at Nicaea, by the emperors.

At times the popes would deal with certain leaders in society, but basically they exercised their power rather locally. They were chosen locally by the clergy and laity of Rome, who never chose someone who was a bishop elsewhere. It was only with the election in 882 A.D. of Pope Marinus I, who was already a bishop in Tuscany, that this precedent was broken. This ninth-century novelty ultimately paved the way for Karol Wojtyla, a bishop in far-off Poland, to become the Bishop of Rome and Pope John Paul II.

Even up to the modern age, the pope appointed very few bishops. In fact, less than a hundred and seventy-five years ago, out of the six hundred and forty-six Roman Catholic bishops in the world, only twenty-four were directly appointed by the pope. The rest were appointed by kings, emperors, local synods, and so on. Historically, laypeople participated in the decision-making process. Bishops were autonomous in their own dioceses, which were under the purview of local chapters and councils. In fact, so peripheral was the papacy that the first catechisms, issued in early medieval times, do not even mention it.

And so, for some fifteen hundred years, very few people even knew about the papacy, and hardly anyone thought it had anything to do with the way they lived their lives. All this is a far cry from our times of mass communications, when the press reports on every papal utterance, encyclicals are routinely issued, churches display the papal flag, and Catholics, along with the rest of the world, equate the Church with the pope and the pope with the Church: Ubi Petrus, ibi Ecclesia ("Where Peter is, there is the Church"). The world views bishops, dioceses, and parishes as franchises of Rome and of the papacy, much as we view the local Chevrolet dealer as a franchise of General Motors.

What moved the localized papacy from a position of respect to a position of power, that of universal overseer? For one thing, historical books tend to tell the stories from the top down and so they become a record of leaders—think of all the "history of the popes" books that dot our shelves—giving the impression that, from the beginning, the popes were pivotal for the whole Church. As we have seen, this is simply not true. Indeed, history writers gave more press to the popes than reality warranted. Second, starting with the invention of the printing press in the fifteenth century up to the latest technological marvel, it is now possible to keep tabs on every president, congress-person, celebrity, and leader, including the pope. That in itself has transformed the latter into a composite media figure for Catholicism, heightening the identity of the Church with the pope.

Finally, there was, in fact, a definitive event in history that set the stage for the sovereign papacy we have now, and it was called the Investiture Controversy. At the start of the eleventh century, a bishop, like all clerics, was a vassal of a feudal lay overlord and usually had been appointed by the overlord. When the bishop was to take title to the land donated by that same overlord, the latter would "invest" him, that is, give him the crozier and the ring signifying that the land now belonged to the bishop, although he remained the overlord's vassal, his man. Yet there was an unsettling ambiguity in this gesture. By handing over the crozier and the ring, the overlord might be seen as conferring ecclesiastical power and therefore, in effect, running the Church.

In the latter part of the eleventh century, Pope Gregory VII, forti-fied by powerful and popular reform movements, came along and declared that this "usurpation" was quite intolerable. Only another bishop, he maintained, could give the crozier and ring. Pope Gregory and others in the reform movement argued strongly for bishops to be elected by their clergy and not simply appointed by the local mag-nate or king. Moreover, they knew that if the reforms begun earlier against clerical immorality and simony were to succeed, it was im-perative that the overlords keep their hands off the appointment of priests and bishops.

The pope and the reformers were at loggerheads with the kings and emperors. (This conflict, by the way, spawned one of history's most colorful pro-pope tableaux: the emperor Henry IV, who had appointed bishops, was excommunicated by Gregory VII for this practice. Sensing [rightly] that there were not a lot of people who supported him, Henry stood barefoot in the snow at Canossa, Italy and submitted to Gregory VII.) The point of the Investiture Controversy was to gradually expand the pope's power and prestige, take away any royal appointment of bishops, and move into papal hands what had formerly been in the hands of the emperors and kings. This would take centuries to become the norm, but the process had been started.

Pope Gregory VII, often called the father of the modern papacy, wove the theory that would give rise to the centralization we know today. He held that the papacy was primarily a governmental institution and as such needed laws which would implement justice. (Of course, what was considered justice would be determined by the Roman Church.) Yet turning to the law gradually introduced a heavy legalism into the Church, making it more of an institution and less of a mystery—a condition that would not begin to be reversed until Vatican II. Gregory argued forcefully that his position was founded on the papal doctrine of binding and loosing, even in temporal matters. The pope, he went so far as to say, exercises a universal role over all of Christendom, which included emperors and kings. Every Christian, serf or king, owed unconditional obedience to the papacy. Gregory even made the novel claim that he could excommunicate and depose kings. Naturally, this did not set too well with royalty, and was hotly contested even by other bishops.

Gregory was the first pope to begin sending his legates throughout the empire in order to make a connection to the Roman See. He also wanted all bishops to visit the Holy See, although this practice did not catch on until much later. There is no doubt that this intelligent and energetic pontiff did much to rescue the Church from secular control, but in the process he unwittingly laid the foundation for a different kind of Church: one of laws, centralization, and a budding bureaucracy.

By the fourteenth century, an effective papal bureaucracy had been put into place, building on what Gregory had started. Then, in the sixteenth century, the Reformation's attack on the papacy ironically brought it into more prominence. Catholics were derisively called papists, which inadvertently forged a solid connection and focus on the person and power of the pope. Strong Protestant leaders like Luther, Zwingli, and Calvin also promoted the novel assumption that indeed, truth is established through individual genius.

Up to this point in history, theology was very much a communal enterprise, a give and take among theologians until a consensus was reached. Now the theological tradition was subsumed as the reigning pontiff became regarded as the most authentic interpreter of revelation in Scripture and Tradition—which, in turn, produced the tension we see today between the magisterium and the theologians. In reaction to the Reformation, the Catholic Catechisms of the time began to define the Church as "under the governance of Peter and his successors, the vicar of Christ," although the Council of Trent found the exact nature and extent of papal authority too imprecise to even address. Two centuries later, popes began to write encyclicals, the first one being issued by Pope Benedict XIV on December 3, 1740. This signaled the fact that popes would no longer be merely judges of doctrine, but had become teachers. Popes succeeding Benedict XIV wrote few encyclicals, but they became a regular staple with Popes Pius IX and John Paul II, while Pope Benedict XVI wrote three.

As we read before, the reform popes wanted the kings to keep their hands off the appointment of bishops, instead directing the clergy to elect them. Now even that was suppressed, as the pope took over the task of appointing all the bishops himself. Yet in actual fact, the papacy remained remote for most Catholics. Even the great missionary ventures of the sixteenth and seventeenth centuries went on with little involvement of the papacy.

The Italian Revolution of the 1870s brought a definitive change. This conflict caused Pius IX to flee from an encroaching army and lock himself up as a voluntary prisoner in the Vatican. This dramatic gesture was widely reported, and brought forth both publicity and sympathy. Because of the development of photography during the nineteenth century, pictures of the pope accompanied newspaper stories relayed around the world. And in this we have the beginning of the cult of the popes, which was in fact encouraged by Pius IX, who went on to make the first papal definition of a dogma (the Immaculate Conception) and preside over the council which declared papal infallibility. From that point on, the rest literally was history. Movie cameras were admitted into St. Peter's, and ultimately millions of people could see Pius XI, Pius XII, and John XXIII along with the colorful happenings of Vatican II. Aided by the sophisticated technology available today, the very visible presence of John Paul II in his many public appearances and unprecedented travel confirmed the identity of Catholicism with the pope.

When, over eight centuries ago, Gregory VII set all of this in motion, he was fighting for reform and wrestling control over the clergy from the local feudal lords and emperors. There is no doubt that, in centuries to come, what he initiated and the theories he pushed forward would culminate in the high centralization of the papacy as we know it today. In fact, it took only a century to move from Gregory VII being regarded as the "vicar of Peter" to Innocent III's self-designation as the "vicar of Christ"—not to mention Innocent's declaration that he was even above the Church, seeing himself and the papacy as "set midway between God and man, below God but above men, given not only the universal Church but the whole world to govern." This assumed sole leadership of the whole Christian world gradually overshadowed the collegiality of other bishops and found its high point in the First Vatican Council, which declared Pius IX and all future popes infallible. It has produced the Church of laws and centralization we have today and for which John Paul II has called for reform.[1]

The issue of centralization

Papal and curial centralization presents a challenge to the Catholic world. To begin with, there are the questions of collegiality and collaboration, principles that are found in theory, but not in fact.

Centralization has swallowed up all local initiatives, charisms, and independent authority. It has all but obliterated collegiality and the standing of the other bishops as equal partners. They have effectively been reduced to second-class lackeys carrying out Rome's orders instead of being collaborators in those orders. Likewise, centralization has bred control, secrecy, censure, suspicion, and a certain small-mindedness.

A prime example of the negative effect of centralization is seen in the case of Archbishop Rembert Weakland of Milwaukee. A few years back, Weakland held hearings with women to listen to their views on abortion, and even criticized some of the more overt tactics of the anti-abortion movement. For this, the Vatican punished him by persuading Fribourg University not to award him an honorary degree which had already been promised to him. Other examples are found in the Vatican applying pressure on a Catholic university in Holland to withdraw its plans to name a chair of theology after the Dominican priest Edward Schillebeeckx; or the Vatican's silencing of Fr. Bob Nugent and Sr. Jeannine Gramick for their work with homosexuals. These types of action without open public discussion rub people the wrong way.

A more current irritation is the way the Vatican handled the new translation of the Mass in the new Sacramentary that took effect in Advent of 2011. The polls show that almost 80% of the priests dislike the translation. The archaic, churchy words no one understands, the long Ciceronian paragraphs, the clumsy phrasing that makes public prayer awkward, and the lack of any spiritually nourishing ideas are all irritants. Bishop Donald Trautman, for example, the former chairman of the U.S. Bishops' liturgy committee, complains: "There are 64 words in one sentence with only two clauses. It's not English, it's not pastoral, it's impossible. I couldn't make sense of it." My take is that the Mass canons were written by someone for whom English is a second language.

The translation was imposed without American input. The Association of U.S. Catholic Priests has sent a resolution to Rome for permission to use the old 1974 edition of the Sacramentary, but it has little chance of being heard. Yet, other counties such as Germany and Italy have refused to use the new missal. The point is a top-down bureaucracy, a lack of collegiality.

The thing is that Vatican has a hard time with the tendency of Americans to at least dialogue with the "opposition," to openly discuss differences. As we saw in the Preface, trying to suppress dialogue in an electronic age is both futile and foolish. When will the Vatican realize that the Internet has flattened all hierarchies and that information has been democratized?

Then there was the wish of the U.S. bishops to appoint Sr. Sharon Euart as General Secretary of the National Conference of Catholic Bishops. After all, not only is she a respected canon lawyer, but she had been Associate General Secretary for more than ten years. She knew the ropes. The bishops asked Rome about this prospective appointment and Rome said no, the Secretary has to be a priest and the NCCB must change its bylaws to reflect that requirement. The fact that the national bishops felt obligated to seek Rome's permission is, as we have seen, a novelty. That Rome could interfere and be heeded is another. And that a competent woman was found to be ineligible solely because as a woman she cannot be a priest gives centralization a shamed face.

There have been cases where bishops have not known in advance about some matters concerning their own dioceses, such as finding out that one of their own priests had been made a bishop. And they are ignored. The Curia does not respond to bishops' repeated calls for a married clergy. Worse, especially for those bishops from democratic countries, Rome closes discussion on certain subjects, saying they cannot be discussed. The suggestions that come from regional conferences of bishops are routinely ignored by the Curia. Even at the worldwide synod of bishops with the Holy Father, the agenda is rigidly set. Certain issues like divorce and celibacy are not allowed to be put on the table. Theologians are silenced without redress and seminaries are controlled.

Garry Wills, a distinguished layman, scholar—one of the best intellectuals around—and a practicing Catholic (whose sarcastic remark on gay clergy we quoted in chapter ten), was frustrated enough to write a book provocatively entitled *Papal Sin*, in which he takes papal centralization to task. In an "angry and sometimes ill-tempered and on occasion, savage" book, as Andrew Greeley characterizes it—indeed, it is a good and powerful book, although unbalanced in some areas—Wills castigates papal coercion, saying it has reduced councils to impotence and everyone beneath the pope to passive receptors of his wisdom. As an example, he cites Pius IX's disregard of his advisors, ramming through his embarrassing "Syllabus of Errors" in which he condemned reason, freedom of religion, democracy, and modern life, among other things. Pius IX shamelessly maneuvered the passing of the doctrine of papal infallibility by bullying his opponents, and when one of them had the temerity to suggest that no such doctrine could be justified by tradition, Pius yelled at him, "I am tradition. I am the [C]hurch."

Unilateral Actions

To bolster Wills's thesis that some papal actions are unilateral, we can point out that Pius IX—who in no way was or is the object of popular devotion, one of the criteria for canonization—has now been beatified by John Paul II. Ironically, John Paul II, if he lived in Pius' time, would have found himself in the papal prison for his kindly approach to the Jews (Pius instituted anti-Jewish laws), his advocacy of human rights and religious freedom (Pius condemned the thesis that everyone is free to adopt and profess the religion that he holds to be true), and commitment to ecumenism (Pius denounced Protestantism). And so it would seem that the pope or a small group has put forth for beatification an unpopular conservative pope and advocate of centralization without the consent or approval of the whole Church.

Wills is also utterly dismayed that Paul VI took the question of birth control out of the hands of his own lay commission, which had approved the use of birth control, and condemned it for the simple reason that he was fearful of contradicting Casti Connubii, the encyclical issued by Pius XI. (Paul VI was both surprised and chagrined at the opposition Humanae Vitae, his encyclical addressing this subject, evoked from the hierarchies, bishops, and priests, and its rejection by the laity, and he never wrote another encyclical again.) Wills cites the condemnation of birth control as a unilateral decision that burdened the rest of the Catholic world. "The pope alone, we are now asked to accept, is competent to tell Christian people how to live....The Holy Spirit now speaks to only one person on earth."[2]

There is no doubt that there are unilateral pronouncements and condemnations made within the papacy, as well as a lack of due process and consultation. On June 30, 1998, for example, John Paul II issued an apostolic letter, "To Defend the Faith," citing canonical penalties for those who dissent from "definitive but non-infallible teachings." (An example would be his letter on forbidding the ordination of women.) But surely this letter raises more questions than it solves. Does that mean that any "definitive but non-infallible" teaching— which in fact is neither revealed nor clearly established as infallibly proclaimed, but simply given on papal authority—is now considered off-limits? You can't question or discuss such a teaching any further? And under penalty, at that. How can you close off discussions about, say, women's ordination without large consultation? A Gallup poll taken in June 2000 shows that seven in ten people favor seeing women ordained. This doesn't mean doctrine should be defined by head count, but it does mean that careful consideration should be given to a consensus of the faithful. In any case, pronouncements such as "To Defend the Faith," coupled with practices of denial and secrecy, are always ill-formed strategies in an era of cyberspace, the Internet, hidden microphones, eavesdropping technology, an open society, and investigative reporting.

Here is another instance of insensitivity. In July 2000, the Pontifical Council reiterated the strictures of Canon 915, that those who remarry after a divorce and without an annulment cannot receive the Eucharist. Moreover, the Council added the claim that such a prohibition was based on "divine law" and could not be modified. Yet people wonder, where does God say that? And people who have remarried without having obtained an annulment wonder how a repentant yet convicted mass murderer can receive Communion, but they can't because they are considered "unrepentant" because they're still living together? Further, priests should not only refuse to give Communion to those remarried without an annulment, but also instruct their Eucharistic Ministers to do likewise (which conjures up images of a weekly blacklist complete with photos of the offenders).

Finally, it is an open secret that many bishops and priests throughout the world would like to see the strictures of Canon 915 relaxed, and in fact do not enforce it. Many European bishops have pushed for a reconsideration. In the early nineties, for example, the German bishops issued guidelines for cases in which divorced and remarried Catholics might be admitted to the sacraments. In 1998, a group of German bishops proposed that those who are divorced and remarried be allowed full participation in the sacraments after a period of repentance. In 1999, Godfried Cardinal Danneels of Belgium opted for a change, citing the stand of the Orthodox Church on this issue. Why do the various bishops and priests feel that the restrictions must be eased? Perhaps because they, like the rest of us, feel the truth of these words:

> Pastors must know that for the sake of truth, they are obliged to exercise careful discernment of situations. There is in fact a difference between those who have sincerely tried to save their first marriage and have been unjustly abandoned, and those who through their own grave fault have destroyed a canonically valid marriage. Finally, there are those who have entered into a second union for the sake of the children's upbringing

and who are sometimes subjectively certain in conscience that their previous and irreparably destroyed marriage had never been valid.

Surprisingly, it was John Paul II who wrote these words back in 1981.

Another area deeply affected by centralization and secrecy is the incidence of AIDS in the priesthood. In a previous chapter, we noted the treatment of priests who die from AIDS. There seems to be no open attempt on the part of the hierarchy to admit that this situation exists, much less ask hard questions about it. When an archbishop in Rome died of AIDS, those responsible for his body had his legs broken so that the cause of death could be listed as accidental.[3] A priest in my own diocese died of AIDS, but it was never publicly acknowledged or talked about. Necessary questions are not being surfaced, such as, how many priests are infected with HIV/AIDS? Is there any relationship between the clerical lifestyle and this disease? Does the presence of gay teachers and students in the seminary affect the kind of education received by men studying for the priesthood? Does the Church's official understanding of homosexuality contribute to the problem?

There is a small silver lining in all of this. The public scrutiny of the Church, the widespread exposure of pedophilia among priests, and the existence of AIDS among clergy have all moved the official Church, after much stonewalling and denial, into formulating an extremely creative, honest, and pastoral response. For the most part, the Church is now dealing far more openly with HIV-infected clergy, as well as listening attentively to the stories of gay clergy, providing care and formation, and giving much attention on the seminary level to the psychosexual development of persons.

It comes down to this. So much of the current crisis in the Church is squarely centered on the question of integrity. The official Church sometimes places its image ahead of truth, and behaves more like a worldly corporation than a community of disciples. On too many occasions, it denies obvious crises and stonewalls investigations.

Worse, it puts a lid on open discussion, acting as if everyone in the world did not know about clerical sexual abuse and AIDS, double-dealing, financial scandals, and the priest shortage. It embraces secrecy, punishes questioners, and retreats to authoritarianism. Within the hierarchy, there is a lack of candor along with intellectual dishonesty. This is no way to run a Church, a community of people no longer called servants but friends (see Jn 15:15).

Attempts at reform

Now and then there are signs of reform. The matter of papal centralization is one area up for discussion. The Curia has been twice reformed since Vatican II and there are further proposals on the board for reform. In December of 1998, the Congregation for the Doctrine of Faith published a significant but little-known document titled "Reflections on the Primacy of Peter," which clearly states that the papacy should recognize the Church's communal and collegial structure. The document squarely places the Bishop of Rome within the college of bishops and notes that all bishops are also "vicars and ambassadors of Christ," and that the pope does not have absolute power: "Listening to what the churches are saying is, in fact, an earmark of the ministry of unity, a consequence also of the unity of the episcopal body and...of the entire people of God." That is a pretty forceful official statement for collegiality and against unilateral papal or curial decisions.

Furthermore, and even more remarkably, "Reflections on the Primacy of Peter" says that the way the papacy has worked in the past was historically conditioned, which means it does not necessarily need to work the same way today. Moreover, the bishops and the pontiff must collaborate on working out what the papacy might mean today. This approach is in sharp contrast to the traditional insistence that the scope of the papal office was divinely willed and therefore could not be tampered with. The document goes on to say, therefore, that no papal decree should be made without the participation of the bishops—who, in fact, must join in the formulation of official dogmatic decrees. The bishops should contribute even to the ordinary papal magisterium that are addressed to the universal Church. The document follows its own logic by also declaring that obviously, the Curia must no longer act on its own above the episcopacy.[4] All this is aimed to recover the Church as a communion of communities. It is obvious that this forthright document is rightly trying to balance the strengths of both centralization and decentralization, for the extremes of neither serve the Church well. The primacy of Peter must be preserved but it must be collaborative, as it "protects legitimate differences, while at the same time it sees that such differences do not hinder unity but rather contribute to it" (Dogmatic Constitution of the Church, no. 13).

These points were never followed through and implemented, and Pope Francis faces the challenge of doing so. No one is holding their breath. The Vatican bureaucracy is deeply entrenched, susceptible to ambition, greed, and manipulation. It's riddled with intrigue. It lacks coordination. A tell-all book, *Your Holiness: The Secret Papers of Benedict XVI* shows complaints of corruption by a senior Vatican official. The letters reveal a medieval Vatican culture of "Eminences" and "Excellencies" with Benedict himself leading the way by reviving the custom of wearing red shoes and ornate brocades—something immediately discarded by his successor. Cardinals, addressed as "your lordships" (Pope Francis used "brother cardinals") enjoy immunity from the law. Favoritism is rampant. Secrecy reigns. Departments move at a snail's pace. The Curia has yet to embrace modern communications technology. Pope Francis faces a formidable job.

Another area ripe for reform is the appointment of bishops. The whole process in shrouded in secrecy. At times, it seems as if the criteria for appointment rests on one's orthodoxy and on whether the candidate has made any critical public announcements on celibacy, married priests, or contraception. In secret, each bishop sends in three names for episcopal consideration—usually men from administration with little or no pastoral experience. Safe men. Very few prophets. No doubt he consults his confidants, but the Catholic community on the whole is not tapped, the very people who could assess and bear witness to the candidates' pastoral sensitivity, compassionate ministry, and effectiveness as a pastor. After all, this is the tradition, enshrined in the second-century Apostolic Tradition of Hippolytus, which flatly declared, "Let him be ordained as bishop who has been chosen by all the people." This sentiment was echoed by Pope St. Celestine in the fifth century, who said, "Let a bishop not be imposed upon the people whom they do not want" and his successor, Pope St. Leo, who declared, "He who has to preside over all must be elected by all. Let a person not be ordained against the wishes of the Christians and whom they have not explicitly asked for."

Several suggestions to reform the process: First, I would suggest that all episcopal candidates must have spent at least ten years in parish work and not just as weekend help. They must have experienced the people firsthand. Second, the people in every parish where the candidate worked should be polled as to his pastoral style and sensitivity. Finally, like the old threefold publication of banns of marriage for engaged couples, every diocesan paper throughout the land should be required to publish the banns of candidates for the office of bishop and list their names online. This way we might avoid another situation like the one that occurred in the Diocese of Palm Beach, Florida, where the bishop who succeeded an accused abuser had a history of abuse himself. We badly need to replace careerists and bureaucrats. Pope Francis early on had sharp words to say about career clergy.

In this sound-bite age of Catholic culture wars, there is the danger that opening episcopal appointments to the community at large might be to introduce popularity contests or unseemly campaigning. No doubt, there should be some higher authority to screen out eccentric candidates put forward by eccentric communities. Yet even if, for very good reasons, candidates' names are kept secret, we need to develop a way to tap the wisdom of the people and their experience of potential episcopal leaders. There should be a more widespread and inclusive way to gather information about a man's pastoral sensitivities, sense of justice, and healthy absence of careerism, which, according to then Cardinal Ratzinger before becoming Pope, are as important qualities for a bishop as is orthodoxy.

Finally, there is ongoing reform in the identity and mission of the parish priest, and the laity must learn to appreciate this. The profound changes wrought by Vatican II and its new theological vision of the Church demand new skills and virtues from priests, who struggle to cast off old mentalities and engage in a long, hard, soul-searching process of becoming someone, something, new. At one time, of course, the priest's life was stable and secure, unquestioned either by himself or others. He was the expert, the one deferred to, a moral force, a revered and sometimes feared figure. He was defined by what he could do and the laity could not. Because the Bible does not in fact offer a clearly defined view of the priesthood, throughout history the priest has had various roles. But even as the roles changed, he remained well defined. During different epochs he was always defined as a mediator, the man set apart, a leader of the community, a representative of the larger Church. All of these were valid, yet all somehow not fully accurate. But they defined him.

Now the priest is in a dilemma: he simply does not know who he is anymore or what he is supposed to do, mainly because the gap between what he can do and what the laity cannot has become narrower and narrower. True, he still has three unique functions: he can offer Mass, hear confessions, and anoint the sick. As to confessions, hardly anyone comes to the Sacrament of reconciliation anymore. As to Mass, what does the priest do after Mass is over? As to anointing the sick, laypeople have largely taken over this ministry.

One among many

The priest once had a lot to do, but now he perceives that laity have moved in and taken over all of his previously understood duties.

He has been forced by social changes to move from his old authoritarian stance as cultic priest who presided over everything, from
the sacraments to the community, with undisputed moral authority,
to a servant leader or collaborator with many folk, who are sometimes more theologically educated than himself. He is seen less and
less as the one who "brings God," and more and more as one who
helps discern God already present. He has become one among many,
demystified, not automatically given credence or respect. He has
seen his unquestioned authority vanish, his moral standing eroded.
(What was it Vatican II said? "Let the laity not imagine that their
pastors are always such experts that to every problem which arises,
they can readily give a concrete solution, or even that such is their
mission."[5])

Clerical dress, once a sign of prestige and unique status, is worn
uncomfortably since the pedophile scandals. The priest used to be
the exclusive minister of baptism, sole visitor of the sick, designated
by anointing as the singular handler of the Eucharist, reader of the
sacred Scripture, proclaimer of the Gospel, spiritual director, pastoral leader of the parish—but no more. He used to have companions
to share the clerical culture in a rectory of high architecture, but they
have since left: deceased, married, become Anglicans. His move from
authority figure to ground-level coworker has led him to move out
of the isolated grand rectory to apartments or regular houses. He is
more and more separated from his declining confreres. He is alone.
Celibacy hangs heavy here, not as a sexual outlet but for intimacy.
Archbishop Rembert Weakland says it for many:

> The trick in dealing with celibacy is to understand that there
> is no true substitute for the intimacy of marriage. We were
> taught that the Divine Office, your community, your prayer
> life were substitutes, but they are not. Travel, an intellectual
> life, and, in the case of a bishop, a measure of authority, power:
> these are not substitutes either. I'm over sixty—for me, it's not
> about sex. When it hits me hardest is not when I'm in trouble
> or want to pour my heart out because I'm depressed. It's when

I have a great idea I'd like to share with someone, when I've heard a new piece of music and want someone to sit down and listen with me.[6]

Usually, these days, the priest is all alone in a large parish where people, well taught that they are the Church, feel that they have less and less need of him. Even with multiple well-organized lay ministries and perhaps one foreign priest to help out, he is overworked and undervalued. How can he function effectively? And when you come right down to it, how important is his job when the bishop substitutes Communion Services for Mass, when deacons baptize, when laypeople visit the sick, when nuns witness marriages, and when the parish administrator writes out his check? There are few rewards (outside of an occasional monsignor robe) and fewer words of affirmation and encouragement from his bishop.

Like most priests, he finds the core of his satisfaction in simply being part of people's lives. But even here he discovers tension. For one thing, he is caught in between. He wants to be loyal to the Church and its official teachings, but since he identifies with the people he knows that some teachings and rules don't fit in with their lives. And perhaps it is here, in the painful battle to maintain his integrity, that the priest feels his personal crisis. Further, in the face of the pedophile scandals, he is hurt at finding himself suspect, not ever daring to put a comforting or encouraging arm around a kid; and he knows that even parents who like him don't want their children alone with him. Statistically, he is moving inexorably towards the age of seventy, when retirement (and more loneliness) looms, along with the insecurities of aging. He is, as Karl Rahner once put it, "dying in installments."

Vatican II was of no help at all in resolving the priestly tensions of today. In a most creative way, the council reformed the role of the laity, the role of the bishops, the place of religious men and women, the enhancement of the role of deacons, and the relationship with other churches and religions. But incredibly, it left the role of the priest unheeded and unresolved. At the time, some council fathers did call for a fuller treatment of issues concerning the priesthood; some even wanted to introduce a debate on celibacy. Celibacy was, of course, a delicate issue because the council would have to publicly argue the old standard that celibacy "is required by the very nature of the priesthood itself" in front of all those Eastern Church observers, other Christians, and Jews. And so, in October of 1965, some of the more conservative cardinals had Paul VI withdraw the topic from discussion altogether. Thus, the debate on the Decree on the Ministry and Life of Priests did not bring up the issue of celibacy.

When it was promulgated in December of 1965, the decree moved the priest from being seen as a cult figure to being a servant figure drawn from among the people. Furthermore, much was made of the fact that the priest was critical to the celebration of the Eucharist, the center of Christian life. But when all was said and done, the decree was basically a traditional, pious recipe for the priesthood. Bill Huebsch perhaps gives the best critique concerning this decree and the lack of action that followed it:

> What it does not do is take into account the fields of sociology and psychology. There is, in fact, no real reform here at all, only a restatement of the place of priests in the Church as it has been known since medieval times. And no synod or other gathering since the close of Vatican II has offered any more reform than the Council did. How will priests fit into the newly reformed role of laity and bishops, not to mention religious and deacons? How will they work in today's culture? How will their own sexual, financial, and psychological needs be met when they must live (mainly alone) in their offices, work (too many hours per week) for a mere stipend, dress in black, and be on call 24 hours a day? In suburban parishes, they are running medium-sized corporations complete with complex human resource issues, insurance headaches, and fundraising nightmares. They get little credit and less praise and most of the time, when they read about the priesthood in the newspaper, it's about clerical sexual misconduct.

Who would want the job? Even if he or she had a sense of vocation to priesthood, these unreformed features of the priesthood would keep most people away. Most would seek a life of ministry in a near-priesthood vocation such as religious education, pastoral ministry, or liturgical leadership. Others will become professors or artists or counselors or parents. Some will seek ordination in a brother or sister church where these difficulties are more nearly resolved. Meanwhile the world is starving for salvation, for a taste of the Eucharist, for the intimacy of agape. Parishes have grown to unbelievable sizes. We once knew and were in awe of parishes "in other parts of the world" with four and five thousand families. Now that size is common in the United States. In many places, the numbers are there on the books but the people aren't. We desperately need a holy, whole, and numerous priesthood for today's world.[7]

Crisis and Cross

It is a time of crisis for the priesthood, and undoubtedly the time of the Cross. Yet here may be the seeds of the priest's recovery. Devoid of privilege—perhaps a subtraction long-overdue—he must now be St. Paul's "imitator of Christ" and complete Christ's work in his own here-and-now reality. He must share Christ's pain in his current state of devaluation and suspicion and, like Peter, be led where he would not go, to new and surprising situations where he can offer his leadership to the faithful as one like them. In a word, the priest can successfully transition to a new way of being only to the degree that he assumes more and more the stance of a true disciple, a true follower, a true imitator of Jesus. Like Jesus stripped of everything, he now has nowhere to go but to the Father. "Father, into your hands I commend my spirit." The new priest will arise from the ashes of the present crisis. In his weakness he will eventually be made strong.

So the priest must start to draw closer to Christ. He must be seriously committed to continuous learning (this is important), and he must begin to redefine himself as one who is out to build consensus in a highly fractured and diverse world. Moreover, in this new world, he must be accountable to his parishioners, who, sensitive to the growing emphasis on their own performance and accountability at work, have similar expectations of him. And not only must he be a storyteller, but he must be the story:

> In a recent book on leadership, Howard Gardener sought to identify the common characteristics of a wide range of leaders—in politics, education, business, and religion. Included among them were Martin Luther King, Jr., Mahatma Gandhi, and Pope John XXIII. He suggests that true leaders achieve their impact through the stories they relate and through the way they embody these stories in the way they live their lives. Their stories are powerful because they make sense to their audiences and create a clear feeling of identity among them. They also stimulate people to action. What better example could we have than Jesus—who taught through parables and whose life of love and service to God is the model to which we aspire? What I have been suggesting here is that, in their own particular way, it is these qualities which we find in the priests who inspire us, people who can reinterpret the story of the good news in a way which makes sense to our lives now and who can demonstrate the meaning of God's love in the way they live their lives. Such priests are able to connect with us and to put us in touch with God and with each other as we make our pilgrim journey.[8]

Finally, the priest who labors in the brave new Church must work hard to mobilize the people to keep the overall vision intact, to hold the center together, and to clarify the parish's identity and mission. This is the critical mandate of pastoral leadership today and the proper use of authority in a post-Christian world. Why? Because the center will hold only if the identity in mission is clear. Discovering that identity is the challenge right now, not only for the parish but for the priest himself.

A necessary postscript. Focused as we are on the priesthood, we must understand that we are talking about the parish priests and the parish. And rightly so, for that is where most of us spend our lives and celebrate the important moments of life's journey, from Baptism to burial. We should not forget, however, that for almost a thousand years there have existed religious orders that have courageously filled in the gaps, so to speak.

The parish is necessarily a stable, geographic community that serves those faithful who come to it. It reflects the bishop's presence locally. But there is a large world beyond the parish that transcends geographical boundaries and is filled with the so-called "unfaithful"— the heretics, nonbelievers, infidels, the unchurched, the ignorant, and so on. Along with large numbers of laity, the ones who serve this larger world include the priests, brothers, and sisters of the religious orders. And most of their congregations are experiencing dwindling numbers. The members of these religious communities have long traversed the planet, entered the schools, evangelized the nations.

So we have a nice division of labor, with both parish priests and order priests, critical to the mission of the Church. Needless to say, the special ministry of the religious orders is needed more than ever today even as their numbers fall. But they too will survive to the degree that they can articulate a clear statement of mission and purpose.

PART TWO

Temporary Transitions

13

THE FALLOUTS

We have examined twelve challenges to the Church as we attempt to move from turmoil to trust. In the next chapters we will examine the current responses to some of these challenges, along with their strengths and their weaknesses. We will, however, frame our discussion primarily within the context of the priest shortage, since first of all this shortage is a collective symbol for many of the challenges we have to meet, and also, the effects of this shortage are what the average Catholic is most likely to experience firsthand. So let us turn to six easily discernible fallouts from that shortage.

First: Parish closings

Most people, as I have suggested before, are vaguely aware of the priest shortage on an intellectual level, but have not experienced it in a tangible way. For the 75% of American Catholics who do not go to church regularly, there is no opportunity to miss the clergy except at sacramental times when they go looking for a priest. Most of the 25%–40% of Catholics who do go to Mass, who are rooted in the old doctrines and ways, still have a priest at Mass, even though, in some places, the Mass schedule has been combined.

Some dioceses facing a severe shortage have yet to use sustained and sensitive public relations to reach out to the public and prepare them for the reality of shortened services and parish clustering—not to mention broadcasting the critical need for vocations. Other dioceses have been more forthright in maintaining contact with their constituencies simply because the realities of the priest shortage have forced them into closing parishes. For example, since 1986, the Archdiocese of Boston has been forced to close at least twelve parishes and has merged eight others. Diocesan officials predict that by the year 2005 it will see up to forty parishes closed, or "suppressed" (the canonical term for closing). Citing the priest shortage, the Diocese of Fall River has recently merged two parishes.

Second: Priestly overload

Recently, Roger Cardinal Mahony of Los Angeles, in a plea for more vocations, sympathetically described how overloaded the present clergy are. We all know that parishes who formerly had two or three assistants are down to one or none, thereby increasing the workload on those who remain. With the shortage they are called upon to double their efforts, and many are doing this heroically. Some are on the circuit, being pastors of two or three parishes. Some function as little more than chaplains to parishes run by nuns or laity.

At the June 2000 bishops' meeting referred to in Chapter 9, Bishop Stephen Blaire of Stockton, California, summarized the findings of eighteen focus groups comprised of priests throughout the country. In these groups, many priests reported they feel inadequate and exhausted, and that there are too many expectations of them, too much paperwork for them to do, and too much isolation in their lives. This overload has a great effect on one's inner life and morale. Too often separated from relaxation and companionship, workaholic priests, who are taken for granted by a workaholic public, soon deplete their inner lives.

More than once I have heard priests express the fear that in taking on the demands of understaffed parishes they will no longer have lives of their own. These demands erode most of their free time, as well as time when they could explore academic ventures, special ministries, or just plain creative pursuits. No wonder some turn to alcohol or absenteeism. No wonder bishops look on their shrinking middle management with a combination of alarm and compassion. There is a high price being paid on a human level for the priest shortage, a fact that is very much underrated and under-attended to.

An irony to be considered here is that, because of the priest shortage, many priests will want to retire early. This flies in the face of the logic of most bishops, who plead with their priests to stay on as long as possible. A document from Rome chimes in by stating, "The presentation of resignation at the age of 75 by a parish priest does not of itself terminate his pastoral office...[and] it should be noted that having reached the age of 75 does not constitute a binding reason for the diocesan Bishop to accept a parish priest's resignation" (Regarding the Collaboration of the Non-ordained Faithful in the Sacred Ministry of the Priest, article 5, paragraph 2). Really. What other organization puts a man of seventy-five or eighty in a management position? In reality, priests will want to retire early not only because they do not want to drop dead in their tracks but also, and most realistically, precisely because of the shortage, which means they won't have associates to help with the everyday, nitty-gritty work. At their age, why should they go it alone?

Thankfully, there are younger priests in the Church—though they are, as we have seen, in the minority—and they are potent signs of vitality. Still, we have to consider that most of the overload is being shouldered by middle-aged priests, whose median age is estimated at fifty-eight—although we know that many pastors are well into their sixties or seventies. And even though studies show that middle age is probably the happiest and most productive time in one's life, priests who have the responsibilities of large parishes without help and support qualify less and less as feeling fulfilled. Even for the most vigorous men, most of the energy of running a parish goes into maintenance, not mission. You have to work hard just to stay where you are.

This is where Protestant and Catholic clergy differ. The former are bent on increasing membership while the latter are so consumed by the huge numbers already in their congregations that they really don't want any more. Even assuming an active lay ministry, the demands of a parish—serving the 25–40% of Catholics who attend Mass, paying attention to the eclectic demands of the 75% who don't, presiding at the growing number of funeral Masses (in New Jersey, where I live, we have the largest segment of senior citizens in the nation, after Florida), witnessing weddings, attending parish council meetings, and so on—leave the priest little time for evangelization, for tracking down the lost sheep, for visiting the sick, for cultivating a Christian intellectual life and, most of all, for the personal contact that might provoke vocations. Fr. Richard Martini, the vocation director of the Archdiocese of Los Angeles, asks the obvious question, "Why are priests reluctant to invite young men to follow in their footsteps? Put simply: we are tired. Fatigue plagues us....What does the potential prospect for the priesthood see? A priest's sense of fulfillment or his expression of exhaustion?"[1]

Third: Lowered standards

Desperate for clergy, some dioceses accept candidates who are almost "brain dead" (as one perceptive layperson put it). Priests who obviously are not fit for parish life are pressed into pastorates. Inexperienced priests, ordained only five years or less, are made pastors—some quite competent, though others very green, to say the least. As the pastor of a parish of 4000 families wrote me, "Today it is less demanding to have no priest associate than one of the highly dysfunctional ones who are often all that personnel boards have to offer. With some priest associates, the volume of work increases geometrically in resolving disputes and doing interventions!"

Fourth: The need for more and smaller parishes

Because of the shortage of priests, the need for more and smaller parishes goes unfulfilled. In many parts of the country, especially in the South and the West, a large parish consists of three or four hundred families. People in such small parishes find it hard to comprehend that in many urban and metropolitan parts of the country, parishes are very large. In my own diocese of Trenton, New Jersey, some parishes are larger than some dioceses elsewhere. For example, one parish with three resident priests claims some 5700 families; another with one resident priest, 4000 families; two others, each with one resident priest, have 2500 families and 3400 families each. According to Bishop Thomas Curry, some parishes in Los Angeles have 18,000 households due to immigration!

And so it goes, especially in the metropolitan areas. Many large parishes have schools, nursing homes, hospitals, and large senior citizen developments. As the diocesan population continues to grow, more and more housing developments are erected and a vast number of Catholics simply fade into oblivion to mingle with the vast army of nominal Catholics. Very large parishes are ultimately counterproductive. No matter how gifted a pastor and his associate (if there is one) are, they must dedicate their time and energy to maintenance over and against mission. Not by choice, of course, but by necessity. Parishioners can get sick and even die without any church person knowing about it. (I recently read that today, a Catholic has a 90% chance of dying without a priest. Sounds exaggerated, but it makes a point.)

With growth in the Catholic Church plus the existence of many oversized parishes, there is an urgent need for more parishes. Everyone admits how much stronger the Catholic presence could be, how much more effectively we might stop the leakage (there are as many former Catholics as there are Southern Baptists) if there were more local, neighborhood parishes. But as urgently as we need them, the priest shortage prevents these parishes from taking root. That, as much as anything, is a fearful fallout with far-reaching consequences.

Fifth: The loss of the celebration of the Eucharist

We will explore this more fully further on in this book, but for the moment no one can deny that the saddest result of the priest shortage is that people will be denied the Eucharist, many for months at a time, some even for years. This is already happening in some countries, and it is happening here, where over 2000 parishes are priestless. My instinct is that if the Catholic laity are increasingly exposed only to the Liturgy of the Word, they will soon migrate to the Evangelical or Pentecostal churches, which may well have a better Liturgy of the Word to offer.

Sixth: Vocations suffer

We have read about the paucity of vocations in previous chapters. In this context, I will just mention the truism that most vocations come from one-on-one contact, from the idealism that a young man projects onto his parish priest. But fewer priests mean fewer contacts and less inspiration. More overworked priests, as we mentioned above, mean a more exhausted and unattractive clergy.

14

CURRENT APPROACHES AND SOLUTIONS

In general, there are six approaches to the priest shortage, ranging from the practical to the daring. Several have already been tried and all affect the Church in the post-Christian era. We will list them, giving the pros and cons of each.

First: Clustering and closing parishes

On the positive side, there are always parishes that have lost their viability. For some this is due to shifting demographics or the flight to the suburbs. Some parishes have lost their ability to financially maintain the buildings, especially those large, grand churches that served a large and churchgoing congregation of another day, but which are now mostly empty on Sundays. Some ethnic parishes face shrunken congregations as the next generations have moved into the American mainstream. It makes sense to close or merge or link some of these parishes and free up a few priests. Parishes can be revitalized through merging, gaining a more substantial and viable congregation. It would seem wise, however, to begin to alert people to such possibilities now, through a long-term and sensitive public relations campaign.

There are, as one might expect, high emotions connected with closing parishes. Old-timers have vested interests in a parish.

Feelings can be bruised, and there can be resentment over the loss of a sense of intimacy as the merger shapes the smaller parishes into a larger configuration. Some may feel that small parish faith communities, like the local Mom and Pop stores, are being sucked up by the large "conglomerates." These types of moves can be beneficial for efficiency, but they are not always so for community. Additionally, clustering parishes will lead to the collapse of the small parish. As Tom Sweester puts it:

> The pressure to make the Eucharist available to all will create a new configuration of megachurches that offer only a few Masses which are attended by large congregations...The tragedy is that in the effort to provide Eucharist to the widest population possible the system of local worshipping faith communities will be destroyed. The combining and closing of parishes in some situations does make sense....On the other hand, if a parish of 200, 500, or 1000 families is asked to combine with another one of even greater size, then the possibility of feeling "at home" and in close personal contact with one another, along with the rich traditions associated with each parish, will be lost forever. This is a great tragedy.[1]

In any case, there is no question that, as we saw above, the priest shortage fuels the decision to close or merge parishes.

Second: Seeking foreign clergy

Dioceses today are trying to import priests from India, Africa, the Philippines, Poland, and other countries. The positive side of this is the genuine help they offer in taking up the slack in this country. Many of these priests make fine contributions to our parishes. The negative side is that, with the renewed importance of preaching, a priest who speaks broken English or who is hard to understand is a liability. Furthermore, some bring backgrounds, values, and attitudes towards authority, women, and sex that are not always compatible with the American experience. It might be sensible to offer a program which, like the Peace Corps, provides training, acculturation, and apprenticeship to prospective foreign externs.

Third: Priestly rearrangements

Another possibility is that deacons can take over some parishes. In this case, priests could live in or share an apartment, and from that base, go out and celebrate Mass within a locally designated cluster of parishes. This way, each parish could have its own Mass. Of course, the normal curve of declining numbers would eventually take its toll here, too.

Priestly rearrangements may be broader in a much more literal sense, as well. We find this statement in a document from the Congregation for the Clergy, published in 1999:

> Numerical shortages of clergy, experienced in some countries, coupled with the mobility of the contemporary world make it particularly necessary to be able to call on priests who are willing to change not only pastoral assignments but also cities, regions, and countries in response to various needs and to undertake whatever mission may be necessary while renouncing personal plans and desires for the sake of the love of God.[2]

Here the world is viewed as one big grid with Vatican leaders moving priests around globally, like admirals moving their toy ships around a flat map. The desperate shortage of priests and the even greater shortage of solutions to this problem provoke suggestions like this.

Fourth: Building larger churches

To compensate for the declining clergy and fewer Masses, dioceses are encouraging parishes to build larger churches, ones that can hold from 1000 to 1500 or more parishioners. The positive side to this strategy is that gathering more people into any particular Mass is a sensible approach. The negative side is that in large buildings, a sense of intimacy and community is lost both during the liturgy as well as after, because the priest cannot possibly greet everyone at the many exits. Also, in large congregations, it is far more feasible for people to drop out of parish life without anyone noticing. The seventeen million Catholics in the United States who are inactive can easily get lost in the shuffle.

Fifth: Promoting vocations

As we have seen, this is not only a mixed venture with meager results, but also inextricably bound up with both the homosexual issue and the attitudes of women. Until these areas of conflict are resolved, vocation recruiting is a fragile and uncertain way of dealing with the priest shortage.

Sixth: More involvement of the laity

Involving more laity is already an established practice. Most parishes have a notable cadre of laypeople on staff and in various positions—almost 30,000 of them, according to the Study of Parish Ministry put out by the National Pastoral Life Center in June of 1999. In fact, a survey taken in May of 2000 found that while the number of priests serving our parishes is down 28% in the last fifteen years, the number of lay ministers is up 54%.[3] Moreover, this same survey shows that the average parish has grown 32% in the past fifteen years, while the number of priests serving parishes declined 28%; the number of deacons and religious are both down 33%. Only the number of lay ministers has grown.

This is why, for the first time, the Church in the U.S. celebrated Jubilee Day for Lay Ministry on November 26, 2000 (significantly, the weekend of Thanksgiving and the feast of Christ the King), with a theme of "Together in God's Service." As much as anything, this was a public bow to the enduring reality of lay ministry, an acknowledgment of the fact that "through Baptism and Confirmation, all are appointed to this apostolate by the Lord himself" (Lumen Gentium, 33).

Along with this, it must be noted, there has been a profound change of attitude. Formerly, as an act of piety, laypeople helped Father run "his" parish. But now, for such laypeople, not only is there a sense of ownership (Father, who is temporary, enables them, the permanent parishioners) but of commitment, of vocation. In fact, the National Conference of Catholic Bishops' subcommittee on lay ministry, established in 1994, convened various groups to discuss what they came to officially call "lay ecclesial ministry." The topic of vocation was explored with some members, suggesting that ecclesial lay ministry be considered the fourth vocation, along with the priesthood, religious life, and marriage. The committee's 1999 report picked up on this idea, and stated that such lay ecclesial ministers be distinguished from the general body of the faithful precisely "by reason of a call to service made possible by certain gifts of the Holy Spirit....Lay ecclesial ministry is experienced by many to be a call to ministry, a vocation" (16, 17).

In addition, the subcommittee went on to describe the characteristics that mark such ministers, though not all apply in every case. A lay ecclesial minister in a parish, it said, is:

1. a fully initiated member of the Christian faithful who responds to a call or invitation to participate in ministry after adequate discernment;

2. one who has received the necessary formation, education, and training to function competently in a particular ministry;

3. one who has personal competencies and gifts for ministry and uses them with community or parish recognition and support;

4. one to whom a formal and public role in parish ministry has been entrusted by a bishop or local pastor;

5. one who has been installed in a ministry through the authority of the bishop or his representative;

6. one who commits to performing the duties of a ministry in a stable manner for a certain length of time;

7. a paid full-or part-time member of the parish staff or a volunteer who has responsibility and the necessary authority for parish leadership in a particular area of ministry. Truly, as Thomas O'Meara reminds us in his book, *Theology of Ministry*, the old image of the pyramid has been replaced by that of concentric circles which move from leaders to full-time and professionally trained ministers, out through levels of part-time ministers to all the baptized.

On the positive side, then, lay ecclesial ministers have nobly taken up the slack from a declining clergy and have proved an asset to parish life. The use of lay parish administrators can lighten the priest's workload—or, truth to tell, he can lighten their workload, for they are the ones "called and gifted," to use the happy phrase of the U.S. bishops. Many thousands of laity are currently in ministerial and professional training programs which often produce a laity more theologically sophisticated than the clergy, and there are proven ways to recruit and train these people on the parish level.[4]

Enlightened dioceses are putting their financial resources into training and supporting laypeople to be parish administrators, pastoral associates, directors of catechetical programs, teachers, principals, youth ministers, liturgical coordinators, and so on, to take the administrative burden off the diminishing clergy while freeing them to do more pastoral work of a spiritual nature. Truly the laity are essential to parish life; having them as collaborative ministers is a blessing long overdue.

And so one of the more positive fallouts from the priest shortage is the breakdown of excessive clericalism. In fact, there have been too many priests doing too many things for too long; the priest shortage has forced the retrieval of lay charisms and rights. A wise parish makes good use of the baptismal mandate and gifts of the laity, and there is no doubt that the successful parish in the post-Christian era will possess a fully shared and collaborative ministry. As we have seen, this movement has already started. Lay ecclesial ministers, in collaboration with the ordained, form the new pattern in the Church.

Ramifications of lay involvement

It is crucial, therefore, to note that the reflections on the following pages are centered precisely in the balancing of such collaborative ministry; that is, baptismally gifted people colaboring with the charism of the priest. Just as the solo priest is a sign of community imbalance, so the solo laity is equally. Thus, the following chapters are predicated on a shared and collaborative ministry which includes the charism of leadership and Eucharistic presider—the priest. And where such a person is lacking, let the Church provide that person through extending ordination. Let's take a look at what this might involve.

First of all, take the matter of liturgy. Many, like the bishops of Kansas, have noted that the protocol for Sunday worship in the absence of a priest found in the 1988 Vatican Directory for Sunday Celebrations in the Absence of a Priest is a stop-gap measure with enormous problems. Furthermore, the publication of an official ritual book for deacons, nuns, and laity gives the impression that SWAP (Sundays Without A Priest) is a permanent, reasonable alternative to the Sunday Eucharist, not a reluctant emergency measure to be eliminated as soon as possible. After all, the faith community is defined as a Eucharistic community. The Second Vatican Council said that the Eucharist brings the Church into being; in fact, it constitutes the Church. A Communion service is not the Eucharist, and its long-term existence endangers the identity and presence of the local Church. Moreover, with SWAP in place, there is the strong tendency to objectify the Eucharist into something you bring in a box—Jesus via UPS, as one wag said. It becomes a "thing," not an action of the whole community.

Then there is the constant danger that if SWAP becomes the norm, people will be satisfied with it and lose all sense of the communal celebration of Eucharist, along with the sense of the role of the celebrant. The situation is open to abuse, as noted in the introduction to the Vatican document on SWAP. The normal coordinator of the parish understandably feels it is his or her right to be quite visible when the priest does come around to celebrate Mass and so often stands at the altar with the priest, which confuses both their identities.

As Archbishop Weakland said, "If the distribution of Communion were to replace the fullness of the Eucharist for any length of time... we would become a different kind of Church that would not be based on gathering around the Eucharistic sacrifice." Msgr. Phil Murnion adds that with SWAP, "You miss the sense of participation across time with the action of Christ at the Last Supper. You miss the transformation of the elements into the presence of Christ among us." Pastoral administrators of priestless parishes are a welcome presence, but as the seesaw tilts, as these administrators multiply and as the clergy decrease in number, both the demands of being an inherently Eucharistic Church and the people's desire that it be so will force the ordination of that administrator.

Secondly, with a parish run by deacons, nuns, or laypeople as parish coordinators, you have the theological dissonance of separating jurisdiction from orders. For one thing, the whole image, the whole perception of the parish community changes because it no longer experiences the role of the priest as the symbol of Christ's initiative for the Church. Vatican II stressed that there is a very close tie between the Word, Sacrament, and governance of the community.[5] Worship that becomes separated from the Word and the whole life of the community eventually leads to the priest's ministry becoming defined as doing whatever the laity cannot do.

The heart of the matter is the time element. If "temporary" parish coordinators stay in their positions for years and years (a situation that has happened and continues to happen more and more), it becomes a fiction as to who really is in charge. In effect, the priest becomes the stranger. He has sacred power but is no longer pastor. In the early Church such a priest would be dismissed and his ordination voided because the pre-Nicene Church was insistent that a priest be attached to a community.

In fact, the origins of the priesthood seem to be rooted in the reality that the one who presides over the community is the one who should preside over the community's highest form of worship, the Eucharist. (Even weekend help are theological extensions of the pastor, who invites the visiting priest to preside at liturgy in the pastor's name, much as the vicar general confirms in the name of the bishop). Thomas Aquinas comes at this issue from the other direction. He says that the one who presides over the Eucharist should also preside over the community. In either case the connection between priesthood and community is firm. That is why the Council of Chalcedon (canon 6) voided any absolute ordinations, that is, ordinations not linked to a specific community.

But long before the Second Vatican Council, through the loss of the village community and the growth of Church bureaucracy, ordination gradually became separated from the community, and jurisdiction from sacramental orders, leaving an unhealthy, lopsided identity of the priest as one with the power to consecrate the bread and wine. It historically led to the distortion of seeing bishops not in terms of sacramental power, but in terms of having greater jurisdiction separate from such power. Vatican II tried hard to dismantle the notion that ordination is simply a transfer of power unrelated to ecclesial community, but splitting the Eucharist from daily pastoral leadership does precisely this. Even in the early days of our country, when there were "circuit rider" priests who traveled from settlement to settlement to celebrate the sacraments, they were nevertheless attached not only to the service of the diocese, which served as their wider parish base, but often they were pastors of a parish from which they sallied forth on their arduous rounds.

So the bottom line is this: where one of the partners in collaboration is missing, the healthy equation collapses. In any social group the absence of the community leader for too long is debilitating. In the Church, where we celebrate the high point of the faith community at the Eucharist, the absence of the Eucharistic leader is likewise debilitating. The point of collaborative ministry is to use the gifts of all to build community. Where a crucial gift is missing for too long, healthy community won't happen.

15

MINISTERIAL CONFUSION

Nuns in Alaska witness marriages. Lay catechists in Africa baptize. Lay ministers preside over Communion services, laypeople are parish coordinators. Some might suggest, why not? A wise priest, they maintain, does not try to do all things himself but works hard to empower the laity. This is certainly true in many areas, but here we are not merely in the administrative, teaching, or pastoral areas. We are into the sacramental and leadership life of the Church. If the priest shortage continues or worsens and there will be no priest in the foreseeable future, it would seem sensible to ordain the parish coordinator because, as Norman Provencher wrote:

> Catholic tradition has always understood that in sacramental celebration it is only a baptized, ordained person who shows that the principal agent is Christ acting through the Spirit. Sacramental ministry is never given by nomination, assignment, or mandate, but by ordination. This highlights the fact that the source of the minister's pastoral activity is the Spirit, who builds the body of Christ for the praise of God the Father. In entrusting a sacramental ministry to lay persons, even if we stress the temporary nature of the situation, are we not undermining sacramentality and reducing it to an organization that simply has to be kept running?

> Currently we have a new kind of ministry, distinct from that of the priest or deacon, and thus two separate and sometimes

competing ministerial bodies. If laypeople continue to lead parish communities and if the supply of priests continues to diminish, the church will soon face a dilemma similar to Peter's when the Holy Spirit came upon the gentiles: "Can anyone withhold the water for baptizing these people who have received the Holy Spirit just as we have?" (Acts 10:47). In a few years some communities being led by lay pastoral workers will ask their bishop to lay hands on those among them who are exercising a ministry fruitful with the Spirit. And the bishop I hope, will react as Peter did—the one on whom Jesus founded his church.[1]

He is saying something we keep proposing: ordain those laity to keep the balance. Consider this:

> To a traditional Roman Catholic, Sunday at St. Mary's of the Assumption parish would come as a shock. The morning services are mostly run by Sister Virginia Welsh, who greets the worshippers, directs the choir and offers "reflections" in lieu of the sermon that under Vatican rules she is not allowed to preach. On hand to say Mass itself is an elderly priest who divides his time between this parish and another.
>
> Later, as Sister Welsh chats with the congregation, hatches plans for the parish school, and presents prospective church members at a regional ceremony, she leaves no doubt that she is the parish leader, and a popular one.
>
> Yet this is no renegade group: Sister Welsh, 45, was appointed to leadership of this struggling inner-city parish by the Toledo bishop. Today, even as theorists debate the future of the Roman Catholic Church, a deepening shortage of priests is already forcing a transformation of Catholic life in the United States, among other things handing vast new responsibilities to women.[2]

Psychologically, the finger-in-the-dike invention of parish coordinators can obviously produce great tension. On the one hand you have the daily, everyday coordinator who does "all the dirty work," the one

who is visible, the one with the keys, who technically is under the direction of the priest. On the other hand you have the one with no practical ties to the parish community except on paper. The latter technically has the power of decision, the former no power. How long can this last agreeably, especially when it comes to disagreement? And how long, as we saw in the quotation above, before the coordinator himself or herself and the savvy people are going to ask: if he or she is good enough year after to year to preside over the community, why isn't he or she good enough to preside over the Eucharist? And they will clamor for his or her ordination.

In the instruction called "Certain Questions Regarding the Collaboration of the non-Ordained Faithful in the Sacred Ministry of the Priest" issued in August of 1997, the Vatican thought it necessary to try to check the blurring of roles, as pastoral coordinators—once considered an emergency solution to the priest shortage—become more commonplace. As the National Pastoral Life Center's study "Parishes and Parish Ministries" puts it:

> We do recognize that the increased service of laypeople in parish ministry positions will keep raising questions about which activities are proper and permitted to these ministries, and which must remain restricted to the ordained. It is important to appreciate that by resorting to certain practices such as Sunday celebrations in the absence of a priest and appointing laypeople to be responsible for the pastoral ministry of a parish because there are fewer priests, expectations are raised both among parishioners and in the parish ministers themselves. These expectations, for example, that laypeople are equally appropriate in these roles are hard to dispel when priests resume activities that had been entrusted to laypeople. Considerable care and education are required.

> In the case of persons charged with pastoral care of a parish in the absence of a resident pastor and commissioned to conduct Sunday celebrations in the absence of a priest, there is indeed a danger of diminishing the significance of both the ordained ministry and the eucharist. We did not address this directly

in this study, but do recognize how important it is to monitor pastoral developments, being open to those that enhance the life of the [C]hurch while being attentive to others that quite inadvertently confuse or diminish certain important elements of Catholic tradition. The instruction also directs the use of terms or titles. Specifically, it cautions against overextending the use of the term ministry and prohibits laypeople from assuming the titles pastor, chaplain, coordinator, and moderator. It is difficult for us to use any term other than ministry or minister when describing the subjects of our study. We resorted to the term pastoral coordinator when referring to those assigned by the bishop in accordance with Canon 517.2 of the Code of Canon Law to pastoral ministry in a parish without a resident priest pastor, for this appears to be the most commonly used term.[3]

The necessarily neutral language of the study should not hide the more passionate problems. "Expectations...that laypeople are equally appropriate in [the clerical] roles are hard to dispel when priests resume activities..." doesn't quite sound the urgent note that as priests become fewer and fewer there will not only be a blurring of roles but also a preference not always in favor of the priest. As an instance, take the current practice of the pastoral care of the needy and sick and terminally ill. Priests who used to handle these people exclusively have, because of the shortage, pretty much withdrawn from routine pastoral care. Laypeople (remember: with a sense of mission, not charity) now commonly visit the needy in hospitals and in nursing homes, and bring Communion to the shut-ins. Pastoral care arrangements, in other words, are becoming increasingly institutionalized under lay leadership.

Again, I want to emphasize that, in one sense, this is as it should be. It represents a successful use of the laity's gifts. The problem lies in the psychological and theological fallouts associated with a long-term absence of the circuit priest; namely, with lovely reconciliation services, compassionate outreach, and comforting rituals being led by laypeople, how long before either the need or the desire for priestly confession and the Anointing of the Sick will fade into irrelevancy? As laypeople, especially women (the predominant ministers by far), acquire professional certification, prepare liturgies, and give "reflections," who will notice the absence of the priest? Or eventually care if he ever returns? Yet, according to a recent poll, between 60% and 65% of Catholics thought it imperative to have a priest visit the sick, and 80% considered it desirable to have a priest for the last rites.[4]

Or take prison ministry. One writer asks, "As the number of Catholic priests dwindles and prison ministry becomes the province of professional lay ministries, will the ministry lose its Catholic character?" Today we have 1.86 million people in prison, soon to be two million, suggesting that prison ministry is more needed than ever. Yet sadly, there are fewer priests to meet it. True enough there are those dedicated lay ministers (now popularly called chaplains, though technically they are not), but the fact is they cannot celebrate Mass— nor can they hear confessions, a critical sacrament in prison ministry or, most of all, in a place rife with mental illness, HIV, and AIDS, can they give the sacrament of the sick. So even with the dedication typical of lay ministers, a specific Catholic sacramental presence where it is most needed for the least among us is slowly being drained away because of the lack of priests.[5]

Once more, not only can collaborative ministry not long sustain itself if one of the collaborators is missing but also, neither can the very sacramental life of the Church.

16

LAY MINISTRY:

Glories and Perils

In this chapter, I take a more cautionary approach to the wonderful explosion of lay ministry. I would suggest, as others have done, that with the nearly 30,000 official lay ministers working in the Church, along with countless volunteers, there may unwittingly occur a very subtle subversion of the very thing Vatican II has tried (unsuccessfully) to promote: the proper vocation of the laity. By this I mean that the laity are not to find their calling primarily in the workings of the Church, but are called to seed the world in which they live with the life of Christ, "to renew the temporal order," to use the words of Vatican II.

As is abundantly evident from the Vatican II documents, liturgy is supposed to be the primary place where this mandate is proclaimed and given. In short, Vatican II was not directly about renewing the liturgy or the organizational structures of the Church; it was about forming and sending forth people into the world to evangelize it, to be "Eucharist" to the world. In one of the Council's most radical moves, the bishops recognized that the apostolate, defined as "announcing to the world by word and deed and action the message of Christ and communicating it to the grace of Christ" (*Apostolican Actuositatem*, the Decree on the Apostolate of Laypeople, #7, hereafter AA), belongs by right of Baptism to the whole Church and each of its members.

Thus, laypeople were told that "from the fact of their union with Christ, the head, flows laypeople's right and duty to be apostles..."(AA #2). In the document "Constitution on the Church in the Modern World", the people are charged "to discern in the events, the needs, and the longings which they share with other people of our time, what may be genuine signs of the presence or the purpose of God" (#11). And it goes on to say that it is the duty of "bishops to whom has been committed the task of directing the Church of God, along with their priests...to preach the message of Christ in such a way that the light of the Gospel will shine on all the activities of the faithful" (#43). And it is up to the laity "to animate the world with the spirit of Christianity and to be witnesses to Christ in all circumstances and at the very heart of the community of mankind" (#43).

The mandate to change the world, in other words, belongs to the laity. As Gordon Truitt puts it, "Religious and especially members of the clergy are allowed to take a step back from that frontline activity in order to teach, train, and form those who carry the chief responsibility for implementing this vision [of Vatican II]."[1] Yet what happened to the vision? We have to admit that it has woefully failed. What happened is that we wound up concentrating so much effort on activities such as the development of parish councils, the creation of good relations with other churches, and the renewal of the liturgy that in the process we lost sight of just why we were doing these things; that is, to empower the laity in their proper vocation to engage the world. In the words of Msgr. John Egan, we failed "to acknowledge the essential connection between liturgy and society, much less liturgy and social justice."

The point of this exploration into the role of the laity is not to say that indeed laypeople do not have a role to play in internal Church matters. After all, "The lay apostolate, in all its many aspects, is exercised both in the church and in the world" (AA #9). Rather, I want to point out a subtle psychological effect resulting from the combination of a dwindling clergy with a growing and very visible laity in Church leadership roles. This effect is that people today—lacking a firm catechesis on their role in the world, not having been schooled on the connection between liturgy and social justice, living in a spiritual vacuum in regard to their proper vocation in the world—unconsciously may identify holiness with in-house service, with "churchy" work. As they see the growing number of fellow laity in church roles, critical Church positions, and high profile liturgical functions, they may conclude that this is where "real" sanctity lies.

In other words, the combination of an exceedingly poor education regarding the laity's role in the Church and the very visible activity of a large number of laypeople in key positions, especially as parish coordinators, might foster a new attitude towards these "clerical-ized" laity as a model to follow, an ideal to be achieved. Not to mention that all those in-house laity might be seduced into thinking that what they are doing is the pattern for the lay vocation. Furthermore, there is a serious deflection from the laity's "role in the world" when people identify with and gravitate toward what goes on at the parish, rather than feeling a call to penetrate the world beyond the parish. "What's going on in church?" usually brings comments about the RCIA program or the drive to raise money to build a new church. In addition, many lay ministers, returning from their training programs, find that there are already more than enough Eucharistic ministers or lectors or members of the liturgical committee, and wonder how they can serve.

Surely a legitimate response to both "What's going on in church?" and "How can I serve if not within church ministry?" might be, "Two of our members have just been elected to the local school board," or, "A few of our retired, seasoned CEOs are helping poor people work through the corporate red tape when their phones or electricity have been turned off." In a word, as much legitimization and effort should be placed into bringing Gospel values and witness to the external workplace, schoolrooms, and corporate boards as is put into training people to be parish administrators and ministers. There is nothing wrong and everything right in sending certified lay ministers into the marketplace as the arena of their ministry. To connect lay ecclesial ministry solely with internal Church workings is a truncation of the mission of Christ.

That the bishops are aware of this issue is indicated by the "state-of-the-question" report given by them at their November 1999 meeting on lay ecclesial ministry. One sentence in the report reads, "Lay ecclesial ministry should not be seen as retreat by the laity from their role in the secular realm. Rather, lay ecclesial ministry is an affirmation that the Spirit can call the lay faithful to participation in the building of the [C]hurch in various ways."

That is what it says. A firm catechesis is certainly called for to make this warning viable. In practice, however, as seminarians and priests more and more decline and disappear from the ecclesial scene, this conviction will be hard to sell. To offset this, it seems that it would be far, far better to ordain these lay leaders than to muddy the vocational waters because identifying the laity with clerical doings, especially highly visible liturgical functions, will surely devaluate the priesthood. Everything is to be gained by the appearance of a viable and strong lay ministry. Equally, everything is to be lost by the disappearance of a viable priesthood.

Summary

With that being said, let me summarize. With a firm recognition that all share their various gifts in the one priesthood of Jesus Christ, the parish of today and tomorrow looks like this: one pastor, a married lay associate (a woman, perhaps), a permanent deacon, a business manager, and a large staff of laypeople—both volunteers and the full-time ecclesial lay ministers. The latter would include a full-time director of liturgy, a lay principal of the parish school, a director of religious education, and a social concerns director. The former would include catechists and the couples preparing parents for baptism, those preparing the engaged for marriage (whose wedding, more and more, will be witnessed by a deacon), and those directing the RCIA, as well as programs for evangelization and ecumenism.

The staff will meet among themselves for prayer and reflection, and with the parish council for advice on daily pastoral matters. Yet all this is done no longer to fill the shoes of the declining clergy and religious, but from a deep grasp of the common baptismal call that all be Church and the need for all charisms to work together for the sake of the Kingdom. This kind of parish works wonderfully; those of us who have experienced such a parish know how satisfying it is.

While acknowledging and supporting this ideal, we must now return to (and belabor) our premise: one of the necessary charisms in the parish is that of ordained leadership and presider of the Eucharist. If that is in danger of disappearing because the requirements are too narrow, then we must simply expand those requirements rather than pretend we can spread the ordained ministry around to lay folk who must stop short of celebrating the Eucharist. This whole dilemma was given focus almost twenty years ago, when the formidable Karl Rahner wrote these words:

> There is no point in upholding the theoretical principle that the ordained priest is and must remain the proper leader of the congregation if the increasing shortage of priests means that without laymen as leaders the congregations will cease to exist....If leadership of the community is an intrinsic and essential element of the priesthood, in which this function and that of the presidency of the Eucharistic celebration are mutually dependent, then the very people who in fact in the future will be leaders of a priestless community should themselves be ordained priests and thus sacramentally recognized for what they are and what they accomplish as actual leaders....
>
> If in practice, despite all sublime theological distinctions, the pastoral assistant [non-ordained parish coordinator] in a priestless community exercises all the functions of a priestly community leader (apart from the two sacramental powers), we are faced with a dilemma. Either the functions actually undertaken by the pastoral assistant are regarded by no means specifically priestly. Then what is truly priestly about the ministerial priest is reduced to the two sacramental powers

reserved to him alone; the priest becomes a purely cultic functionary. It has been said often enough that this interpretation of priesthood is no longer acceptable today...or it is admitted that the functions actually undertaken by the pastoral assistant are at bottom specifically priestly....

If in practice the leadership of the community is entrusted to pastoral assistants and this commissioning can be distinguished from a priest's community leadership only by subtle theories; if in a modern theology of priesthood the two sacramental powers [confession and Eucharist] reserved to ordained priests are basically articulations and extrapolations of the priest's fundamental task as leader of a local church and official representative of the episcopal major church and of the church as a whole, by what right are these two powers denied to the pastoral assistant as community leader in a priestless community? If someone as pastoral assistant is in fact appointed community leader, he is granted in this capacity the basic nature of the priest and at the same time refused the sacramental powers that flow from this basic nature. Is this theologically consistent?[2]

Right now, closing parishes and having laypeople pastor parishes is a short-term solution to the priest shortage, a long-range problem. The "solution" of having people lead a Communion service without a priest; the "solution" of having the laity administer the sacrament of Baptism, as well as witness marriages, preach, and catechize; the "solution" of having the non-ordained pastor a parish; the "solution" of making the parish "priestproof" through vigorous lay ministry— all are but stop-gap solutions for the short run. But, apart from the logic of ordaining such non-ordained leaders, I think it is obvious that these "solutions" have a tendency to confuse the calling of the laity and to undermine the ordained priesthood. At least, they blur the lines of identity when the priest is absent for a long time, which becomes more of a possibility as the priest shortage expands. Furthermore, if some kind of order is to be maintained in a diocese, an ordained person will be needed to provide an effective link to the bishop. Otherwise, the danger of congregationalism grows in proportion to the absence of the priest.

So once more I return to my thesis: in the context of the severe and growing priest shortage and its effects, I am saying that, if the priest shortage continues and unless we ordain key lay leaders, married or single, all will suffer: the ecclesial lay leaders who increasingly live in an in-between world of not-quite-laity/not-quite-clergy, who have the power but not the title; the priest who has the title but not the power; and the laity who, unschooled as to their proper role, tend to see the increasingly visible in-house laity as ideal spiritual models to emulate, and are thus deflected from their proper vocation.

I maintain that as laypeople in Church positions multiply, especially women, and ordained male clergy decrease, the product will be confusion, imbalance, and harm to the Church as a whole. As a firm and earnest believer and promoter of shared and collaborative ministry, I want to be sure there are priests to collaborate with. Simply put, my premise is that shared and collaborative ministry is a reality whose time has come and must be embraced fully and joyously by all. And I am saying that such collaboration should be along with, not instead of, the clergy. Our leaders need to see this and to do the only sensible thing: widen the conditions for ordination.

PART THREE

Responses

17

A MARRIED CLERGY

As we have seen in previous chapters, the priest shortage is more severe than most people realize. Consequently, if the current trend continues, our grandchildren have a good chance of never being at a Mass. Right now, bishops are desperate and are crying to Rome for relief, as they have been for a while.

It is in this context that we begin this section by thoughtfully considering the issue of a married clergy, a subject mentioned several times in the preceding chapters. Indeed, the possibility of a married clergy, unlike the ordination of women, is clearly in our tradition. (The ordination of women may also be in the tradition, but this has yet to be fully teased out and explicated from another hermeneutic.[1]) In fact, a married clergy, the ordination of married men who have the gift of leadership, would be a return to the earliest tradition of the Church, a tradition testified to by St. Paul, who, in his first letter to Timothy and in his letter to Titus, urges that presbyters be "a man of one woman," able to manage a household and have believing children, whose lives are in order and are not rebellious. What about Paul's very strong statement, "Do we not have the right to be accompanied by a believing wife, as do the other apostles and the brothers of the Lord and Cephas?" (1 Cor 9:5).

Most Americans do not know that, in fact, the Church has always welcomed the married priests of the non-Latin East. Rites like Ukrainian

Catholicism or Maronite Catholicism that are fully Catholic and obedient to the pope ordain married men, although they do not allow unmarried priests to get married. Not to mention the fact that right now in our tradition we do have a married clergy—they are called deacons—and that in January 2012 the Vatican announced the formation of a nationwide ordinariate for married Episcopal priests and their congregations who want to move into Roman Catholicism.

The ordination of married men, I repeat, is not an aberration, a novelty, or a heresy. It has been solidly in place from the very beginning of Christianity with the choice of Peter, a married man, to lead the apostolic band—the first of thirty-nine popes, by the way, who were married.[2]

The restoration of a married clergy rests on an appeal to Scripture, to the tradition of the Church, and to the dictates of pastoral needs. Celibacy, on the other hand, is a tradition rooted in church discipline, not revelation; this is a fact admitted by all. We are well aware that in the early centuries the hermits and monks were celibate, but this was by choice, as an alternate lifestyle. Marriage remained an option for the clergy, and for some twelve hundred years celibacy was not considered essential to the priesthood, as even John Paul II has declared. Remember, Paul admonished Timothy that a bishop should be kind and peaceable, a man with a family, for "if someone does not know how to manage his own household, how can he take care of God's Church?" (1 Tim 3:5).

By the fourth century, however, for political, cultural, and cultic reasons, some popes (for example, Damascus and Siricius) tried to enforce either a celibate priesthood or clerical marriage with no sex. The political reason for this was so Church property would not pass on to the priest's children. The cultic reason stemmed from Old Testament times, when the Levitical priesthood demanded that the priest be ritually pure (sexuality had many ritual taboos). In keeping with this tradition, it was felt that it was not fitting for a man to have intercourse and celebrate the Eucharist. Typical of this line of thought was the admonition of St. Peter Damien, who said that since a virgin brought forth Jesus, only virgins should bring him forth on the altar, as well as the words of Innocent II at the Synod of Clermont in 1130, to the effect that since priests are supposed to be vessels of the Lord, they should not have sex with their wives.

The cultural reason for a celibate priesthood came from the early Church, when the great desert ascetics were the celebrities of the time, held in high esteem and dearly sought after. These ascetics were fiercely disciplined and celibate; the priests back in the cities paled by comparison. So in order to shore up the clergy, the bishops took two strategies: either they enticed the celibate desert ascetics to become priests or they had the priests imitate the lifestyle of the celibate desert ascetics. (Later, that would include even the monastic practice of saying the Divine Office daily, although this never really fit in the life of the busy secular priest.)

In later centuries the continuing denigration by the hierarchy of sex and married life, along with the need to contain Church property and control the clergy, propelled a growing emphasis on celibacy. In 1074, Pope Gregory VII legislated that anyone who was to be ordained must first pledge celibacy. In 1095, Pope Urban II ordered that married priests who ignored the vow of celibacy be imprisoned, and their wives and children sold into slavery. Mandatory celibacy was finally legislated at the Second Lateran Council in 1139, under Pope Innocent II, though most of the Eastern Rites have kept the tradition of a married clergy.[3]

Priorities

Fundamentally, one reality should guide us in this sensitive and provocative issue of restoring a married clergy: the primacy of the care of souls. When seeking a solution to anything, it is necessary to give great focus to the goal, to the object to be achieved. Thus, two compelling themes must concern us. The first comes from a phrase in our Sunday creed: *Propter nos homines et propter nostram salutem descendit de coelis* ("Christ came for us and our salvation"). The other is the primacy of the Eucharist. The Constitution on the Sacred Liturgy is explicit:

> For it is the liturgy through which, especially in the divine sacrifice of the Eucharist "the work of our redemption is accomplished" (2). Every liturgical celebration...is a sacred action surpassing all others (7). The liturgy is the summit toward which the activity of the Church is directed; it is also the fount from which all her powers flow. For the goal of the apostolic endeavor is that all who are made sons of God by faith and baptism should come together to praise God in the midst of his Church, to take part in the Sacrifice and to eat the Lord's Supper (10).

What could be more explicit? As the title of a popular book written by the notable Cardinal Manning put it, "it's the Mass that matters." If we hold these two expressed goals in mind—that Christ came for all, and that the aim of the Church is for the faithful to come together to praise God and have access to the Lord's Supper—then everything else must be subservient to these goals, including celibacy. The proper focus is enshrined in canon law: "the salvation of souls...is always the supreme law of the Church" (*Salus animarum suprema lex*, Canon 1752).

One who knew that law most keenly was Cardinal Kim, president of the 1998 Federation of Asian Bishop's Conference, who confessed to a change of heart on ordaining married men. The bishops of the Asian conference told the cardinal that some of their dioceses were as big as South Korea. They "recounted how they walked for days and days in order to make pastoral visits, and they showed me their legs battered with cuts and abrasions in their trips across the roadless forests." The Cardinal added, "When I saw those wounds on a bishop's legs I was profoundly moved by the level of pastoral love, and I understood why the Indonesian bishops had repeatedly asked permission to confer sacred orders on *viri probati* [men of proven worth]."[4] The late Cardinal Hume of England, in a June 1985 speech in Belgium, called for married men to be ordained to the priesthood "in certain parts of the world as the only way to bring the sacraments of Eucharist and reconciliation to the people." His successor, Archbishop Cormac Murphy-O'Connor, said the present discipline of celibacy is open to change.

Some of the bishops of the Oceania synod, which oversees the farflung islands and the vast, distant lands of the Pacific and is faced with a diminishing cadre of clergy to care for their eight million Catholics, have appealed for a married clergy. They wanted to make the pope aware of the "gradual spiritual starvation of our Catholic people and their moving away from us to find spiritual nourishment elsewhere." The leader of a missionary order, Fr. Patrick Moroney, adds:

> It would be a great grace if...another look could be taken at the situation of ordaining committed married men to the priesthood, and also the possibility of a more compassionate assessment of the situation, of priests who have left due to their inability to live the celibate life.

Clarifications

The need, then, is to ordain married men, and in particular local married men who can serve in their own communities, the *viri probati*, those men of proven worth testified to by the community, many of whom are already highly involved in parish life. So that you don't think this is a novel idea, we should note this issue was in fact raised during the time of Pius X, as well as at the Second Vatican Council. It was also the subject of the 1971 World Synod of Bishops, where about 45% of the delegated bishops voted in favor of ordaining married men. Yet, for reasons we shall discuss, this issue remains on hold.

We should recall that ordaining married men will mean that we will not only return to an earlier tradition, as we mentioned before, but to an earlier philosophical position. In the current system, a "stranger" goes to the seminary, gets trained to be a priest, and is sent by the bishop to a parish that does not know him. In effect, this tells the local parish communities that they can only celebrate the Eucharist when somebody from outside the community who has been ordained is sent to them. Ordaining married men of the local community, however, is an organic process. The people propose one of their own for ordination. He arises from the community and remains in the community, earns his own livelihood, and may practice his ministry either part-time, as weekend celebrant, or full-time.

The point of this is deeper that you think. The concept of the community proposing its own Eucharistic leader takes the focus off an emergency response to the priest shortage and moves it toward a more basic point of community-led clergy, which was the system in the early Church. The current system focuses on only one charism: celibacy. Because of this, lots of other charisms are necessarily excluded. But with the community-based concept, the fundamental issue will not be the priest shortage but, more basically, how can we find those who are willing to accept fully the responsibility for the Gospel? Who can best give us an example of living the Gospel? Who can best help us live out the Gospel in our community? In other words, the idea would be to replace a clerical kind of priest, fortified with his portable, monopolistic "power to consecrate" apart from any community (this would have been a horror to the early Christians) with a community-based priest. The scenario would be to ordain those men who already work within the parish, whether paid or volunteer (although that might simply continue another form of clericalism).

Many, if not most, of the ordained married men would work part-time in the parish and while continuing to work at their secular jobs. They may even be used solely to help with a few Masses each week. Perhaps they could say an early Mass before they leave for work or, like the married deacons, give a few evenings a week to the parish. This part-time schedule should not put us off, since there have always been part-time clergy, the ones we call "hyphenated priests," for whom ritual and parish life play a very small part. These are the priests who come to our parishes, say a few Masses, then return home to their full-time jobs as professors, scientists, administrators, sociologists, college presidents, and so on. This same situation could apply to the ordained community leaders. Some, of course, may work full-time in a parish, but this presupposes a financial system that can support them and their family.

The reality of married priests will come, but no one, in considering a married priesthood, would deny that there are formidable adjustments to be made. I would suggest that these might be initial adjustments, which eventually would fall into routine acceptance. Let's examine some of these adjustments.

One major hurdle, especially for those in third and fourth world countries, would be financing. If one of the married clergy became disabled or ill and could no longer work, would the diocese be obliged to take financial responsibility for him and his dependents? If this type of situation happened often enough, the diocese simply could not handle the financial burden. This is one reason why the bishops have put the notion of a married clergy on hold.

Here is another problem: if you seek out *viri probati*, you are going to have a stampede of angry women asking about the *mulieri probatae*, parish women of proven worth who often form the majority of those involved in parish work. True enough, many women are not interested in ordination until the whole clerical image of the priesthood is abandoned; only then would they want to be priests. On the other hand, perhaps what Fr. Gerald Sloyan writes is the most realistic comment: "Many women of the Catholic West do not want to see even more men in the sanctuary and pulpit than there are now, but they are outnumbered by people of both sexes who wish to see someone there."[5] Still, the choice of proven men would lead to such confrontations by women, a situation which would be gleefully exploited by the media.

Celibacy

Another highly sensitive problem would be the celibacy requirement for the existing clergy. If you have married priests ordained for their own communities and engaged in their secular occupations, where does that leave the celibate priest? Will he, too, be given a choice of marriage or celibacy? Why should he remain celibate? The priest, as we have seen, already has an identity problem. Who will he be when he is surrounded by others who are called priests but who live a very different lifestyle? What would be the role of the celibate priest? How will he feel if one parish is served by a married priest and another by a celibate priest?

Celibacy is a valued charism; I don't think anyone denies that. The value goes astray, however, when celibacy becomes more important than the Eucharist and more honored than fundamental justice. In her book *The Cloister Walk*, prize-winning poet and spiritual writer Kathleen Norris has this to say:

> Celibacy is a field day for ideologies. Conservative Catholics, particularly those who were raised in the pre-Vatican II church, tend to speak of celibacy as if it were an idealized, angelic state, while feminist theologians such as Uta Ranke-Heinemann say angrily that "celibate hatred of sex is hatred of women." That celibacy constitutes the hatred of sex seems to be a given in the popular mythology of contemporary America, and we need only look at newspaper accounts of sex abuse by priests to see evidence of celibacy that isn't working. One could well assume that this is celibacy, impure and simple. And this is unfortunate, because celibacy practiced rightly is not at all a hatred of sex; in fact it has the potential to address the sexual idolatry of our culture in a most helpful way.

> One benefit of the nearly ten years that I've been a Benedictine oblate has been the development of deep friendships with celibate men and women. This has led me to ponder celibacy that works, practiced by people who are fully aware of themselves as sexual beings but who express their sexuality in a celibate way....

I've seen many wise old monks and nuns whose lengthy formation in celibate practice has allowed them to incarnate hospitality in the deepest sense. In them, the constraints of celibacy have somehow been transformed into an openness that attracts people of all ages, all social classes. They exude a sense of freedom.[6]

There is much truth in Norris's words, especially where celibacy is tied in with asceticism. On the other hand, where it is not—and this seems mostly to be the case—it loses its context. Celibacy falls short of the ideal and so does the justification for celibacy, which suggests that, freed of family concerns and demands, the celibate priest can 1) be more available, and 2) display a powerful witness for asceticism, which is so needed in a consumerist society. In practice, most priests live a quite comfortable lifestyle and are hardly known for their ascetical lives. And the issue of availability is a problem in this era of clergy shortage. Besides, does this imply that we should deal only with unmarried doctors, dentists, therapists, politicians, and so on because they are obviously more "available" than their married counterparts?

Then, too, celibacy today is placed in wider social and psychological contexts. As Jesuit priest Robert Egan expresses it:

I believe we should see this [the priesthood becoming a gay option] as one aspect of something broader: a crisis in the public meaning of religious celibacy. The celibate life of priests has had its "witness" value considerably muddled by studies that indicate a high percentage of sexually active priests; by perceptions that half or more of our priests are homosexual, whose choice of celibacy therefore has multiple and undecidable meanings; by serious psychological, philosophical, and theological criticism of the traditional rationales for mandatory priestly celibacy, especially for the celibacy of diocesan priests; and by the deep disappointment and shock caused by sexual scandals and lawsuits involving priests, brothers, and bishops....The aura of emotional immaturity among some members of the clergy can make their celibacy look like a flight from intimacy and commitment.[7]

Tensions

In all candor, a married clergy does have its own built-in set of difficulties, and it's worth looking at our Protestant brethren to see what these are. The major one is the high tension between one's clerical life and one's personal life. Patricia Dixon, whose husband was a Protestant minister before entering the Catholic Church, writes in favor of a celibate clergy.[8] She rightly notes that a married man must give priority to his family while the celibate can give his full-time attention. The average parish could not financially support an entire family or the individual houses each married parish priest would need. She cites the emotional burdens in the average family of a Protestant minister, where the needs and demands of the family and the needs and demands of the congregation compete.

The experience of clergy in the Catholic Eastern Rites, as well as the Protestant clergy, is instructive. They openly say that their wives must be mother, sacristan, sexton, chairperson, and sometimes even choir director—roles that modern women, keeping their own names, are less and less willing to undertake. Married Eastern Rite and Protestant clergy speak of how the family is closely watched and of how the children of a priest or minister are expected to behave all the time. They all speak of the tension between ministry and marriage. As one minister frankly writes:

> After 17 years in the ordained ministry, I still struggle to find a balance between the unending demands of pastoral ministry and the ongoing needs and desires of those closest and dearest to me—my family. But the following has become clear to me: as church members' lives have grown more frantic, they have come to expect more from their ministers. One of the expectations is that clergy be constantly available....Overtime can be

required at a moment's notice. Emergencies develop. In a culture in which family crises abound and where people are pager
or beeper or cellular phone ring away, availability has become
the new form of codependency.

Technology has made the pastor available 24 hours a day, 7
days a week....Clergy families sometimes call the church "the
other woman" (perhaps today "the other lover").[9]

The strain shows up in the uncomfortably high divorce rate among
Protestant clergy, both male and female. Imagine the effect marriage
might have on the Catholic clergy. Surely, even a ten or 20% divorce
rate among Catholic clergy (less than half the national rate) would be
devastating. Catholic priests divorcing, getting annulments, remar-
rying, arguing over joint custody of the children would be an unsettling novelty. Moreover, Catholic people not only tend to see their
clergy as special, as men set apart (even though that stance is resisted
by modern thought and some priests themselves), but want them to
be this way.

In Old Testament times, before entering the inner part of the
Temple, the Jewish high priest had to separate himself from the
community and have no relations with his wife so that he would be
worthy to enter the Holy of Holies and offer sacrifice. But after the
fall of the Temple in 70 AD, and the end of the Jewish priesthood and
animal sacrifice, Christians gradually began to appropriate Temple
terminology. Thus Jesus' actions came to be seen as a sacrifice, the
Eucharistic table became an altar, and the presbyter (the leader of the
early Christian community) became a priest. The separation mentality of the Jewish high priest was also passed on to the Christian
priest, and celibacy became a natural aspect of being apart from the
community, including a family.

In any case, Catholics have never really wanted their priests to be
just "ordinary Joes." Likewise, Protestant ministers have never had
quite the aura of the Catholic priest, who is considered set apart from
the people. The attraction and power of the Catholic priesthood

(despite whatever negatives there may be) has been precisely this separateness, of which celibacy was a potent sign. The priest seen as the married man next door with a couple of kids doesn't quite cut it. Yet this does not mean that there ought not be a married priesthood, just that something will be lost in the Catholic tradition.

Then, too, as Andrew Greeley has pointed out, optional celibacy would eventually mean pressure on a priest to marry, for, in today's atmosphere, if he is not married, dark suspicions of homosexuality or predation may follow him. Nor must we be indifferent to the sincere dismay of the more conservative Catholic, who will see the ordination of married men as one more sign of the wicked effects of Vatican II and the denigration of the clerical priesthood they love and admire.

And, finally, will the removal of celibacy really help in the long run? As one letter to an editor commented:

> Thank you for your excellent series on seminaries and the crisis in the Catholic priesthood. I acknowledge the problems, but despair of solutions. Would the abolition of compulsory celibacy make the Catholic clergy more chaste? Have the Protestant and Anglican solutions done away with pedophilia and homosexuality in their clergy? Given the fact that most sexual abusers of children are married and are usually relatives, studies indicate that Catholic clergy are no more likely to abuse a child than anyone else. And a married clergy and married seminarians would also bring the challenge of sexism, promiscuity, adultery, and divorce. My own formation was at Catholic University (where lay students were the norm), Graduate Theological Union (Berkeley, California), which is an ecumenical consortium, and Oxford University. I did not see fewer problems in these different environments, only different ones.[10]

Ultimately, we must have married priests because our identity as a Eucharistic community and the sacramental life of the Church demand it. I don't think there is any doubt about that. We simply must not underestimate the sensible concerns that surround this issue, as well as the gains and losses that will come with a married priesthood.

Other concerns

Will ordaining married men lead to a two-tier or a two-class system? Right now, the Catholic priesthood is a fairly well defined category. But with a married clergy, all this will disappear. Some priests will have a family, some will not. The old camaraderie that existed, where one priest could freely walk into the rectory of another, will go by the board, for a priest just can't walk into the family home of another married priest. He will no longer be able to mix so freely. And how will diocesan meetings take place when some priests have jobs and families that prevent them from working within a firm diocesan schedule?

As a practical answer to all this, some have suggested that the full-time celibate priest adopt a new role of supervisor, dean, or coordinator engaged in the task of formation and overseeing the married priests. Then, since celibate priests have no family and tend to seek and enjoy the company of other priests, they should eventually form a kind of religious community of priests. After all, most of them would be available to work full-time within the parish while the married priests may still work at a job outside the parish, and so be available only on a part-time basis (like the married deacons). In effect, the existing celibate clergy can be like Paul to the married presbyters of the early church communities. This would also give their celibacy a firmer foundation, as the role of coordinator would truly be a full-time commitment.

As the celibate clergy take on the task of supervising the part-time or full-time married clergy, they would establish a more direct link to the bishop, with the understanding that the full-time celibate priest receives his vocation for a wider area, for the whole diocese, wherever the bishop needs him. In this, those who are currently priests would have a visible, sorely needed sign of identity, as they would come to be seen as the "bishop's men," as "episcopal vicars."

These distinctions might be one way of introducing a new kind of priest without losing the existing ones. Whatever the case, it seems that when and if a married clergy is introduced into the Church, in no way should it be done before a long dialogue commences with the existing celibate priests.

A side problem in all this is the existing diaconate, which will certainly have to undergo some radical changes if full-time or part-time married clergy become a reality. The diaconate might then be in danger, once more, of disappearing. And deacons, who already have a severe identity problem (there is nothing they can do that a layperson can't do) will have to find a new way to be meaningful to the Church.

Finally, what about seminarians? When candidates for the priesthood hear of the possibility and actuality of a married clergy, how will this affect them? Most, I suspect, will continue with their formation, but others will drop out and wait until they get married. But they, too, must fully explore the charisms of both the full-time, celibate priesthood and the part-time community priesthood. Those who choose the former must be specially trained in formation and coordination. Their role will be like that of Paul as overseer, but also like that of Peter, mandated to "strengthen the brethren."[11]

Options to consider

It is conceivable that a stroke of the pen from a new pope could open the gates to all married men, and that would be it. But this would be impractical, inopportune, and insensitive. Because the ordination of married men is, as we have seen, fraught with practical and emotional ramifications, yet the need for them is so pressing, perhaps what would work best is a slow, "organic" approach. This would mean opening the door to a married clergy on a graduated, one-on-one, petition basis, something like this: a bishop would petition for the ordination of a specific married man on the basis of a real pastoral need. Rome, while hard-nosed on its principles and law, has always been open to pastoral emergencies. And surely such an emergency exists. This one-on-one request, therefore, preserves Rome's principle of ordaining only celibate men, while the individual dispensation fulfills a real need for the good of souls.

The selection of such candidates could be proposed by the congregation (or actively sought out by the bishop upon various recommendations), and be based on five practical criteria: age, financial independence, private housing, a stable marriage, and minimal family responsibilities. First of all, as we all know (and can immediately mention several) there are those *viri probati*, mature older men of outstanding character and spiritual development who own their own home, have sound medical plans, whose long-term marriages are secure, and whose children are grown. In short, their finances are in order, their homes secured, they are not likely to divorce, and their family commitments are more regular at this stage. And many of them retire early from mainstream jobs, leaving the possibility of many years of service as full- or part-time clergy. Younger men, of course, are certainly in the running provided they are financially secure or the community can afford to compensate them in some way.

So the question remains: why don't we ordain such men for weekend help and daily Mass when needed? Currently, the weekend supply is augmented by retirees and religious order priests, but the former are mathematically due to disappear through death or disability and the latter, as well, have their own replacement problems. Looking down a short road of ten or fifteen years, the weekend supply will dry up. Surely, then, a contract of some kind could be made with mature, ordained married men offering a stipend for their clerical training and restricted duties while letting them maintain the expenses of their own homes and families through an outside job. The "as needed" ordination of worthy and settled married men, based on a genuine pastoral approach for the sake of the salvation of souls, offers one way of relieving the priest shortage.

The simplex priest

There is, in the history of the Church the category of the Simplex Priest. This is a candidate for the priesthood who is determined by his superiors not to be too bright. But because priests are needed, they will ordain him with the restriction that he can only celebrate Mass; he cannot preach or hear confessions.. For us Americans, we have a celebrated case. Barney Casey, born in 1879 in Wisconsin, was from a large immigrant Irish family. A fairly non-descript kid, he knocked around on various jobs before winding up as a streetcar driver. On one rainy afternoon, he witnessed a drunken sailor who had assaulted and stabbed a woman. He could not forget the incident. He prayed for the sailor and the woman and felt called to pray for the whole world.

At 21 he quit his job and applied to St. Francis seminary in Milwaukee. Five years later he joined the Capuchin order in Detroit, where he got his religious name of Solanus. But he was not that bright. Or at least appeared not be, because the classes were conducted in German, which he didn't know. Some seminary professors opposed his ordination, but an old priest spoke up for him and he was ordained in 1904 at age 33. But only under one condition. He would be a "simplex priest." He could celebrate Mass and that was all.

Father Solanus became sacristan and a doorkeeper, first in Yonkers and them in Harlem. But ordinary people were discovering something about this doorkeeper. He was a wonderful listener and insightful counselor. He became known for his compassion and insight. Miracles began to happen. At night he was found in the chapel praying. He died at 86 in 1957. Some 20,000 people passed his coffin. His cause is now up for canonization.

I mention this holy man because it raises the possibility that a parish community, unwilling to forgo the Eucharist because of the priest shortage, can propose a goodly man who need not have all the learning or degrees required but a good heart and be there for the community to preside at its Eucharist. What a boon that would be.

Deacons

Another approach would be to ordain selected married deacons to the priesthood. I suggest this with much hesitancy because deacons truly do have a separate, independent vocation, and I certainly don't want to devalue it by reviving the old notion that the diaconate is but a stepping stone to the priesthood. Because we are in an emergency situation, however, there may be some deacons who in fact have discerned a further call to the priesthood. If that's the case, then ordain them to that office. Deacons have many advantages in this regard. They are already ordained clerics and have gone through extensive training in ministry. The parish community is used to seeing them function liturgically and pastorally. They also can follow the criteria listed above, which relieves the diocese of a heavy financial burden—they are usually mature men, homeowners with intact insurance plans.

Even now, married deacons are serving as interim heads of parishes. In St. Paul-Minneapolis, for example, two married deacons are acting as interim parish administrators while the pastorates of these parishes are waiting to be filled. The way things are now, it is likely to be a long "interim" because in this diocese, as in so many parts of the country, the Catholic population is growing faster than the number of priests available. In fact, St. Paul-Minneapolis has had parish vacancies last for as long as fifteen months. The solution is obvious: instead of playing around with the fiction of a long-term "temporary" administrator while waiting for priests who are less and less there, it would make much more sense to ordain these married deacons to the priesthood.

And then there is the obvious possibility of reinstating married priests. On a recent edition of the Religion and Ethics series on television, the subject was married priests. The segment was full of interviews with former priests, and what came across most strikingly from each of these men was a deep longing to celebrate Mass and the other sacraments. They were still faithful Catholics and, as one said, if offered a chance to come back to the exercise of full ministry, they would do it "in a heartbeat." They all expressed a reverence for the charism of celibacy, but simply noted that it is a charism, a free gift, and not everyone—themselves included—is granted it. They noted that in fact they found themselves more human, more sensitive from the experience of marriage and they deeply desired to bring those gifts back to active ministry.

These were the men who fell in love and discovered a wholeness in marriage that the celibate life simply did not give them. They were happier, reveled in the support and affection of a wife and eventually children, found satisfaction in open sexual expression with their wives (rather than clandestine yearnings or liaisons), and often found that they had a partner in practical church ministry. Many of these priests and their wives (some of whom are former nuns) are engaged in challenging ministries: education, counseling, prison ministry, religious education, social justice, and church work of all kinds. They often show a dedication that simply was not there when they were celibate priests. The fact of their having left the priesthood to enter a married state, as so many of their predecessors did in previous times in history, should not disqualify them. Rather, the satisfaction of their lives and the richness of their ministries should recommend them most fully to be once again present at the altar as an ordained priest.

The whole issue of reinstating married priests becomes painfully acute when the laity and resigned married priests see married clergy from other denominations who have converted to Catholicism being fully accepted as priests both by the Church and by the people. (Every poll shows a high percentage, 70%, of acceptance by the faithful.[12]) The Vatican has allowed the ordination of over 100 married Protestant ministers and so has, in effect, concretely proclaimed that celibacy is not essential for the priesthood. It has effectively reestablished a married clergy through the back door. Ironically, some of these married priests have replaced those priests who married and were forced to leave.

Consider this excerpt written by a priest's daughter:

> My father is not conveniently a doctor, a solicitor, or a bank manager: he is a Catholic priest. Quite a conversation-stopper, or starter, at the best of times. I cannot and will not say that he *was* a Catholic priest, as that would be an untruth. He is no longer a practicing priest; but the sacrament of ordination is indelible and cannot be undone. He is therefore still a priest and will always remain a priest....
>
> The story I am about to tell you is not a tale of deceit and dishonor but one of love, vocation and honesty, the story of a man whose vocation to the priesthood was very real indeed, but whose vocation to love a woman was as great a reality.
>
> My father, the hero of this story, gave many years of faithful service to the Church he loved—and loves, for he has not ceased to love the Catholic Church and is still as active a member of it as he is allowed to be—before he fell in love. It was an unimaginably difficult choice, between the woman he loved and his priesthood, but after months of soul searching and prayer, he made it....
>
> The fact is that the more I learn about him, the more aware I become of his priesthood. He still says his breviary faithfully every day, and his vocation as a priest has grown throughout his married life....Far from reeling under the burden of his family, he finds his wife and children a joy. He was a good priest, and good priests, I believe, make good fathers. Contrary to popular belief, married Catholic priests are not embittered against anything that remotely smacks of Catholicism. My father today is as devout a Catholic as in the days of his active ministry as a priest, and he has brought up his children to love the Catholic traditions and beliefs he holds so dear.

It is not always easy being a Catholic in a secular world, and young Catholics in post-Christian society need all the courage and conviction they can find. Those are the qualities my father has provided for me as I have grown to adulthood. There is only one discordant note. I wonder how long I will have to watch other married priests who were formerly Anglicans saying Mass while my father is forbidden to do so, simply because he was born and brought up a Catholic, has always believed in Catholicism and always will. If he had been brought up a Protestant and crossed over a couple of years ago, he would be a parish priest by now. It hurts that I am allowed to be a [E]ucharistic [M]inister and he is not, despite the fact that he is an ordained priest and theologian.

Times, however, are changing and I still maintain hope in my Church's mercy and justice. It would be a wonderful celebration of 2,000 years of Christianity if the Vatican were to allow married Catholic priests to take part actively in church ministry once again, instead of leaving them wasting on the sidelines when they have so much to offer the Church. Until that time, however, I will continue to wait and pray that one day I will be able to go to Mass and see my father where he truly belongs, at the altar, saying the words of consecration as I know he longs to do.[13]

To repeat, the laity are extremely desirous not to have any reduction in services that priests typically perform, such as Mass, confessions, and anointing of the sick. All indications are that they treasure deeply these ministrations. That is why they have no trouble with a married clergy, which they deem as very preferable to having no clergy at all. Recent polls (NCR-Gallup) show the laity are most willing to extend ordination to married men (71%), formerly active priests (78%) and women (if married, 54%; if celibate, 63%).

Among the 110,000 married priests worldwide, there are over twenty thousand married priests in this country—or, to put it in perspective, one out of every three priests in the United States is married. (Some of them, as we know, are in our parishes: there is a large pool of help out there!) And they remain priests forever (Canon 290), if not clerics. Some are not interested in resuming the clerical state and duties. But many are, and they form an impressive resource for a Church whose current dwindling clergy are aging and overburdened, and whose people, in growing numbers, are being denied the Eucharist.

Rent-a-Priest

Some readers may be aware of the program called Rent-a-Priest, whereby married clergy are invited into a parish to perform clerical duties—sometimes with the knowledge of the bishop, who discreetly looks the other way, grateful for the help. It should be noted, however, that some resigned priests will have no part of this irregular program as part of normal ministry, arguing that they do not wish to be part of any noncanonical, freelance ministry that separates them from the authorization of the local bishop. As one resigned priest put it, "I don't want to be part of yet another schism."[14] But since the very existence of such a program makes an ironic point, it is worth looking at.

Rent-a-Priest was started in 1992 by a traditional Catholic lady who couldn't find a priest to visit her mother, who was in a nursing home. (Remember the polls: people do want the ministrations of priests.) Thus, she started the Rent-a-Priest program, calling on married priests to perform clerical duties, so that all Catholics, especially the elderly, would never be without a priest. The program features a list of married priests, many of whom are in our own counties and even our own parishes. This list can be accessed on the web at www.rentapriest.com. (My list of Rent-a-Priests includes many men from my local community.)

Canon law, rightly keeping the pastoral needs of the people ever in mind, allows many exceptions in emergencies. For example, priests without faculties can hear confessions in danger of death (Canon 976 or 884:2), administer confirmation in the same situation (Canon

883:3), or anoint the sick (Canon 1003:2). We are in an emergency situation where, because of the shortage of priests, the spiritual needs of the people go wanting and where people are turning to other religions because of our lack of shepherding. In such pastoral emergencies, would the same pastoral reasoning apply? If not, we have to ask ourselves if we have moved celibacy away from being a charism to being an idol.

Here is an intriguing question which brings up a nice practical issue: does the parish have a moral obligation to print in its bulletin the Rent-a-Priest list—not, of course, as an act of defiance but as an act of compassion? Consider this: your mother is dying and you need a priest, but due to the shortage of priests or to the burdens of the resident priest, none are available. Would you not want a resource for priestly ministrations for your loved one who is in extremis (at death's door)—especially if you knew that, in such an emergency, Church law allows precisely such an action? There is no question what a parish must do, both from a moral and pastoral standpoint, since "the salvation of souls...is always the supreme law of the Church." And once that not-too-far-fetched scenario begins to become commonplace, then a married clergy will indeed come in by the back door. It is like a previous situation, where the early Church positively forbade the Irish practice of private confessions over public confessions, until private confession became so popular that the Church had to accept it. In this same way, the Church will be forced to accept married priests.

Returning to the ancient tradition of ordaining local community leaders (such as St. Paul did) is a practice whose time has come. We must always keep in mind that in the early Church, it was unthinkable that a settled community would lack a priest. They would simply choose one. Period. Raymond Brown, a conservative Biblical scholar, writes:

> A more plausible substitute for the chain theory [of apostolic succession] is the thesis that sacramental "powers" were part

of the mission of the Church and that there were diverse ways in which the Church (or communities) designated individuals to exercise those powers—the essential element always being church or community consent (which was tantamount to ordination), whether or not that consent was signified by a special ceremony such as the laying on of hands.[15]

Bishops who agonize over the shortage of priests, who see their current priests overworked and overextended; the priests themselves who would welcome help and know that their parishes are much too large for one man and need to be divided; the people who, as all the polls show, are hungry for the Eucharist and thereby open to a married clergy—surely bishops, priests, and laity constitute a *sensus fidelium*, a movement of the Spirit, who tells us it is time for history to repeat itself.

18

THE HUNGERING AND THE HOPE

We know that organized religion today is in crisis. There abounds in many quarters a marked disaffection for institutional religion and a clear affection for personal spirituality. Social scientists point to our global, free-market economy as well as our high social and geographic mobility as the cause of this crisis. People, always traveling, always moving, are more and more cut off from their extended families and value-laden local traditions, making it difficult for people to be socially or religiously anchored. Add to this the fact that people these days are forced to live in a very homogenized and depersonalized high-tech society produced by the global corporate economy, and you get a double bind.

On one hand, people are being cut off from the stable, traditional sources of belief and ritual; on the other, they are awash in endless value-neutral diversity. Where can they go but to their own inner resources in order to find answers to their questions about life? In the context of this world, people simply can no longer relate to any kind of institutional Church that comes along with a set hierarchy, a codified way of worship and belief, and precise rules. They find that this is an affront to the diversity they know and cherish.

In short, there is no longer an accepted and public moral framework for any kind of meaning or direction in life. As a result, people are forced to choose and construct their own spiritual journey. They design, not a spiritual life, but a spiritual lifestyle. And they find this quite compatible with the fast moving, multicultural world they live in because it gives them precisely the flexibility, space, and ability to flow that no rigid or uptight (as they see it) formal religion can offer. Hence, they are spiritual but not religious.

So the number of professed church-affiliated believers continues to drop. And it's just as bad elsewhere, if not worse. We have been concentrating on our own country, but all statistics show that Christian Europe is really Christian no longer. Mass attendance, ordinations, baptisms, and Church marriages have fallen steadily in Britain. The Belgian Jesuit Fr. Jan Kerkhofs has tracked thirteen European countries over the past twenty years, and his research shows the same trend in those countries.[1] In former Communist East Germany and the Czech Republic, for example, 74% of the population does not belong to any church. Denmark and Sweden are famous for their lack of a churchgoing population. David Martin, an English sociologist, says that the departure of Christianity in Europe has reached unprecedented proportions: "Europe has become the only really secular continent in the world." Sociologist Peter Berger says that Europe has become "a church catastrophe," while a *Herald Tribune* survey concludes that today Europe is "the most godless quarter on earth." A poll conducted by the German newspaper *Der Spiegel* finds that "the Germans have lost their belief in God, and with it their Christian philosophy of life."[2]

So concerned are some that Giacomo Cardinal Biffi, the Archbishop of Bologna, created a major uproar when he summoned some 300 priests and a bevy of journalists to call, in effect, for a crusade against Muslim immigration. Such open discrimination is embarrassing at a time when the Church has reached out to non-Christian religions. (John Paul II met with Muslim leaders more than fifty times during his papacy and called them "brothers in Abraham.")

But in one sense, Cardinal Biffi has reason for alarm. The reality is that the Muslim population in Europe has doubled in the past decade while Judeo-Christian populations have declined. For example, there are more Muslims in Italy than Protestants or Jews. Islam is the number two religion in France. Moreover, in contrast to the nonpractice of the European Catholics, the Muslims are enthusiastic practitioners of their faith. Evidence of this is seen in the opening of the first mosque in Rome in 1995; about a hundred more have opened in Italy at large since 1989.

Furthermore, the Muslims have more children than the Europeans, whose family size has shrunk drastically. The birthrate in Italy, for example, is now below replacement rate and other countries, like Spain, are fast catching up. Finally, as the Cardinal pointed out, the Muslims are less easily integrated into the Italian culture with their differences in diet, holy days, family structure, treatment of women, and most of all, their deep belief that there is a unity between politics and religion. While some saw the Cardinal's call as a form of discrimination, all were made aware that Muslim immigration is a potent sign that the Church has collapsed on a continent that once was called Christendom.

Then, too, science seems to go on undermining religion.[3] Technology awes us. Consumerism and celebrity continue to define what and who we are. Urban sprawl, the rape of Earth's land and the extinction of its wildlife, the collapse of marriage and family life, an ongoing cycle of drugs and crime—all of these situations are part of our own lives. The Catholic faith continues to lose adherents. The numbers of priests and seminarians are in decline.

It would seem that the old prediction of the Enlightenment has come true; to wit, that modernization would lead to secularization and a total decline of religion. It is true that secularization has made inroads even into the mainline religions, whose numbers have declined dramatically. (As the old saying goes, when the Church marries the culture, it soon becomes a widow.) But it is equally true that secularization has provoked powerful counter-movements, creating religious subcultures such as the Amish or the Hasidic Jews. (But even they have been invaded by the secular world, for example, as their children buy and sell drugs.) Secularization has also spawned an increase in membership in powerful, conservative religious movements such as Islam, Hinduism, and Buddhism. With the collapse of the atheistic Soviet Union, the conservative Russian Orthodox Church has had a remarkable revival. The evangelical churches (like Islam elsewhere) are in the midst of one of the great religious revivals in history in China, South Korea, the Philippines, and especially and most spectacularly, in Latin America.

In the United States, the number of religious groups active today has multiplied, while interest in the paranormal and the supernatural is epidemic. Look at the ongoing proliferation of movies and TV shows about angels, life after death, superheroes with extraplanetary powers, and all the rest. We seem to be on the verge of another "Great Awakening"—though observers have noted that the "fire and brimstone" that accompanied the previous Great Awakening has been substituted with "Christianity lite," a kind of low-calorie religion that embraces sentiment and resists institutionalization.

Still, there is a great awakening at hand, and all this turning to religion or to superhuman beings, even in a backdoor way, is understandable for two reasons. First of all, secularization undermines the certainties that are taken for granted, and many people (outside of university professors) simply find this hard to bear. Thus, anything that promises to renew certainty, to suggest meaning and purpose to life, has a ready market. That is why strong religious movements will always arise to run counter to a culture that tries to get along without any transcendent point of reference. As Peter Berger puts it:

> The religious impulse, the quest for meaning that transcends the restricted space of empirical existence in this world, has been a perennial feature of humanity....The critique of secularity common to all the resurgent movements is that human existence bereft of transcendence is an impoverished and finally untenable condition.[4]

Second, the average person, especially the average parent (as we have seen previously in this book), deeply resents the cultural elites who attack their cherished beliefs from their bully pulpits in the universities and in the media, and who have nothing to offer their children but the bread and circus of money and sex. They know there is more available with which to nourish their children, and they will seek it. And this is why—outside of Europe which is, as we have seen, the one truly secular spot on the globe—religion is flourishing. (But even there, rather than having disappeared, religion has more likely shifted from being an institutional belief system to a more personal belief system.) Indeed, the revival of religion is everywhere.

Revival

Item: In one twelve-month period it was estimated that approximately five million people purchased books about angels (none of which, by the way, were published by churches or written by clergy).

Item: Half of a recent *New York Times* nonfiction bestseller list contained books about spirituality.

Item: The findings of a survey entitled "Religious Beliefs, Spiritual Practices, and Science in the 21st Century" conducted by the Gallup Poll Organization indicate that the twenty-first century could become the most spiritual and religious century in the last 500 years.[5]

Item: Note the ubiquitous presence these days of retreat centers, holistic health organizations, self-help groups, and psychic boutiques.

Item: A very large percentage of popular TV shows and movies deal with the supernatural, from *The X-Files* to movies such as *The Matrix*, *The Sixth Sense*, and *Being John Malkovich*, both of the latter nominated for Oscars.

Item: The enormous popularity of the Harry Potter books among both children and adults testifies to the keen interest in the paranormal, which is always a backdoor entrance to the world of the spirit.

Item: Top scientists make statements like this, from Nobel prize winner Carl Rubbia: "A higher intelligence exists here—over and above the existence of the universe itself."

Item: The Princeton Religion Research Center reports that "religious faith continues to be important to teens" and "67 percent of people say religion can answer today's problems— the highest since 1957."[6]

Item: More public soul-searching goes on among the affluent bene- ficiaries of wealth, and in an open-ended culture where people are now asking questions such as "Is technology making us intimate strangers?"[7] A new, lonelier crowd has emerged from a study of Internet users, people who are seeking community. In other words, in a booming economy, people are asking, "What's it all about, Alfie?"

Item: For many people modern society means "an emptiness, a void that has rendered life meaningless." Scientific rationalism discredits myth but offers nothing in its place; in its worst form, rationalism has led to totalitarian states.[8] Many folks, overwhelmed by their buying binges in affluent times and drowning in their accumulations, are sensing a deep dissatis- faction with so much materialism.

Item: The median size of a new house in the United States is over 2,000 square feet, 25% bigger than two decades ago. Ford's $45,000 vehicle, the Expedition, is selling out as soon as it reaches the dealer; when purchased, it is stored, along with the family's other vehicles, in a garage the size of a gymnasium. Half of all U.S. households invest in the stock market. And yet even with all this prosperity, people sense they are falling be- hind. They do not have enough time for their families, and they are more stressed. "People are looking for more than material values," says Glen Chilstrom, a psychologist who started a group for people trying to have better balance in their lives. "They realize they're overspending, and they're dissatisfied. They're looking to develop their spiritual values."[9]

And concerning Catholic matters:

Item: Over 100,000 young people from Eastern and Western Europe flocked to Vienna for a meeting with members of Taizé (an ecumenical Christian community), and in 1997 almost a million young people came to World Youth Day in Paris to meet Pope John Paul II.

Item: Tens of thousands of young people turned out for the papal Mass at the Sea of Galilee when John Paul II visited Israel— as happens in every place and every country he visited.

Item: There is a proliferation of groups like RENEW that focus on prayer, Scripture, and the spiritual life. More than four million people have participated in these movements in this country. CARA reports that in an overall evaluation of RENEW, the participants and their leaders give very high ratings to the communal aspects of RENEW, expressing the positive feelings they have in these small faith-sharing communities and the spiritual growth they have experienced.[10] A significant proportion of the 500,000 participants in the RENEW 2000 report are being encouraged to consider lay ministry (21%) or the priesthood or religious life (10%). Add to this the increase of vital parishes and the successes of the RCIA process.

Item: There are an estimated 37,000 small Christian communities (SCCs) in the United States with an estimated number of 45,000 to 50,000 participants.[11]

Item: After 140 years of suppression the Church was allowed to celebrate an open-air Mass in Mexico. It was attended by hundreds of thousands in the sprawling plaza known as Zocalo.

Item: Africa and Asia show a marked increase in the number of Catholics. Every day the Church in the West loses 2,000 members. But every day there are 16,000 new Church members in sub-Saharan Africa, showing an annual growth of 33%.

Item: At the Easter Vigil around the United States the Catholic Church welcomes tens of thousands of new members through the RCIA process. In the past five years in this country more than 160,000 adults annually have entered the Church. During Easter 2013 in the top twenty U.S. dioceses, 17,839 people became Catholic through the RCIA process.

Item: While the number of religious is declining, the number of lay associates all over the world who are involved with religious orders is rising. A recent study shows that 25,000 laypeople around the world are formally attached to religious orders, volunteering their time for everything from prayer to paperwork to caring for the sick and poor. That's a steep increase from the 4000 lay associates in 1989.

Item: While nine major mainline Protestant denominations lost 22% of their membership between 1970 and 1997 and evangelical denominations gained a startling 40%, Roman Catholics, contrary to the popular impression, are nearer the latter than the former. Its membership has increased during those years.

Item: In his book *American Catholics,* Charles Morris studied American Catholics on two levels, one national and the other local. He saw considerable turmoil on the national scene, with divisions among Catholics whom he grouped into liberal, radical, traditional, and conservative camps and whose squabbles provide fodder for the news media. On the local level, however, he found a very different story. He found parish life to be thriving. He found core parishioners who are educated, intelligent, and liberal-minded with a lively interest in their religion. These people spoke of the liturgy as central to their lives, and they were actively involved in parish life. And they are legion.

The seeking

It is clear that even when people look in the most bizarre places and indiscriminately read the most awful "spiritual" nonsense, they are hungering for direction, purpose, and meaning to life. They are seeking rituals to express spiritual feelings that are routinely denied or suppressed in our culture. They are desperately seeking God, especially the young—for even here, in the fast lane, underneath it all there is a search. Listen to author James Gleick, who writes in his aptly titled book *Faster*:

> Today we just don't do one thing anymore. We multi-task. In the car we drink coffee, listen to self-improvement tapes, talk on the cellular phone and floss. We're on the run. Cars advertise themselves as the vehicle for busy families as the videotape shows the car screeching to pick up family members—and the dog—dashing here, there and everywhere for "a good time." We use shampoo that cuts down drying time 30 percent. Honed by video games, workers function at "twitch speed." Politicians are coached to speak in ten-second sound bites, and a three-minute television news segment is considered long....We are speeding cartoons, cloud puffs scutting behind our heels. There is no time for contemplation. We live in the crisis lane.

Seeing all this, seeing us glued to our cellular phones and our screens, Gleick has an astute comment that is germane to our chapter here. He says:

> It is a way of keeping contact with someone, anyone, who will reassure you that you are not alone. You may think you are checking on your portfolio, but deep down you are checking on your existence.

The point here is that more than ever, even in counterfeit ways, people are "checking on their existence." People are in search of belief. All of us are on a quest for meaning and purpose in our lives, and the fact that some people insist that neither exists is intolerable. Neither science nor the vague agnosticism prevalent in our culture can give answers to the unresolved mysteries of life. As far as we know there has never been a people or a tribe that had no religion. Religion is simply a part of being human.

We have this terrible longing for God, and yet there is a departure from the institutional Church. We can satisfy that longing because, in spite of everything, we have kept the essential Christ, and must find ways to proclaim him anew once more. There are small signs of hope. For one thing, Catholicism has survived 2000 years precisely because it has shown a most remarkable capacity to renew itself. We must tap into that genius again. Think, for example, of the recent progress of the Church: since Vatican II, many inter-Christian po-larizations and divisions have disappeared, especially those which caused the Protestants to break away in the sixteenth century. Also, people are returning to the Catholic Church because they can now find their protests resolved and the fulfillment of what they already believe.

Think of the stunning apology for the sins of the Church, made by Pope John Paul II as he knelt before a fifteenth century crucifix in St. Peter's Basilica. No one has done that before on such a scale. This is unique in the Church. We might remember the image described in a previous chapter, that of Emperor Henry IV standing barefoot in the snow, begging the forgiveness of Pope Gregory VII in 1077 at Canossa; or Pope Urban II rallying Christian Europe to the cause of the Crusades at Claremont in France in 1095; or Pope Pius VII reluctantly officiating at Napoleon's self-crowning in 1804 at the Cathedral of Notre Dame. But there has never been a pope on the receiving end, so to speak. Never has a pope humbly apologized for the sins of his own Church.

This unprecedented act was admirable, moving, and humbling. The pope was breaking new ground. It was, as he knew, a symbolic action. In this it was similar to the time when Paul VI donated his papal tiara to the poor people of India during the 1965 Eucharistic Congress, or the ceremony of reconciliation between Paul VI and the Patriarch of Constantinople, regretting the sins of the eleventh-century division between East and West, or the welcoming of Protestant observers to the Second Vatican Council, apologizing to them for Rome's part in Christian divisions. And so it was with John Paul II. No longer the very embodiment of medieval politics, power, and triumphalism, here was a very old man bowing low on behalf of the Church, saying "mea culpa." It was indeed an historic moment, causing Lance Morrow to write in *Time Magazine*:

> An apology must be made with a good heart. It must also be re-ceived with a good heart....In the apology, the Pope does what a leader ought to do. He sets an example. Only by apology on one side and forgiveness on the other—acts of moral clarification and of collaboration—can the dead weight of the past be lifted. The apology was an admirable way for an old Pope to start a new millennium.[12]

But there was more to it, as we know. To put action to his words this bent, frail figure visited Israel and the Holocaust memorial. Who was not moved, both friend and foe, Christian and Jew, by the sight of John Paul II with head bowed in a long silence, standing alone before a granite slab with the world looking on, honoring the graves of unidentified victims of the Holocaust. Nor should we fail to take note of the symbolism of another action. The pope, who usually sits in an armchair while people file before him, did not do this at the Holocaust memorial. Rather, like Jesus getting up from the table to wash the feet of his disciples, John Paul II got up from his chair and shuffled humbly across the darkened room alone, between the inscribed words "Buchenwald" and "Auschwitz," to shake the hands of six Holocaust survivors including several Jews from his Polish hometown, a very touching and emotional high point of his trip.

Never had a pope been so humble. Never had a pope moved the world so deeply. Never had enemies shaken their heads in awe and respect.

This was the papacy's finest hour.

Yes, there were naysayers, who said he didn't go far enough. And there were others who still vigorously do not agree with his policies, people from Catholic theologian Hans Küng to Pulitzer Prize nominee and Presbyterian minister Frederick Buechner. But the pope's policies weren't the issue here. Rather it was his example; it was the fact that he sought healing among Catholics and Jews, taking a stance of humility rather than arrogance, saying we were wrong when we always said we were right and others were wrong. His apology caught the world's eye and opened up new avenues of tolerance and unity.

All this shows that the Church, even as it still carries an unconscionable burden of bureaucracy inherited from the counter-Reformation and the hubris of the eighteenth and nineteenth centuries, is really endowed with a capacity for renewal that is difficult to find anywhere else or in any other church. And many people are finding that attractive.

The power of the sacraments and the Mass

Finally, we should never, never underestimate the power and attraction of the sacraments and the Mass. In spite of very real defections among the general Catholic population along with the religious illiteracy among young adults which we discussed in chapter three, the latter nevertheless are drawn to the sacraments—as evidenced by the significant number of Baptisms, First Communions (an impressive 85%) and Confirmations (59%) received by their children. These numbers have remained remarkably stable indicating that young people, although attached to Catholicism in their own way, are nevertheless attached.

As for the Mass—and the community of the people who celebrate it— it remains a powerful draw (which is why doing liturgy well should always be a priority). In a book entitled *Why I Am Still a Catholic,*

Kevin and Marilyn Ryan gathered responses to that question from twenty-five well-known people. What is remarkable is how often the authors cite the Mass as the central reason why they are still members of the Catholic Church. Novelist Jon Hasler is one of those persons. He writes:

> I'm still a Catholic because I love the Mass. It punctuates my life like a semicolon; it's a pause, a breather, in my week, my day. I don't pray very well at Mass; in fact I often don't pay much attention, yet sixty years of church-going has left me with a need—it's more than mere habit; it's a deep-seated need—to be lifted up and carried along time after time, by the familiar words and rubrics. It's like boarding a boat and standing out from the shore of my life for a half-hour or so, viewing it through the refreshing air of a calm and scenic harbor.[13]

And as for converts, listen to this woman, a feminist who left the Church and has returned:

> I continue to get angry at what I see as the hypocrisy of the hierarchy; sometimes it seems to me they don't have an inkling of what Jesus is really about....But I've come to understand that this is my church too, and I intend to reclaim it for my own.... We are the church. When my friends ask me, why the Catholic church?—why not one of the other Christian churches?—I can now easily answer them. I have come back to the Catholic [C]hurch because nowhere else can I celebrate the liturgy with others on a daily basis. Nowhere else can I daily receive the body and blood of Jesus Christ. The Eucharist is the primary reason I'm a Catholic.[14]

Another feminist, an English Protestant, writes:

> It was personal factors which provided the catalysts. My mother died in 1996, followed three months later by my beloved godmother. Moving from a job with the Council of Churches to a highly commercial publisher was proving more

of a culture shock than I had expected. Distressing problems had arisen in the East End church which had been my spiritual home for twelve years. We had moved to a village (not the one where we now live and worship) where the rural church was a liturgical desert, where Easter was reduced to the sun and the flowers and the darling baby rabbits, and where I never heard a woman speak or read. On top of it all, after months of anxiety, doctors had put a name (but not a treatment) to a tiresome health problem. I lost two stone in weight, and began to think I had lost God as well.

Longing for peace and liturgical coherence, I decided, one Sunday, to go to the little stone church attached to the Augustinian priory in Clare, Suffolk, some miles from the village where we lived. For the first time in months, I found myself freed to encounter God. Oh the relief! The next week, I came again.

And the next. Looking back, I suppose it was a bit like being on holiday: feeling better for the break, but knowing you'll have to go home in the end. It is inconvenient when you start to identify with a Church which is not your own. You become a traitor in your own eyes, one who flirts with "another," self-indulgent whims taking precedence over lifelong commitments. But surely, I thought, the love affair we have is not with the Church, it is with God. The Church is there to provide that love affair with the best possible chance of bearing fruit.

Two things happened. On the Tuesday of Holy Week, my Jewish-born husband and I joined in the parish celebration of the Passover meal, and towards the end of the evening I found myself part of a cheerful group doing the washing up in the kitchen. I had a sudden revelation. "I'm fed up with being a visitor," I thought. "If I'm washing the dishes, I want to be part of the family." The second was the Easter Vigil: a service of extraordinary beauty and grace, during which I found myself, at last, able to make friends with the various problems in my own life, and to say goodbye to the two "mothers" I had lost so many months before.[15]

A minister who became a Catholic priest adds his testimony:

> Of course the real home of Catholics is not to be found in any city [Rome], for here we have no abiding city, but it is to be found in the Mass at which the pilgrim people gather to "proclaim the Lord's death until he comes" (1 Cor 11:6) to lead us to our final home. In such gatherings I see again and again the Lord who has compassion on the hungry crowd and feeds them, the Lord who invites to his table tax-gatherers and sinners. I challenge any other organization, sacred or secular, to be able to produce, week by week, such a cross-section of humanity. Here is the reality of Catholicism—not a uniformed army but a motley mob of all sorts, ordinary people whose faith mingles with doubts and tears, who with often heroic courage, try to be followers of Christ.
>
> When I was in Oxford I used to say the 9 am Mass at the university chaplaincy at which a local judge would often be a [E]ucharistic [M]inister, and I would then set off down the road accompanied by a few students to celebrate the same Mass for that judge's clients in the prison. Two different worlds you might say—a world of the gifted and privileged young and a world of the failures, the broken and defeated— but the presence of the one Christ in the Mass embracing them both. And I have seen the same in school and parishes, the Catholic Church providing a home for all sorts and conditions. Of course that makes it a messy and muddled Church, not at all the ideal Church fit only for heroes and zealots, but content to be the net which catches all sorts of fish, the field in which wheat and weeds have space to grow together. It is here that the real drama of faith takes place, amongst flawed imperfect lives that the torrent of the Holy Spirit flows, God working amongst people who often seem to have to face insurmountable difficulties, yet God working triumphantly in almost every community to produce that thin red line of real but unobtrusive saints whose goodness is attractive because it is unselfconscious.[16]

Finally, read this testimony from an unusual American lady, a feminist and a minister, a woman of vast pastoral experience and power named Patricia Carol who became a Catholic in September of 1999. Why? She answers:

> My heart got stuck in the daily Mass, and I cannot leave. Some 15 months ago, I came through the doors of the Catholic [C]hurch in spiritual crisis. My marriage had ended. My complicated life of being married to another minister had led to a train wreck of my personal, professional and faith life, and I couldn't find God.
>
> I felt the need to be with people praying but didn't want to have to explain myself or my inevitable tears, so I went to a daily Mass. I didn't know the first thing about a Mass. But that first day I knew I needed to learn the words, the prayers, the saints. I knew I had to see Advent and Lent, Christmas and Easter. I felt the need to see the year's cycle unfold. I feel that I am hearing the stories of Jesus as if for the first time, though I've heard them my whole life. I feel that I am not to set this down for the security of my position, prestige or paycheck.
>
> Why do I want to join this [C]hurch? Because I have felt more prayed for than at any time in my life. The prayers are for the injured, the depressed, those with back pain, those addicted— not me, and yet definitely me. Me as connected to everyone. Why do I want to join this [C]hurch? Because the saints and the examples of faithfulness are so real and compelling that they remind me to be faithful. I find myself wondering, "Who wrote that call to worship? Who combined these words so gently and beautifully? Who wrote that song? Who put these readings together for this day, just when I need them?"
>
> Why do I want to join this [C]hurch? Because the people come every day. Young and old, with babies and walkers, with business suits and rumpled T-shirts. They sing and say together, "Lord, hear our prayer," and move with focus to the Eucharist. I stay in my pew and feel the currents of the air around me, created by the movement of their bodies, perhaps by the movement of the spirit.

Why do I want to join this [C]hurch that "no thinking person" would join? It is true that I see contradictions and flaws. I do not understand why people are silenced for reaching out a hand of love. I believe Jesus also reached out with a radical love, and the dissonance created by such silencing is deafening.

I regret that women are not able to serve the [C]hurch as priests. I wish I could simply transfer my ministerial credentials and preach. I suspect I would have some things to say. But I have come to realize that waiting for a church without contradictions, a church of perfect justice and consistency might keep me from the most important thing. The most important thing is to follow the call of Jesus, the call of God. I want to join this [C]hurch that has brought me so close to that love, to the vision of justice and to a deep personal peace and joy.[17]

Parenthetically, we cannot resist reminding ourselves that all these testimonies, both from born Catholics and from converts, point out the urgent need to provide celebrants for the Eucharist. The people have a right to "have their hearts stuck at daily Mass" and, even more, at the Sunday Mass. The fact that celibacy, noble as it is, should continuously subvert the Eucharist would never have been tolerated by the early Church. Nor should it be now.

The power of example

Notice in all these testimonies the power of the Mass and the example of the worshipping community. As it has always been, we have here a wonderful force for renewal and hope. One of the problems we face is the temptation to fixate on high profile issues that the media pushes as the essence of Catholicism, that is, the sexual issues: premarital sex, homosexual unions, sexual scandals involving priests, and so on. These are the preoccupations of society and they deflect us from understanding and proclaiming our real strengths as a Church. We will not win people over with endless arguments and defenses about sex. We will win them over with the beauty of our liturgies and with communities that care. People are touched through a sense of the sacred and a sense of authenticity in life. That is why the Mass remains a potent and powerful example of our faith.

I have the opportunity to visit many parishes. I am awed over the vital ones, the ones where the people are so vocally in love with the Church and such a part of it. They all speak of "the spirit," by which they mean the care, compassion, and deep sense of community that abounds in their parish. Needless to say, the leadership of the pastor is crucial to creating such feelings. One city parish I visited has a full-time visiting nurse on staff; she alone has made a tremendous difference to the parish and to the neighborhood as she makes her indiscriminate rounds. In another parish, the people donate so many cans of Spam for the people of Haiti with whom they have a covenant that they cannot handle the flow. Another parish has a truly compassionate outreach to the poor and shut-ins.

Finally, there is this example. When John Cardinal O'Connor, the prominent bishop of New York, died in May of 2000, there followed a tremendous outpouring of love and appreciation for this man even from those who disagreed with him on almost every issue. The New York Jewish community, the most populous in the world, could not say enough about O'Connor's empathy, understanding, and ability to reach out to people. The former mayor of New York, Ed Koch, another member of the Jewish community, was a personal friend and grieved over his death. Some members of Act-Up, the group of gay activists who had shamefully desecrated St. Patrick's cathedral some years back, praised the cardinal for starting one of the first and most comprehensive AIDS help programs, and they admired his almost daily visits to AIDS patients, caring for them and emptying their bed pans. Opponents who resented his unbending stands on moral issues were effusive over this man's kindness and charity; they spoke feelingly of his firm stance and were happy to have met a man who stood for something. O'Connor was constantly praised as a man who held his ground as a representative of the Church but, while doing so, washed the feet of the poor and needy. In the wake of his death, countless little people came forth to reveal his Christlike charity. The Church was seen in a better light because of him.

And so in some ways we can sense a turnabout in the perception of the Church. This vaunted individualism, this do-your-own-thing business is showing signs of wearing thin. Going it alone has proved to be risky, self-serving, and ultimately unsatisfying. That is why respected commentator Martin Marty predicts that, "all those people who say they're spiritual but not religious, who encounter the Divine while meditating or at weekend retreats, and who find their 'Bibles' in the spirituality section at Barnes & Noble, are going to start seeking community."[18]

Conclusion

A reality check. For all that has been written in this chapter, we return to the stubborn fact that the world does grow steadily more secular every day as science continually adds more natural explanations and subtracts the need for supernatural ones. We are at a point in history where we can now construct our own universe as well as our own faith or lack of it.

And that remains the problem. As "masters of our own fate," as free-floating atoms of self-definition, people nevertheless continue to feel adrift. They feel a profound, often unarticulated, unease. Once people used to feel connected to each other by a spiritual bond, by a transcendent world of spirit and enchantment, but now? Now the social and spiritual landscape is segregated (the haves and have nots), flat, one-dimensional, confined to one's own ultimately self-constructed interpretation. For all of the advantages, all the modern social and scientific progress, things don't set well and we can't get our house in order. Society is at once more open and more dangerous, more liberating and more captive to the corporations and their advertising auxiliaries that turn wants into needs and define people's worth solely in terms of consumption. People, deep down, simply do not want to live in a world closed off from the transcendent, a world that is merely material. Witness, as we have noted before, the insatiable fascination with zombies, vampires and aliens. There remains a spiritual hunger, the yearning for community, for the transcendent.

Perhaps Charles Taylor had it right when he suggested that, instead of decrying and condemning them, we harvest the intellectual and social gains of the past 500 years (for example, we don't burn heretics or pass Jim Crow laws anymore) and rejoice in the pluralism modern life offers. Yes, such pluralism may bring shallowness and endless options, silly and serious, but it beats the stultification and conformity that organized religion has often imposed. Let us accept the fact that the modern world does offer a secular future but one that must necessarily contain pockets of spiritual rigor propelled by religion. People are hard-wired for the transcendent and that is our advantage. In short, it's up to us to embrace the gains of a secular society while offering it the faith it is often unknowingly seeking. For ourselves, we have to learn to live with the doubts that secularism raises and witness while doubting.[19]

19

LINKING LITURGY AND LIFE

To spring from the inspiration of the last chapter and to begin to formulate a response to the challenges that the Church faces today, let me present the centerpiece which will underpin all of the remarks to come—that the parish of the future must link liturgy and life. If there is to be a parish of the future, it must categorically and absolutely be centered around the Eucharist. I know that sounds banal at first hearing, almost trite. But let me refer to a homily I gave this past year on the Feast of Corpus Christi, when I said (among other things):

> The feast of Corpus Christi refers to the whole people of God, the congregation, the gathering of the community of faith. The people are the Body of Christ. And one exists for the sake of the other. In other words, the only reason that Jesus is the Body of Christ in the Eucharist is that we might be the Body of Christ in our world.
>
> To put it another way, the Jesus-presence in the Eucharist is for the sake of the Jesus-presence in the world through us. They are interconnected. As Jesus nourishes us with his body and blood in the Eucharist, we are to nourish the world with our body and blood. The Real Presence in the Eucharist exists only to make us the Real Presence in the world. If you break that connection, you wind up with empty in-house piety and the absence of Jesus' mission in the world.

> What I am saying—what this feast is saying and reminding us—is that we are not here alone. We are here to listen to the same Scripture and break the same bread as our brothers and sisters throughout the world, whether in cathedrals or prisons or households or hospitals, free or enslaved, openly or secretly. We are, through our baptism, in solidarity with all who are the worldwide Body of Christ. This feast, therefore, is not so much a focus on the sacred species as it is a focus on those who eat and drink the sacred species, and what they do with it.[1]

In that homily I was trying to reconnect what has been woefully lost—what, as we saw in chapter fifteen, all the theologians and liturgists bemoan as the worst failure of Vatican II: to effectively connect worship and witness. I wanted to remind the people of our tradition, which speaks of four ways Christ is present in the Eucharist: in the gathered assembly, in the priest presiding, in the word proclaimed, and in the meal shared. Christ's presence reserved in the tabernacle is quite derivative and secondary to his living presence in the celebration, and in that living celebration which we then bring out into the world. Remember, the ideal and the teaching of Vatican II is that we are transformed by the Eucharist in order to transform the world. It is not too much to say, I think, that the core of the message of Vatican II was that the members of the Church should be set "on fire"—the Council's phrase—and to share that fire, the love of God, with the world. They were, the Council said, "to renew the temporal order." The laity were charged with the apostolate, no longer as a sharing in the bishops' mission, but in a mission that is theirs by Baptismal right. Everyone is charged at Baptism with the task of interpreting life in the light of faith.

Derailment

But what happened to separate the liturgy from lived faith? How did we lose sight of the Council's insistence that there must be a connection between liturgy and life? Why has the social dimension of liturgy, so central in the heyday of the liturgical movement, vanished? In a paper written for a conference a few years ago, Juan Hinojosa made some assertions that I would like to reiterate. He says that, although there are many parishes, numerous movements, and large numbers of individuals that are wonderful exceptions, nonetheless, he believes that if one examines U.S. Catholicism as a whole, the following seven statements apply:

1. The vocation and mission of the laity are not a priority in the Church and are generally not understood, affirmed, encouraged, or supported.

2. There is a fundamental disconnection between what the laity experience at church and in their ordinary lives, families, occupations, and civic involvements. They do not find what they experience at church particularly relevant to what they experience in their day-to-day lives.

3. The spiritual resources in our rich tradition—retreats, spiritual direction, discernment, etc.—generally do not serve as the resources people need in order to recognize the sacred in their everyday lives or to become agents of the Gospel in the world.

4. Faith consciousness, defined as a lively sense of God's presence and call, is diffuse in the vast majority of laity.

5. There is a general lack of mission focus and consciousness on the part of the laity.

6. At many parishes, worship is routine and ineffective in providing the laity with the spiritual sustenance and resources needed to be effective in transforming the world in the light of the Gospel.

7. After the Second Vatican Council, the focus at both parish and diocesan levels shifted toward affirming those laity who would serve the pastoral task of the Church in internal

ministries, but almost totally neglected the mission of the laity in the world.[2]

Pretty accurate, I think. Our problem is that we have developed neither the mentality nor the vision to do the real work of the parish, which is the formation of lay disciples who feel a necessary, holy compulsion toward evangelization. After all, as Pope Paul VI noted:

> People today put more trust in witnesses than preachers, in experience than in teaching, in life and action than in theories. The witness of a Christian is first and irreplaceable for mission. (*Redemptoris Missio*, 42)

We simply do not provide preparation and formation for our parishioners for their role as disciples and evangelizers. We do not inculcate a profound sense of the dignity and the challenges of discipleship. Rather, our parishes are all too often thought of in terms of administration and internal survival—some have used the metaphor of a nursing home—rather than a place that calls people to mission beyond it. The fact is, most people who do come to church come to receive its spiritual goods and then depart with little concept of their mandate to evangelize the world they inhabit. There is no internal conviction that "the Church, placed in the neighborhoods of humanity...lives and is at work through being deeply inserted in human society and intimately bound up with its aspirations and its dramatic events" (*Christifideles Laici*, 74). Why is this? We might sum it up this way:

- Catholics widely assume that only the ordained have an official role in the Church and in the Church's mission. The great attention paid to the question of who should be ordained signifies this fact. We must accept that, however ironic, the post-conciliar Church harbors a marked tendency to clericalism.

- Most Catholics experience the parish according to a pre-conciliar paradigm; that is, the parish exists in order to offer the laity the spiritual goods of the Church. That the parish is a "stable community of the faithful" with its own part in the mission of the Church to the world does not enter into the experience of most Catholics.

- The mission of the Church to the world has not yet been sufficiently proposed to most Catholics. Despite the constant teaching of our popes and bishops, it is rarely preached and little experienced by parishioners in our local communities.

- Popular culture renders all belief a matter of individual and subjective preference. Catholics think it wrong to proselytize. They therefore hold the mission of the Church to the world suspect. Such suspicion particularly holds true in the West.

- The secular role of the laity in the Church has been largely ignored; the most that has been achieved is participation in delegated pastoral and liturgical ministries in the parish.

An apostolate of all

In the average parish, then, there is little sense of the notion that "the apostolate exercised by the individual...is the origin and condition of the whole of the apostolate....All lay persons...are called to this type of apostolate and obliged to engage in it" (*Christifideles Laici*, 28). There is accordingly a great need to educate lay Catholics as to their apostolic dignity, to invite them to consider their talents and gifts and the opportunities to witness to what is already present in their lives. In other words, they need to be taught and tutored in discernment: to discern their talents (they are, after all, called and gifted), their personal call through Baptism, and the innate thrust of the liturgy to lead to life.

If you want these thoughts cast in more sociological terms, let me call to mind an article by Robert Bellah where he laments the loss of the concept of the common good, the impulse for social concern. The Protestant regard for the sacredness of the individual—along with a near exclusive focus on the relation between Jesus and the individual—and a prevailing economic belief that a free market is the answer to all our problems have made it hard for Americans to understand and embrace the idea of the common good, much less to engage in conversation about it. In a word, the mission to the common good, Bellah claims, is submerged under self-preoccupation and self-measurement. For an answer out of this social mess, Bellah, a Protestant, interestingly turns to the rich tradition of the Catholic Church. He writes:

> The resources of the Catholic tradition of the virtues and Catholic social teaching as embodied in papal encyclicals are invaluable....I believe we need at this moment to reconstitute our cultural code by giving much greater salience to the sacramental life...and, in particular, to the Eucharist.

Bellah claims that Catholics need to relearn to appreciate the concreteness of sacramental worship, to grasp those very sacraments as actions "that pull us into an embodied world of relationships and connections."

He cites St. Margaret's, a Catholic parish largely made up of Puerto Ricans in the poorest neighborhood of Hartford, Connecticut, which was deeply involved in a justice ministry. What caused this to come about? The answer is that in this parish, a sacramental theology has formed the life and worship of the whole parish. For example, Bellah notes how the people spoke of "being Eucharist for others." One of them said, "That's what life is for me, being Eucharist for others. It is not about martyrdom, it's about life; it's about giving life to others." Another parishioner put it this way:

> The commission to "go in the peace of Christ to love and serve one another" means that this is what the Mass has nourished us to do. And yet, when he says the Mass is ended, that is only true in one sense....It is not ended, it is continuing. It is an

invitation to go out and put it into practice now. To do what you said you were going to do. What you tried to focus yourself on so that you can function as a whole person, united with Christ and then as the whole body of Christ. So now you have to go out and incarnate that, that is what life is about.[3]

We have too long withdrawn from the public square. There is a "political" side to ministry, which has been submerged by the therapeutic side, that must be recovered. (By political we mean the ancient sense that Christians must be engaged with the polis, the city, the community.) Ministry includes but transcends reaching out one-on-one, person to person. It not only feeds the hungry but tries to correct the causes of hunger.

Let's translate this truth close to home. If my mother is sick and I pray that she gets better but do not drive her to see the doctor, I have not been Eucharist. If I see a colleague or friend who looks depressed and pray for her but do not go out of my way to speak to her, I have not been Eucharist. If I pray for a close friend today but do not send him a postcard to tell him I am thinking about him, I have not been Eucharist. If I pray for world peace but do not forgive those who have hurt me, I have not been Eucharist. And, by the same token, if I bring Communion to someone in a substandard nursing home but do nothing to correct the inhumane conditions there, I have not been Eucharist. If I give a piece of bread to a beggar but do nothing to erase poverty, I have not been Eucharist. If I offer mercy but do not work for justice, I have not been Eucharist.

A congregation of adult men and women is not simply a gathering of spouses or parents. These adults are also workers and citizens. They are protagonists of a life beyond the home. Ministers can promote the infusion of a sacramental imagination when they acknowledge the complexity to which that imagination needs to be applied. Ministers also need to rediscover the tools of pastoral care that equip a minister to have a credible political presence. The Scriptures, preaching, the history of the Church, and mission keep the minister aware that an essential practice of pastoral care is public leadership.[4]

We should note that the fault for the disconnection between liturgy and life goes both ways. If liturgists have been too ingrown, focusing far too much on the aesthetics of worship, so at times the social activists have distanced themselves from the liturgy, disdaining it as being too distracting from the "real" world and its needs. Yet the truth of the matter is, each reflects the other and each without the other becomes ultimately sterile.

The bottom line? The parish of the future must remind people to be Eucharist where they are, to be Church where they are. It must help them uncover God in the lives they lead. The parish of the post-Christian era must retrieve its Catholic center by moving beyond private piety and personal cults to the centrality of the Eucharist as both mandate and justification to commit to the common good, to social justice, and to a lived faith in the marketplace. Preaching and liturgy must always give the message that we are here only in order not to be here; that, as we shall see shortly, our arena is the world and the Presence is there.

Parishes really have been too exclusive, too focused on personal piety, personal salvation, and internal concerns. Yet on the parish level, Eucharistic worship, with its witnessing impulse, will go far to revive the Church of the post-Christian era. Let us end with a lovely reflection on the Eucharist:

> The moment in the Christian Mass that fills me with the deepest awe is the "fracture," when the celebrant holds the host up high, for all to see, and then breaks it in half. Our silence is profound at that dramatic moment and I am always surprised at how easy it is to hear the crack as the wafer breaks, throughout the church. Such a little thing, but what a moving sound. The impact of the sound is in what it represents, of course: the irreparable act, the ritual of the irremediable, the confrontation with absolute loss, with death.
>
> And yet the ceremony continues; the celebration of Communion begins. The value of the wafer is not in its form, the perfect circle of our tradition, but in its function, the nourishment of

our beings in community. Break the bread, then, into as many pieces as possible, so that all of us can be fed, so that all of us can be a part of this sharing. So that a new, perfected circle can be formed as we all hold hands, thankful, restored, mindful of loss and suffering, prayerful for the strength to live with our fragility.[5]

20

THE STRENGTH OF THE CROSS

The second response to the challenges the Church faces is that the parish, in the post-Christian era, in a multicultural society, must become the weakness of the Eucharist. Yes, the Eucharist is bread broken and given; therefore, it gives us a stance from which to face the religiously indifferent world we live in today. The Almighty incarnated into a baby born in Bethlehem's cave, bending low to wash the feet of his disciples, becoming present in common ordinary bread—this is the pattern of how we are to be Eucharist today.

I say this because not since the first century have Christians been as weak, as marginalized, as disdained as they are today. You and I know this from experience: Christianity in general (and Catholicism in particular) is increasingly an option. We now daily rub shoulders with many old and new religions. For example, think of those approximately 1600 religions and denominations in the U.S. today including the fast-growing Eastern religions (not to mention the amorphous New Age permutations). We live and will continue to live in a world that is more and more secular, religiously pluralistic, economically monolithic, and most of all, indifferent.

And that is the problem. Not so much people's hatred or anger; the problem is indifference. As one sociologist put it, "People aren't leaving their churches, they just aren't going to them." Certainly, most people you and I know who are not at church on Sunday are not at home brooding about the Church's faults or reading anti-Catholic books. They are sleeping, shopping, skiing, jogging in the park, watching baseball and football games, working on their lawns and gardens, visiting with family and friends, or off to an away soccer game. They do not have huge ecclesiology questions. In regard to the Church, they are on sabbatical. They want a kingdom, but not a Church. Or, as the young people put it, they want spirituality, not the Church. That means we have to face facts and stop operating as if the parish were the centralized medieval parish of the 1500s or the neighborhood parish of the 1950s with a full rectory, a full school with a nun in every classroom, a formidable CYO, and persuasive moral authority. Not so anymore.

Today's Church is characterized by shrinking congregations, a struggling school if it is still open, and a depleted, aging clergy who, like Rodney Dangerfield, "get no respect." We are a minority religion in a secular world whose media images, icons, and corporate story lines dominate our lives. All of this puts us in a new-yet-old position, one characterized by Methodist Colin Morris, who wisely says, "You cannot preach the gospel from the strong to the weak. You can only preach the gospel from the weak to the strong." In other words, we can no longer deal from the pinnacle of power and position. Or, as Clifford Longley put it, "It is churches without privileges, churches which turn privileges down if offered them, which are best adapted to survive and thrive in a pluralistic culture."[1] In short, where diversity reigns, to have influence is to renounce power, not to ally oneself with it.

In other words, linking influence and power will be counterproductive for the parish of the post-Christian era, for people in a multicultural society are drawn to authenticity rather than office or power. We will gather more converts by faithfully living the Eucharist than by strong apologetic arguments (which usually are very logical, prove everything, and convince no one). Therefore, spreading the Gospel, advertising the Church, will take on a new look—the look of a Eucharistic people who have nothing to offer but the bread of their lives. This means—and here is the heart of my remarks—that Catholics of the third millennium should think of ourselves very much like the Christians of the first century.

The first Christians

The Christians of the first century were a small persecuted group with no standing. This fact raises a question: how did an obscure, tiny, Messianic movement from the edge of the Roman Empire displace paganism and become the dominant religion of Western civilization?

For an answer, we turn to a book neatly titled *How Jesus Won the West*, by religious sociologist Rodney Stark. Using the theories and tools of contemporary social science, Stark addressed one of the great historical mysteries of two millenniums ago and came up with an illuminating response to our question. Christians, he said, introduced into a world of hatred and cruelty a totally new concept about humanity: that we had a responsibility to be compassionate and caring toward everyone. Christianity rewarded its adherents not just in eternity but in the here and now. Membership was demanding, but it paid off. Because Christians were expected to aid one another, many of them received such aid. They could feel more secure, therefore, against inevitable hard times. Because they were asked to nurse the sick and the dying, many of them received such treatment themselves. Because they were asked to love, they received love in return. The lot of women improved, as did family life. Men were required to marry and to be faithful, and infant girls were no longer routinely put to death.

In the Roman world, justice was the ruling virtue, and mercy was scorned. Christianity preached a merciful God and proclaimed mercy as the primary virtue. Even more remarkably, Christians taught that love must extend beyond the family and the tribe, even beyond the Christian community. This approach came naturally from their Jewish roots, from which they had not yet separated:

In the cities of the Jewish diaspora (especially Alexandria, Antioch, Tarsus, Ephesus, and Rome), Jews were widely admired by their gentile neighbors. For one thing, they had a real religion, not a clutter of gods and goddesses and *pro forma* rituals that almost nobody took seriously anymore. They actually believed in their one God; and, imagine, they even set aside one day a week to pray to him and reflect on their lives. They possessed a dignified library of sacred books that they studied reverently as part of this weekly reflection and which, if more than a little odd in their Greek translation, seemed to point toward a consistent worldview.

Besides their religious seriousness, Jews were unusual in a number of ways that caught the attention of gentiles. They were faithful spouses—no, really—who maintained strong families in which even grown children remained affectively attached and respectful to their parents. Despite Caesar Nero's shining example, matricide was virtually unknown among them. Despite their growing economic success, they tended to be more scrupulous in business than non-Jews. And they were downright finicky when it came to taking human life, seeming to value even a slave's or a plebeian's life as much as anyone else's. Perhaps in nothing did the gentiles find the Jews so admirable as in their acts of charity. Communities of urban Jews, in addition to opening synagogues, built welfare centers for aiding the poor, the miserable, the sick, the homebound, the imprisoned, and those, such as widows and orphans, who had no family to care for them.

For all these reasons, the diaspora cities of the first century saw a marked increase in gentile initiates to Judaism.[2]

Their steadfastness in the face of persecution earned for them a grudging admiration of their energies: "See those Christians, how they love one another." Tutored by their roots, Christians cared for the poor and the ill. There was also an unintended irony here. When the many epidemics overran Rome in the early centuries after Christ, the elite immediately fled to the safe shores of the Adriatic. The Christians stayed and ministered to their own and to the pagans;

thus, many of them died in these epidemics. But unknowingly, in the process of caring for the sick, they also built up an immunity. When the next round of epidemics came, the pagans died but many of the Christians survived. In one sense, they triumphed because they outlived and outpopulated the pagans. By the fourth century, the Churches of Rome were feeding an estimated 20,000 of that city's poor each week. The Church succeeded, in great part, because it presented a liturgy that seeded the world.

Community and compassion

The first Christians possessed a radical sense of community. There is a book (now out of print) by Baptist historian E. Glen Hinson, called *The Evangelization of the Roman Empire: Identity and Adaptability*. He writes that in the year 30 AD, a number of religions were prevalent in the empire of Rome: the cult of Isis, Mithra, and Judaism, along with a small handful of Jews who believed in Jesus. Three hundred years later, there were still many religions, but one—Christianity—had become so strong that a Roman emperor, Constantine, joined it. Fifty years after his reign, it became the official religion of the Roman Empire. How did Christianity flourish and come to dominate the Roman empire?

Hinson's answer is that basically, if you were a Christian, no matter what else you did, you were first and foremost a Christian. This is precisely what annoyed Rome. For example, its Christian soldiers were not first and foremost loyal to the emperor, but to Christ. Therefore, Hinson maintains, the cohesiveness of this community, its loyalty to Jesus, were major factors in the development of Christianity. In other words, you could not just say "I believe in Jesus." You had to publicly commit to Jesus and publicly join the communities that professed his name. Early Christians simply would not be able to comprehend the divisions Christianity underwent in the second millennium. Nor would they understand the individualism of the previous century or the commonplace absence of religion from the public square.

This community loyalty showed in their attitude toward property, as well as in the impulse to see Christ in the least of the brethren. "Share everything with your brother and do not say 'It is private property,'" advises the *Didache*, an early Christian document perhaps written around the time St. Paul was penning his letters. In the second century, Clement of Alexandria warned the wealthy to use their money to serve justice. The rich were told time and time again that they were the earth's stewards. Private property was allowed (with some misgivings) but its greedy misuse was not.

The motive behind this attitude toward property was to be aligned with Christ's presence and his identification with the disadvantaged. "As long as you did it to one of the least of my brethren, you did it to me." That is why John Chrysostom said that the rich could not dare to make a golden cup for Christ's table if they refused him a wooden cup of cold water.

In succeeding centuries, a Francis of Assisi or a Mother Teresa truly saw Christ in the faces of the lepers they embraced. They caught the message of the early Christian community, and the fact that they are considered exceptions to the rule—untouchable and inimitable saints—is a commentary on how much a sense of solidarity and community within Christianity has been lost. When one looks at Christians—who, like every other American, have many possessions, overlarge houses, three cars (the national average), and expanding stock portfolios—and sees how they exist side-by-side with America's poor, we need no longer wonder why religion has so little impact on people today. The sense that the early Christians had of being one body in Christ, the "we", has given way to "us" and "them," and an ever-widening gap between the rich and the poor. Thus, the formula of the early Church, which linked liturgy and life together with baptism and community loyalty, would seem to be a compelling guidepost for today. Laurence Freeman, the director of the World Community for Christian Meditation, captures what I'm trying to get across:

Why is it that the upbeat talk we heard about Christians making a new beginning in this jubilee year seems to have had little impact outside the loyal congregations that were its prime audience? The malaise of institutional Christianity has not gone away.

It is puzzling and frustrating to try to understand how the main-line Churches, despite all their determination and resources, still seem unable to connect with the profound spiritual needs of our time. For so many young people, ready for idealistic and sacrificial commitment, hungry for inspiration, the Church could give the sense of belonging that they seek as citizens of the global village. But instead of discovering an inclusive vision, a comprehensive philosophy of life, a spirituality, they dismiss what they find as narrowness of mind, intolerant dogmatism, internal feuding, interdenominational sectarianism, medieval sexism, and so on. It seems disloyal to reiterate it all. Perhaps the best way of dealing with it is to ask why—the unkindest cut of all—the most damning criticism is that Christianity lacks spiritual depth. It is all very well for practicing Christians who have the grace to see the Church in a mystical as well as an institutional light to say that this assessment is extreme. Of course it is. It is nevertheless what an increasing number of people believe.

Instead of worrying about the size of congregations, what if we paid attention to the quality of faith that characterizes the Church? We might do this better for the century ahead of us by learning lessons from the beginning of the first Christian millennium.

By the year AD 250, despite successive waves of harsh persecution, it is estimated that Christians formed one quarter of the population of the Roman empire, and of the eternal city itself, where there were at least 40 basilicas. From some of the earliest documents of the Church from this period, such as Hippolytus's Church Order, we can glimpse what life as a Christian was like. It was vigorous, well-organized and bursting at the seams. Catechumens went through a three-year initiation, comparable to that of a strict religious order today. They were accepted finally not so much on account of their theological correctness as of the practical quality of their life. Let their life be examined, we read in one document concerning baptism, whether they lived devoutly while catechumens, whether they honored the widows, visited the sick, and fulfilled every good work. Workers in many professions were excluded or discouraged from joining—those who engaged in the human blood sports of the circus or the sex industry of the theatres, employees of the pagan temples, even soldiers—because their conditions of service were held to be incompatible with Christian values.

As Josef Jungmann, the great Jesuit scholar of the period, once wrote, it is remarkable in such a spiritually and numerically vigorous Church that none of the documents of the time discusses propaganda or missionary activity. Other scholars speak of the unprofessional missionaries of the primitive Church. The Christian lifestyle itself, the way it was lived by those who paid the cost of discipleship, was its own best publicity. Not only martyrs and confessors (those who stood by their faith but were not killed for it) but also the butchers and bakers, the deacons and deaconesses must have evangelized by the simple example of their lives.

A more deeply contemplative Christianity seems the only possible future for a Church which will be smaller, less grand perhaps, when stripped of its secular pomp and prestige, freed from obsessive single-issue theological politics, self-destructive divisions and excessive clericalism, quick to defend the weak and to fight for justice, excited by the challenge of dialogue with other faiths, discerning what is really essential and what is of secondary importance in its customs, able wisely to balance authority and charity, courageous enough for new kinds of martyrdom and, through it all, eucharistically grateful for Christ.[3]

The lesson for us? Two millenniums ago, a few people took seriously the teachings of Jesus. They transformed a brutal, pagan society into the Christian West. When they prayed, "Thy kingdom come" they were not just yearning for heaven; they were determined to reshape the earth as well, to introduce God's Kingdom of compassion into the world they inhabited. Christians say that the Holy Spirit had everything to do with the transformation of ancient Rome. Stark, however, points to another quite valid truth: the benefits of Christianity in the daily lives of people were immediate and obvious. The payoff, if you will, was something tangible, visible in their daily lives. It was not something entirely reserved for the afterlife. This should not surprise us. After all, Jesus told us, "The kingdom of heaven is even now in your midst." Every Eucharist repeats that message.

Moreover, the Christians of the first century were formed out of the writings of the Church Fathers, who were incapable of doing what came in later centuries: that is, separating theology from spirituality. Before theology became a system in the Middle Ages, it was a search both for truth and for God. The writings of the Fathers were forged out of daily challenges and crises, and often from their own blood (one thinks of Ignatius of Antioch on his way to be torn apart by the lions). And so, they have an immediacy and a depth. For these Fathers and for those who read them, believing and living one's faith were two sides of the same coin.

It should be obvious that we Christians on the brink of the twenty-first century are very much like the Christians of the first century. We are to offer mercy in a brutal world, bear a different message from the prevalent culture, build from the bottom up, while gathering around the same Eucharist. We have an imperative, a mandate to build a Church where liturgy becomes life, on the ashes of an old triumphal Church.

This old story from World War II is a good ending for this chapter. A church conference was being held by special permission in the city of Leipzig, East Germany in 1964. It was the custom to ask a high city official to bring greetings to the assembled people. But how could one invite a Communist magistrate to address a church group? Nevertheless, the invitation was extended and accepted. The magistrate, an avowed Communist, addressed this conference of Christian people. In the course of his address, he shared something of his own experience.

He told of being imprisoned under the Hitler regime because he was a Communist. And he told of another prisoner who had been given some work and limited freedom as a "trusty." For his work that man was given a few bits of extra food or an old shirt or other things which he could well have kept for himself. Nobody would have known. But that man, whom the magistrate said was a Christian, would share what he received with the other prisoners. From time to time, he would toss a bit of biscuit or tobacco into their cells. Whatever he had that would make the life of the other prisoners a bit more bearable, he would give them. This was against the rules. It was at great risk to himself that he shared those things.

This Communist magistrate of Leipzig concluded his story by saying, "That was the first time I ever thought the Church might be worthwhile."

21

THE SPIRITUALITY OF
ECCLESIAL LAY MINISTERS

The brave new Church presents a unique challenge to the Eucharistic lives of its growing numbers of ecclesial ministers. It is an ambiguous challenge, particularly for those full-time paid professional ministers in the Church, for many reasons. One is the question of identity.

In 1997, a subcommittee of clergy and laity under the auspices of the National Catholic Conference of Bishops (NCCB) met to discuss the paper "Towards a Theology of Ecclesial Lay Ministry." The only sure thing to come out of these meetings was the validation of the first word, "toward" because the subcommittee couldn't fully answer the question, "What is an ecclesial minister?" Part of the problem, of course, is with the word "ministry." It is a term full of contradiction—although we will continue to use it because it is so common. Dominican Thomas O'Meara points out the contradiction. He says, if the bishop's secretary who is a priest is considered a minister, why not the full-time layperson on a hospital pastoral team? It doesn't make sense to call one a minister and not the other. It would seem that, by and by, we simply have to jettison the clerical-lay, ecclesial-volunteer dichotomies and think rather in concentric circles of varying levels and degrees of service. After all, the Church is built up by many kinds of services from the staff to the volunteers, from the ordained to the lay minister, and they all represent different movements of the one community.

Yet while we are having trouble defining the term, the fact remains that there are indeed ecclesial lay ministers, those full-time, paid people who work in the Church, often in key positions. What's the problem with them? For one, recent surveys have shown that a collaborative and largely lay parish staff led by a priest is rapidly becoming the norm. We spoke of the priest shortage in previous chapters. This time, let's put it this way: the ordained priesthood has declined 12%, while ecclesial lay ministry has risen 30%. These percentages show every sign of continuing in the future: that is, the number of ordained male celibates will go down, while the number of non-ordained male and female, married or single lay ministers will go up. Right now, as you recall from previous pages, 63% of American parishes have lay ministers—some 29,000 of them—and 85% of these ministers are women. Because this is a relatively new situation, one that is changing the face of the American parish, the lines of authority, stability, leadership, and identity are very much blurred and up for grabs.

A second problem is that there is no standardization for competency, although various national organizations like the National Association for Lay Ministry (NALM), the National Conference for Catechetical Leadership (NCCL), the National Federation for Catholic Youth Ministry (NFCYM), and the National Association of Church Personnel Administrators (NACPA) are working to develop just such a resource. (Anyone interested in lay ministry should know about these organizations. Check out their addresses in the endnotes.[1])

Third, there is no background check on these thousands of lay ministers—a rather sensitive point in the light of abuses by some Church employees. The Archdiocese of Boston has pioneered a process to correct this. Starting in the Fall of 2000, it required a criminal background check on current and prospective staff members and volunteers who work with children, the disabled, and the elderly. (This background check will soon extend to priests.) Other dioceses are expected to follow suit.

Finally, ecclesial lay ministry does not as yet belong to any clearly identifiable group. In other words, the spirituality of a lay minister differs from that of a priest or religious. As I wrote in *The Parish of the Next Millennium*:

> Rather, [lay ecclesial ministers] work from the stance of being an openly "churchy" person in and of the world. To the extent that they do work for the [C]hurch and are known as such, their spirituality revolves around modeling Christian commitment in a secular, pluralistic society. It's a difficult and new stance, one in much need of dialogue and investigation. At the very least, [ecclesial] lay ministers need recognition, support, stability, and the acknowledgment that theirs is a genuine vocation, not just a job. Lay ministers are basically forging a new kind of Catholic identity by bridging the clerical and lay worlds. And they are forging a new kind of spirituality.[2]

What might that new kind of spirituality be? Picking up on suggestions made by Zeni Fox, let me present three characteristics that might ground that spirituality. First, Jesus said of himself, "I came not to do my own will but the will of him who sent me" (Jn 6:38). He grounded his ministry in the Father's plan for him, and thus made discernment and following God's will central in all things.

Second, of his colleagues in ministry Jesus said, "I do not call you servants any longer, because the servant does not know what the master is doing; but I have called you friends" (Jn 15:15). A disciple accepts oneself as a friend of Jesus and learns how to be with and work with each of their colleagues.

Third, Jesus showed how ministry is done. Using a visual parable, he got up from the table, put a towel on his arm, poured water in a basin, and began to wash the disciples' feet. When he was finished he went back to the table and said,

> "Do you know what I have done to you? You call me Teacher and Lord—and you are right, for that is what I am. So if I, your

Lord and Teacher, have washed your feet, you also ought to wash one another's feet. For I have set you an example, that you also should do as I have done to you." (Jn 13:12–15)

These three characteristics were central to the ministerial identity of Jesus and his disciples: a ministry focused on God's call, a ministry shared in the spirit of friendship with others, and a ministry of radical service.

Formation

I want to bring up a critical point here. Because, more and more, the laity are highly involved in both volunteer and paid ministry in the Church, it is more necessary than ever that they get some theological and spiritual formation. In their work as ministers, they are on the front line. Lectors, Eucharistic Ministers, heads of parish organizations, the parish secretary, the DRE—all ecclesial lay ministers should spend one year in preparation for their tasks or, concomitant with their time of service or employ, a year in Catechetical and spiritual formation. Surely a diocese and parish could prioritize their budgets to include such training and formation programs. If these programs were to become the norm—much like the extensive training required of diaconate candidates—they might soon lose any sense of being burdensome to either the parish or the minister.

These programs would not have to be very sophisticated, just sufficient enough to give the average person some solid background in Church teaching and service, as well as an opportunity to experience spiritual growth. I can hear the reaction now: "For cryin' out loud! I just want someone to read from the lectionary, not be a theologian!" But this type of reaction seriously underestimates the desire on the part of the average lay minister to know more about the faith, as well as their desire for spiritual growth and access to resources. It also overlooks the fact that these ministers, the everyday, frontline evangelizers, the neighbors-next-door who are associated with the Church, are the ones who will be invitation and example. Obviously, both volunteer and paid ecclesial lay ministers are people of good will; most would be open to and even welcome spiritual formation. That is why even now dioceses and parishes should be forming a cadre of well-trained teachers and spiritual guides to take up the daily task of formation. I can think of no other effort with effects that can be as far-reaching.[3] Roger Cardinal Mahony is correct when he writes:

> There is a need for a clear understanding of the nature of lay ecclesial ministry on the part of the [B]aptized and those who have received the sacrament of [H]oly [O]rders. Finally, there is need for a common foundational theology as the basis of the formation of seminarians, deacons, religious, and lay persons for ministry as well as for the development of more collaborative skills on the part of the ordained so that one and all can exercise their ministry in a collaborative fashion.[4]

Furthermore, since most lay ministers, from choir members to those on the finance committee, are publicly known to be such, they are in a unique position to be evangelizers. And so necessary training must be offered them. We seldom think of that aspect of lay ministry because our approach in this regard is so utilitarian. We need lay ministers to function at their jobs. Period. But the well-rounded Christian needs a spirituality and grasp of the faith that compels him or her to share the good news. It is all part of the lay ministry package.

Pastoral humility

In keeping with our emphasis on the importance of the Eucharist, I want to stress the humility that must inform our imitation of Jesus; that is, in bowing to God's will, in sharing friendship, and in washing feet. As lay ministers, we must never give the impression that we have chosen the better part, that we represent a kind of "clericalized" laity because we are privy to the inner workings of the parish. This kind of attitude can be a temptation.

No. Our whole aim—whether clergy, religious, or ecclesial lay ministers—is to help people to be Eucharist where they are. We are in service to their mission. Remember, Jesus washed the feet of his disciples so they could travel to the marketplace with the good news. Likewise, we humbly give Eucharist to people so they can take it home. We humbly instruct them or their children so the domestic Church can flourish. We direct social outreach so people will find the impetus to do the same in their everyday lives. We offer programs so the people can find meaning in their lives and in the marketplace.

You see, the spirituality of lay ministry invites us to assume a very humble position. We are not the ideal; we are servants to the ideal. We are the lowly distributors of the sacred bread, if you will, that nourishes parents and singles and workers and searchers. Let me repeat: we—clergy, religious, and laity in Church-related leadership positions—need a firm spirituality that supports us in the role we have inherited from Jesus. We must be related to the Father, friends to fellow disciples, and models of bread broken and shared.

Let me share two true stories that catch what I'm trying to say. One is a paradigm, the other a warning.

> Bonnee Hoy was a gifted composer who died in the prime of her life. At her memorial service, a friend said that there was a mockingbird that used to sing regularly outside Bonnee's bedroom window on summer nights. Bonnee would stand at the window, peering into the darkness, listening intently and marveling at the beautiful songs the mockingbird sang. Being a musician, Bonnee decided to respond musically. So she whistled the first four notes of Beethoven's Fifth Symphony. With amazing quickness, the mockingbird learned those four notes and sang them back to Bonnee.

Then, for a time, the bird disappeared. But one night, toward the end of her life, when Bonnee was very sick, the bird returned and, in the midst of its serenade, several times sang the first four notes of Beethoven's Fifth. Then the friend said, think of that now! Somewhere out there in this big wide world there is a mockingbird who sings Beethoven because of Bonnee.

This is our story, too. The fruit of our ministry is that somewhere out in this big wide world there is a Christian who sings the Gospel because of us, someone we sent out full of the Eucharist.

Now, the second story is a warning to those of us who gain competency yet not a proper spirituality in our work. Following a two-day workshop attended by Mother Teresa and some of her sisters, the workshop leader (a clergyman) and the good Mother were having a cup of tea together. Referring to her famous ministry to society's rejects, the clergyman asked, "What is your biggest problem, Mother?" She quickly replied, "Professionalism."

Her strange, one-word answer left the clergyman momentarily speechless. In his words:

> My jaw dropped. I had expected her to say something about the difficulties involved in trying to hold her community of nuns together. Or the difficulty of determining who would be her ultimate successor as the authority figure among the sisters. Instead, I got "professionalism."

> Seeing that I was dumbfounded, Mother Teresa then spelled out her answer, saying, "I have five sisters getting MD degrees and far greater numbers getting RN, LPN, and MSW degrees. But a funny thing happens. They come back from their education, they are concerned about titles and offices and parking privileges. So I take all of that away from them and I send them to the hospice of the dying. There they hold people's hands, and pray with them and feed them. After six months of that, they typically get things straight again and remember their vocation to be a spiritual presence first, and a professional presence second."

You see, it always comes back to us as broken and shared bread, how much we have internalized the connection between liturgy and life, doesn't it? I think this Mother Teresa story should be the "scripture" of every minister.

22

THE POSTMODERN GENERATION

The newspaper is before me. On the front page is a story about a young couple in France, ages twenty-seven and twenty-nine, who, along with many other couples, have just filed for and received a Civil Solidarity Pact. Casually dressed in baggy sweaters and slacks, they went to the court clerk, filled out a paper, and in a few minutes were declared legal partners. Originally intended for gay couples, this partnership is not marriage, but it gives some of the benefits of marriage. The partners are responsible for the financial support of each other, as well as for purchases and debts (unless they specify otherwise). They have the ability to file a joint income tax return and get the same tax breaks as married couples. And they can dissolve the arrangement quickly and easily and, most importantly, without a lawyer or the long process that divorce entails, simply with three-month's notice. The couple in the story is using the Civil Solidarity Pact as a trial run for marriage.[1] Of course, this kind of arrangement will not in itself prevent breakups. Actually, if the statistics on living together continue to hold, the arrangement will, in fact, increase their chances of splitting up.

In any case, this process may strike some readers as more evidence of the paganism of the young and their distancing from religion and the Church. But put yourself in their place. Both of the partners mentioned are the offspring of Baby Boomer parents. Now, there are many wonderful and solid Boomer parents, those flower children of the '60s and '70s, but for the most part, they have left a terrible, fractured legacy to their children and grandchildren. They have divorced in record numbers—the French couple cited above both come from divorced parents, as do many of their friends—taken drugs, overturned conventions, made "free" love, and broken away from the Church. They had precious little to pass on to their children who, in turn, had even less to pass on to their children. As we have seen in the chapters on religious illiteracy and the loss of "thick" Catholicism, this has left the offspring of Boomers suspicious of organized religion, wary, and rootless, open to the manipulations of the media and the marketplace which confects their vocabulary, their values, and their needs.

Is it any wonder that the children and grandchildren of the Boomer generation are hurt, displaced, and cynical about any kind of commitment? They are living in a culture where Larry King, married six times, interviewed Mike Wallace, married five times. One young man, writing in *Newsweek* (May 8, 2000), says "I had lost my grandmother Mary, and for a while, my whole sense of family because of divorce. My parents split up when I was 9 and my brother 12...My father and mother each married three times, my brother four times, and I married twice....in all, 12 marriages. Seven of these unions ended in divorce, one in death." Another teenager in that same issue writes, "There is a lot of anger in my generation. You can hear it in the music. Kids are angry for a lot of reasons, but mostly because parents aren't around."

The context of their lives, therefore, is anything but stable or promising. They are confused and angry. Scott Appleby adds summary statistics about some of the social and economic circumstances they face:

> Real wages peaked in this country in 1973 and have been declining ever since, yet we work an average of one month more per year than we did two decades ago. Since the mid-1970s, poverty among young adults 18 to 34 has gone up by 50

percent, while the median income for under-30 parents fell by one-third. In 1993 AIDS was the top killer of young adults in sixty-four cities and five states. Twenty-five percent of all African-American men in their 20s are either in prison, on probation, or on parole. Nearly half of the new full-time jobs created in the 1980s paid less than $250 a week or $13,000 a year—below the poverty line for a family of four.

Every day over 2,500 American children witness the divorce or separation of their parents. Every day 90 children are taken from their parents' custody and committed to foster homes. Every day 13 Americans aged 15 to 24 commit suicide and another 16 are murdered. Nearly one in three college graduates between 1990 and 2005 is expected to take a job that does not require a college degree. That is up from one in ten college graduates in the 1960s. Every day the typical fourteen-year-old watches three hours of TV and does one hour of homework. Every day over 2,200 kids drop out of school, 3,610 teenagers are assaulted, 630 are robbed, 80 are raped. Every day 500 adolescents begin using illegal drugs and 1,000 begin drinking alcohol. Every day 1,000 unwed teenage girls become mothers.[2]

Generation X, also called the "postmodern generation," has inherited a very fractured world. One Gen X-er witnessed and commented on Woodstock II, which took place in 1999 and turned into a reckless, rioting, fire-burning debacle:

What I am thinking now is that safety is an illusion that we use to cover up some larger absence in our lives. The real causes of the Woodstock riot, if that's what it was, are larger than personal irresponsibility, or bad music, or poor planning, or greed. The riot is a footnote to a larger story. Thirty years ago something vital and lasting—an idea of the good life and how to live it, what marriage meant, what to eat, what family and community were for, and of who was supposed to take care of the kids when the parents both work—broke apart, and now, thirty years later, that sense of connection, of some overarching narrative frame for our lives, still hasn't been repaired or replaced.[3]

This generation is heir to that. Yet, this generation of today, wary of commitment, is truly searching. They are dissatisfied with all this deconstruction of meaning and purpose and coherence. And so, even in their excesses and mockery, they are looking for God—but they are looking on their own terms. This poses a problem for Church leaders, who must adjust to the reality that two-thirds of people under the age of thirty-five shun organized religion. Also, the emotional and mental landscapes of this younger generation are vastly different from those of current pastors, most of whom are in their fifties, sixties, and seventies. One writer describes these landscapes:

> The analysts tell us postmoderns value relationships, yet they are skeptical because their parents—about fifty percent—divorced. They are delaying marriage. Trust is hard won. They are tribal, sticking more closely to their peers because of a perceived lack of meaningful intergenerational guidance. They expect to be heard, not because of age or experience, but just because they're there. Youth's right to a voice, won in protests by boomers, is the inheritance of successive generations, and they exercise it.
>
> Postmodern people are tolerant of many things, including multiple paths to God. Truth, in this era, is relative, and the standard for measuring truth is personal, individual experience.[4]

The same writer goes on insightfully to offer Church leaders five characteristics that identify the younger generation's quest. The first is authenticity; they value that. This means that they expect Church people and leaders to have conviction and integrity, as well as the intuitive sense to know that they can no longer do ministry *for* the postmodern generation, but must rather do ministry *with* them. Second, the younger generation wants to be known. If the Boomers want to slip in and out of Church unnoticed, the postmoderns want to hang out and be known. (This is another reason why having larger parishes and larger churches as a way to cope with the priest shortage is a bankrupt notion.)

Third, postmodern people, conditioned by relativism and diversity, have long ago given up on finding absolute answers. And so for them, the journey itself is the thing. The challenge and joy of getting there—even if "there" is vague—is the interest, the draw. This means that, for them, the Church will have to be less a depository of a body of doctrine, and more a band of pilgrims who tap ancient resources together.

Fourth, postmoderns, young, energetic, and passionate, want to make a difference. They want to interface (to use their term) with those whom they help. They don't want to be told simply to increase their donations; they want the hands-on knowledge about what that increase is going to do and how it is going to impact them. Finally, the postmoderns want new forms of liturgical expression and ways of participation beyond simply singing four tired old hymns. Remember, these are people who have spent some 23,000 hours watching TV before they turned eighteen.

So the question is, how do we reach them? We have already given some clues in the preceding chapters, but let me review them by turning to an article by a young writer named Jeremy Langford.[5] He ingeniously suggests that the post-Easter story of the road to Emmaus gives us an approach to this question.

The road to Emmaus

What happened along the way to Emmaus? First, Jesus walked with the disillusioned disciples who are just like the postmodern folks: walking and talking constantly with one another about their lives and loves and struggles and the quest for meaning, who have turned away from Jerusalem (the Church) and are headed for Emmaus or Oz or whatever is out there. Jesus didn't reveal himself right away. He just walked along with them. So, walk we must. We must put ourselves in their experience, right down to the ear-splitting music and baggy pants.

This goes back to what we wrote before, about being Eucharist to others. We need everyday people, far more than certified clergy, to walk with Generation X young people. This means that a parish must be one that has forsaken its own self-centered institutional concerns, one that does not wait for the people to come to it but rather, has an outward thrust; a parish that takes seriously the words "The Mass is ended. Go in peace to love and serve the Lord," a place of formation as well as celebration. Why do you think the youth flock to the Taizé community by the hundreds of thousands and sit there at the feet of the monks? Why do you think over 2,000 postmodern young people connect with Chicago's thriving young adult ministry, except to find people who will walk with them? Who will do the Emmaus walk?

Second, Jesus listened. "What are you discussing? What things have happened?" he asked the two dismayed disciples. What has happened is that the market might crash and the youth will be left out in the cold. What has happened is that their parents have split, and they have had to cope with half-brothers and sisters and reconfigured families. What has happened is that some of their friends have died from drug overdose or AIDS or suicide. What has happened is that they have been abandoned by their working single or married parents. What has happened is that they have a lot of consumer toys to play with and lots of sex to indulge in, so why aren't they happy? "Hey, Jesus, you want to listen? Does anybody? I'm trying to make sense out of it all."

Who will do the Emmaus listening? Again, the necessity of theological and spiritual formation comes to the fore, and the wisdom and necessity of joining liturgy and life becomes apparent. The parish must send out people who truly listen, not those who judge or condemn.

Third, Jesus talked with the disciples. We can't talk to Generation X in church; they stay away in droves because there they are only talked *at*, not with. And sometimes, they are talked at with nonsense that has nothing to do with their lives. Yet they have their own secular religious vocabulary, if you will, and their pop culture must be taken seriously, especially when it speaks of the need to find meaning. We have already taken note of the popularity of books and movies on angels and other supernatural phenomena. Young people today can't get enough of stories about people with a sixth sense, outer space aliens, vampires, and all kinds of supermen and superwomen who vanish, dematerialize, and do all kinds of magic stunts. What are these but back doors to the sacred, which they do not know by its proper name? We must talk with them and even sometimes, like Jesus, be blunt. "O foolish men and slow of heart, to believe all that the prophets have spoken!"

Fourth, they knew him in the breaking of the bread. Jesus broke bread with the disciples. Getting together for a meal, for a pizza, is hugely important to the postmodern generation. In their small apartments and with their even smaller budgets, they nevertheless feel a strong compulsion to get together—maybe it is because they have never shared a family meal while growing up. In any case, they sense not only the camaraderie of sharing a meal, but its sacredness, even when unexpressed. For just as the meal on the way to Emmaus was a chance to know the Stranger, so postmoderns find the meal a chance to know each other, and perhaps, too, the Stranger among them.

Once more, the need to have a meaningful liturgy comes to mind, as do all those testimonies we have seen about the attraction of the Mass and the community that celebrates it. Marva Dawn, who writes well on matters of worship, finds that Generation X, which she describes as a media-saturated and "dumbed-down" crowd, are an eager group for genuine worship.[6]

Mission and mentoring

Finally, Jesus gave the disciples a mission. He left them with the urgency to return to Jerusalem to share the good news with the others, to tell how the Lord had appeared to them and how they had recognized him in the breaking of the bread. They were empowered by the encounter, as we empower the people we serve to share the bread of their lives with others.

This is a double challenge when dealing with Generation X-ers. For one thing, they have dropped out. Recent surveys show that they are far less politically engaged, have a low trust in government and a low allegiance to their country or to political parties, and are far more materialistic than previous generations. The external status symbols of income, clothes, material goods, and, above all, "image" are powerful attractions in a world that has ceased to honor the internal virtues of character and integrity. Virtue won't get you noticed, but the latest smart hairstyle or steroid-pumped body will. And maybe they are just cynical about it all.

But one thing can be said: as suspicious as this generation is of rhetoric, it is attracted to action, to service. As a group, they are "roll-up-your-sleeves-and-get-down-to-work"-type people. They are concerned about guns killing children, along with violence in general and the state of education. They will help out at Habitat for Humanity, clean up neighborhoods, and tutor innercity children. They also need the opportunity, the encouragement, and the empowerment to do these things.[7] Thus, a parish that truly celebrates the Eucharist will offer all three to the postmodern generation.

To walk, listen, talk, break bread, and offer a mission; these form the basis of a good mission statement for any parish. But we might add one more element, one that is historically proven and never fails to attract people: the mentor, someone who lives with faith and wisdom and is noticed by the community at large.

Let me share a story that took place some many years ago, in another era when pastors were a lot stronger and sterner than they are today (and parishioners a lot more obedient!). It so happened that a little boy came to serve Mass with dirty boots on. The pastor thought this was very disrespectful and very irreverent, and waited until the sermon to publicly bawl out the little boy. He told the kid, "I want you to come over here and kneel on the top step for the rest of my sermon and the rest of the Mass so that everyone can see how dis-respectful you are. They can see your ugly, dirty boots." So the little boy came up and knelt there, embarrassed, wanting to be anywhere else, wanting to die. After a few moments, he felt a presence next to him. He looked over and saw his father, who had come up from the congregation and knelt beside him and put his hand on his shoulder. "That," says the former altar boy as a young adult, "is when I got a glimpse of what God is like. The God I celebrate and believe in is the God who comes and stands by me."

There were eighty-four million people born in the U.S. between 1965 and 1983. Now their children are emerging, Generation Y, the "millennial generation," those eighty-eight million born after 1980 who are the next big challenge to the Church. They, like their prede-cessors, will be reclaimed not by doctrines and programs as much as by personal witness, integrity, and a community that knows them by name and is willing to do the Emmaus walk with them.

This calls for a new kind of Church, a new style of leadership, and new priorities. And so it seems that we are back to the genius of the first-century Christians, who espoused small, faith-sharing communities whose members broke bread together and shared the events of their lives with one another. These early Christians, as we must, evoked the admiration of non-Christians: "See how they love one another."

23

Pondering the Institutional Church

The institutional Church. The very phrase evokes hostility from the Church's enemies, even disdain from its own members, especially from the more progressive Catholics. The institutional Church. It seems that we can't do with it—and in this book, we have seen ample reasons why—and we can't do without it. The fact is, we need institutions, and even those who pretend to dislike them rely on them.

For example, when the most vocal proponents of free speech, who hurl diatribes and invectives at all institutions, are challenged or curtailed, what do they do? They instantly call the most liberal lawyer they can find to defend them. In short, when pressed, they turn to the institutions of law and enforcement trusting, indeed demanding, that they will be given their due. Moreover, these people put their money in a bank, carry a car license, send in their taxes, demand contracts when necessary, sue their neighbors, pay their cable company, and buy stocks on the Internet. Even when they hate them and think them corrupt, they need, use, and depend on institutions. A society without institutions is simply rootless and chaotic, and lacks memory.

In a larger sense, institutions are valuable because they codify and preserve the initial epiphany, the initial experience, and those who keep it alive. They are repositories of tradition and record, along with the heroes and heroines who preserve both. For example, the independence won by the American revolutionaries gave rise to the institution of democratic government that would preserve it long after they were gone. The same goes for religious institutions. They arise subsequent to a spiritual experience, which in turn births a religion, which in turn spawns an institution. It is an inevitable and noble progression simply because we institutionalize what is valuable to us. We want to preserve it. As the old saying goes, "First the god, then the dance, and finally the story." In other words, first comes the religious experience of a great seer (for example, Moses and the burning bush). Then the dance or ritual, the liturgy, makes the experience present again. Then comes the theology, the official story. Finally, the incipient community gathers around the seer and wants something of what he or she has experienced. Institution has begun.

The original seer dies, but the religion lives on. The institution preserves the message, along with the Saints and the prophets who proclaim it. The institution becomes the collective memory and depository of the vision. It offers support, symbols, rituals, holy places, nurture, theologies, and leaders while the vision, the spirituality, remains at its core. This same dynamic happens whenever people meet regularly to play cards; eventually a card club is formed with formal or informal rules. It happens whenever kids gather for a pickup game at the sandlot; soon after, a league is formed with teams, rules, umpires, and uniforms.

The problem with institutions, as everyone knows, happens when the letter, the format, the envelope becomes more important than the message. Roles can become rigid, leadership can become corrupt, traditions can ossify, rules can smother; this is what we have in mind when we speak disdainfully of the institutional Church.

We have witnessed the credibility of our Church lessened by its unwillingness to listen to those outside the narrow corridors of the Vatican, its unwillingness to dialogue, instead issuing ineffective unilateral statements. Still, we really don't want the institution to disappear. We couldn't survive intact without it, and we would soon invent another one, perhaps even more rigid and controlling. We just don't like manmade traditions supplanting mercy and justice. We don't like the institution tithing mint, dill, and cumin while neglecting the weightier matters of the law: justice, mercy, and faith. It is these which the Church ought to practice without neglecting the others. Straining out the gnat, but swallowing the camel brings disgust, disaffection, and cynicism (Mt 23:24).

Spirituality, yes; religion, no

There is another reason why we should be concerned about the state of the institutional Church. As we have noted earlier in this book, "spirituality," that vague, inner-directed bleached-out faith in self, is preferred over "religion" by many people today. In the cultural sense, spirituality is strictly a private matter between a person and God. As such it does not need—indeed, rejects—any kind of institutional framework, which is deemed a curtailment of individual freedom. Everything is a sacred matter of choice and nothing must be allowed to violate one's personal integrity. People are looking for spiritual nourishment—indeed, they desperately desire it—but they are not looking for it in a church or synagogue.

The transcendent self, as some have called it, reigns paramount. You can see this at work as people flock to secular shrines of their own creation. In New York City, for example, not far from where I live, people from all over the country and abroad crowd around a small shrine commemorating the life of the late John Lennon, one of the members of the Beatles. They leave flowers, notes, and pictures of loved ones at the shrine; they light votive candles, meditate, read poems, and sing. In England, Princess Diana's shrine draws similar attention. All the while, significantly, nearby Christian shrines are ignored and empty.

This self-created spirituality, of course, fits in quite well with our consumerist, individualistic society. A good example of this enshrined individualism is reflected in the new recruiting tactics for the Army, which is scrapping its long-time slogan, "Be all that you can be." The new slogan is "An Army of One," and is intended to appeal to the individualism and independence of today's youth. The TV ads are no longer shown during Sunday football games but on youth-orientated sitcoms. They feature a lone corporal who says, "Even though there are 1,045,690 soldiers just like me, I am my own force. With technology, with training, with support, who I am has become better than who I was. I'll be the first to tell you, the might of the U.S. Army doesn't lie in numbers. It lies in me. I am an Army of One."[1]

There is a snapshot of the attitude of today. And we can say the same about the attitude toward religion; that is: "I am a believer of one." The same day the Army unveiled its new recruiting approach, a study conducted by the Public Agenda published its report entitled, "For goodness sake: Why so many Americans want religion to play a greater role in American life." It found that "so many Americans are strongly religious. On the other hand, they believe that there has to be a tolerance for people of other religions. The study suggests that Americans have faith in faith no matter the doctrine."[2] That says it all.

This combination of a preference for the individual self and doctrinal indifference leads people to find spirituality sufficient and to substitute it for religion. Testimony to the success of this substitution can be found in the best-selling books on spirituality and self-help, on the Internet, on college campus bulletin boards, which are full of listings for tai chi, yoga, sanitized Buddhist meditation techniques, and New Age programs. You can even customize your own spirituality. There is a book out by Bobbi Parish called *Creating Your Own Personal Sacred Text*, which is described as a "step-by-step guide to writing your own scripture" by using selections from various texts of your choice as well as "your own words." More and more, the moral law becomes one's own creation.

This is what organized or institutional religion is up against. It is in the very difficult position of maintaining that there is Someone who counts beyond the self, who beckons; that there are moral and ethical demands beyond one's own creative fantasies that challenge and confront. Contrary to a privately assessed spirituality, religion is unapologetically communal. It promotes beliefs through ancient practices and corporate liturgies. It boldly plunges people into its long history of collective reflection on ethics and, in contrast to a spirituality that offers people a quick fix for their harried lifestyles, offers time, space, and the history of other seekers for spiritual experience.

Religion offers encoded memories, traditions, links to wisdom, and a leveling of self-serving and delusional ideals. It offers a historical, corrective context for our self-indulgence and self-interpretations. It pits our lives against those of our predecessors in the faith and demands a communal listening and understanding of the word, and communal praise of God with our contemporaries. As Donna Schaper writes,

> In a world increasingly populated by Zen-leaning Lutherans, or Buddhists turned Catholic, or Jews turned Quaker, it's not surprising to find highly personal expressions replacing institutional religion. We are so mired in the self that we are losing sight of the sacred. Religion, and its many imperfect institutions and spiritual expressions, promotes belief through its ancient practices and liturgies. Religion steeps people in its long history of reflection on ethics. At its best, religion offers time and space for spiritual experience. Spirituality gives us a quick fix that fits into our fast-paced, insular lifestyle.[3]

We should ponder these realities. Even though we may be exasperated with the way institutional religion sometimes works, we should recognize its validity and be able to offer solid justification for its existence.

Testimonies

There is a certain bravado, but also a certain necessity, in having a chapter that defends the institutional Church. That being said, let's put aside any images of stifling bureaucracy, erratic rule-making, vile suppression, and out-of-touch patriarchy—does that cover it?—and bring on a few witnesses, most of whom are considered very much in the liberal camp, to speak in defense of the institutional Church and its local affiliate, the parish. I'd like to present these testimonies, if you will, in a manner something like the witness talks at a Methodist campground meeting or a Catholic charismatic gathering. So spend some time reading their words and take in what they have to say.

First, two brief appearances provide a context for the speakers who follow. One is theologian Kenneth Osborne, who says, "Any suggestion that originally there was a completely democratic or congregational Christian community cannot be authenticated."[4] The other, theologian Bernard Cooke, writes,

> Among the charism given to individuals by Christ's Spirit for the sake of the community's life and mission is the charism of governance, a clear recognition that able administration of the structured elements of the church's life is a gift to be cherished. This means that those who are in directive positions must possess the power needed to guide and unify the community, and to some extent at least, this involves something like jurisdiction.[5]

Now, let's backtrack and ask for a cameo appearance from Andrew Greeley, who is always ahead of his time:

> The idea of a pneumatic Church is an attractive one and always has been. A handful of dedicated Christians working in a community in almost invisible fashion, exuding good will and love, and unconcerned about mundane things such as finance, administration, and communication, sounds terribly appealing. But even if it were possible for a community of humans to exist without a formal structure (and it is quite impossible) those who would object to a structured Church and would prefer a pneumatic one should take the matter up with the Founder who wanted his Church to be a thoroughly human organization and seemed prepared to accept the fact that in this human organization there would be all kinds of human imperfections....

The trouble with angry, alienated revolutionaries is that they can't win, they really don't want to win. They are what Irving Howe calls the kamikaze radicals who desire to pull down and destroy so that a fresh new start can be made. But they ignore the lessons of history that real growth is always organic, and that true progress usually comes from reforms of existing structures rather than from the creation of brand new ones.[6]

This testimony from J. Neville Ward is right on the mark:

Institutional religion will always exasperate us because it is carried in the words and deeds of inadequate and sinful human beings. Nevertheless, there is no other way of knowing that Christ is risen and really present in this our life than in the only group that believes this and exists to hold this belief before the world....People who attempt to learn Christianity while rejecting institutional religion develop impoverishments and distortions in their spiritual life which are clearly traceable to this rejection....Two familiar dangers dog the footsteps of those who attempt to go it alone, the tendency to settle for a moralistic "Golden Rule" type of inchoate religion, and the likelihood of intellectual superiority, particularly among the educated.

Without organization, without the [C]hurch, the Christian faith must necessarily be left to the private interest of individuals who may easily grow bored with looking for God and may never care whether others find him or not. Its prospects, then, would not interest any insurance company. This is not to say that there is anything sacrosanct about any of the administration or intellectual forms of the [C]hurch which is by definition always under the mercy and judgment of God, always in part usable, always needing reform.[7]

Many people feel that faith can be viable even outside the institutional Church. But consider what philosophy professor William Shea has to say about this:

In addition to my feeling about the Church, I have a view of her. She is vital. She is gracefully engaged in the salvation of the world. Volatile, full of power for the Christian life. Promising, confident, confused, wrong-headed, stubborn, authoritarian, even perverse. But I am unable to make my affections for the [C]hurch a distinction between the Catholic faith and the institutional [C]hurch.

As much as I now spontaneously dislike hierarchs and mistrust ecclesiastical bureaucrats, I think the distinction intellectually almost worthless and even a self-deception. Nor can I bring myself to say I love the [C]hurch when her leaders are correct, and I do not love the [C]hurch when they are mistaken. There is, to my mind, no institutional [C]hurch of unfeeling bureaucrats, on the one side, and a nearly invisible [C]hurch of good Catholics on the other. For me there's only one [C]hurch. Right or wrong, sinful and saved, all at once. What you see is what you get, *per omnia saecula saeculorum.*

I am sad at her sins as I am at my own. I am wary of her penchant for intellectual and spiritual repression as I am of my own fear of power, and my primal resentment of criticism. I find writ large in her life my own struggle, my own good and evil, my own truth, and my own lie. What I'm saying is that for all of the humanness and mistakes and even sinfulness of those of us who are the [C]hurch, we always have to have confidence in the bottom-line reality.[8]

The next to come on stage is Kenneth Woodward, religious editor for *Newsweek*:

One often hears among educated Catholics the phrase, "the institutional [C]hurch" used as a term of derision. How very American and sociological, how naive to suppose that anything of value can survive without institutions. The early Christians would never have begotten a second-generation [C]hurch if the charismatic first generation did not develop institutions, chains of command, and eventually a hierarchy.

Of course, the church is more than the sum of its institutions. But no society can survive without institutions, which are not just buildings or chains of command, but also patterns of behavior. It is only through institutions that traditions are passed on, the young are brought up, the undisciplined disciplined, and society sustained including the society we call the [C]hurch.

I have done my share of institutional criticism. There isn't a religious group, I suppose, that I haven't offended. But what offends me is the romantic notion that all the ills of the [C]hurch reside with the institution so that if only we could reform it, we ourselves would be better Christians. The truth quite often is the other way around.[9]

Rosemary Radford Ruether, a liberal columnist for the *National Catholic Reporter*, was invited to speak at a conference in the conservative Diocese of Lincoln, Nebraska—but not without a great negative fuss and protests from the diocese. She worried editorially whether the Lincoln, Nebraska type of repressive Catholicism, as she sees it, is "the future of American Catholicism." Progressive American Catholics may scoff at such a question, choosing to regard Lincoln as a "freak" situation of a right-wing extremist bishop. But those who cherish an open Church need to remember that the people who control Catholic institutions control the future of the American Catholic Church.

Then she goes on to warn those progressive Catholics who have dropped out of the institutional Church and meet among themselves in a kind of old-fashioned "house church." She says,

Autonomous house churches are wonderful as support groups, particularly for older people whose Catholic identity is long since confirmed. But these informal groups will not deliver church membership in the next generation.

By and large, progressive Catholics are not very successful in getting their own children to become regular churchgoers. If we are interested in having the creativity of the Vatican II generation of progressive American Catholics carried on into the future, it is time to get concerned about younger Catholics, those born after Vatican II. And this means defending the base for progressive Catholicism in Catholic institutions: parishes, religious orders, high schools, and colleges and seminaries.

This will entail a degree of investment of time and effort in Catholic institutions that many progressive Catholics have spurned, preferring to create house churches or independent movements, such as Call to Action. This option for voluntary organizations is not to be dropped. These are the main bases of progressive Catholicism at the moment. But movements such as house churches should not be set against institutional [C]hurch reform. Rather they should become a base for efforts to enter into such institutions and find ways to organize to defend the presence of progressive Catholicism in them. Otherwise I fear that Bruskewitz [the conservative bishop of Lincoln], and not Call to Action, will command the future of the American Catholic church.[10]

Anthropologist Mary Douglas adds to this sensibility:

My point is that we are emphatically not a congregational church. We do not understand the priesthood simply as a special ministry that represents the general ministry of the community. We do not understand the church as a community that simply extends its ministry locally by delegating certain functions to individual ministers; and certainly we do not understand our ritual forms and liturgy as something caused and created by the assembly itself....We are an ecclesial church with connections and differences. However we transmute in the next thousand years, we will remain true to our Catholic genius: connected to the vast Communion of Saints past, present, and to come, connected to each other, the diocese, and the universal church.[11]

Next to speak is a man I admire deeply, a theological Renaissance man and one of the nation's best homilists, octogenarian Walter Burghardt, SJ:

In the course of a half century, I have seen more Christian corruption than you have read of. I have tasted it. I have been reasonably corrupt myself. And yet, I love this Church, this living, pulsing, sinning people of God with a crucifying passion. Why? For all the Christian hate, I experience here a community of love. For all the institutional idiocy, I find here a tradition of reason. For all the individual repressions, I breathe here an air of freedom. For all the fear of sex, I discover here the redemption of my body. In an age so inhuman, I touch here tears of compassion. In a world so grim and humorless, I share here rich joy and earthy laughter. In the midst of death, I hear here an incomparable stress on life. For all the apparent absence of God, I sense here the real presence of Christ.[12]

Why Church?

This "speaker" will deliver the longest commentary. He is Ronald Rolheiser, a respected, bestselling author and spiritual director. Rolheiser speaks more specifically of the parish community and the necessity to be a part of it, but the dynamics of his remarks can also extend to the universal Church. Sit back and read:

> [We need] the grounding, earthiness, and necessary pain that only real involvement within a concrete parish type family can give you. Let me explain. In parishes, as we know, we do not get to pick who we will be standing beside as we worship and celebrate various things together. A parish-type family is a hand of cards that is randomly dealt to us, and precisely to the extent that it is truly inclusive, will include persons of every temperament, ideology, virtue, and fault. Also, church involvement, when understood properly, does not leave us the option to walk away whenever something happens that we do not like. It is a covenant commitment, like a marriage, and binds us for better and for worse.
>
> Accordingly, if we commit ourselves to a church community and stay with that commitment, we will, at some point, have

the experience that Jesus promised Peter would befall every disciple: Prior to this kind of commitment you can gird your belt and go wherever you want, but, after joining a concrete church community, others will put a belt around you and take you where you would rather not go.

And Jesus is right. What church community takes away from us is our false freedom to soar unencumbered, like the birds, believing that we are mature, loving, committed, and not blocking out things that we should be seeing. Real churchgoing soon enough shatters this illusion and gives us no escape, as we find ourselves constantly humbled as our immaturities and lack of sensitivity to the pain of others are reflected off eyes that are honest and unblinking.

We can be very nice persons, pray regularly, be involved in social justice, and still not be fully responsible. It is still possible to live in a lot of fantasy and keep our lives safe for ourselves. This gets more difficult, however, if we start going to a church, most any church, especially one that is large enough to be inclusive. To be involved in a real way in a church community is to have most of our exemption cards taken away....[For] Jesus teaches us clearly that God calls us, not just as individuals, but as a community and that how we relate to each other is just as important religiously as how we relate to God. Or, more accurately, how we relate to each other is part of how we relate to God. For Jesus, the two great commandments, to love God and love one's neighbor, can never be separated.

Moreover, for Jesus, concrete involvement within a historical community of faith (churchgoing) is not an abstract thing. Essentially it means that we must, in our worship of God in heaven, involve ourselves concretely with a worshiping community on earth. Hence, he tells us that anyone who claims to love God who is invisible but refuses to deal with a visible neighbor is a liar, for one can only really love a God who is love if one is concretely involved with a real community (ultimately an "ecclesial community") on earth.

For a Christian, concrete involvement within a historical community of faith (churchgoing) is a nonnegotiable within the spiritual life. This is something that is difficult for our age to hear. As we saw before, our age tends to divorce spirituality from ecclesiology. We want God, but we don't want church. By doing this, however, we bracket one of the primary demands inherent right within the very quest for God.

Already a century ago, a prominent Protestant theologian, Frederick Schleiermacher pointed out that, separate from historical religion, namely, the churches with all their faults, the individual in quest of God, however sincere that search, lives the unconfronted life. Without church, we have more private fantasy than real faith. He submits that real conversion demands that eventually its recipient be involved in both the muck and the grace of actual church life.

Spirituality is ultimately communitarian, even within those faiths such as Buddhism, Hinduism, Islam, and Taoism that are not ecclesial within their essential makeup, as are Christianity and Judaism. Why? Because the search for God is not a private search for what is highest for oneself or even for what is ultimate for oneself. Spirituality is about a communal search for the face of God and one searches communally only within a historical community.[13]

Now listen to premier educator, Thomas Groome:

Even when beset with great abuses and corruptions, Catholicism clung tenaciously to the conviction that the Church is crucial to the faith of Christians and their spiritual well-being. As one contemporary theologian [Schillebeeckx] summarizes this tradition, Jesus is God's primordial sacrament to the world, and then the Church is the sacrament of Jesus. Jesus is the primary means by which God reaches out to Christians and how they respond to God—together! Ever wonder, for example, why Catholics put so much emphasis on going to Mass on Sunday? The theological rationale is its emphasis on being a community of faith, on approaching God together. Thus, the Sabbath mandate includes publicly worshipping God in community. Likewise, Catholic Christians usually do not make claims about their personal salvation—"I am saved" or "accepting Jesus Christ as my Lord and Savior." The undergirding theology is that Christians cannot be content with individual salvation alone, but must commit to living as a people of God in the world—a daily challenge as community rather than a fait accompli of personal achievement.

Incensed at the corruptions so evident in the institution of the Church at the time, the Reformers tended to downplay its role in the work of salvation, emphasizing instead people's immediate relationship with God—rather than mediated through the Church—and the call to personal salvation. Although they rendered a crucial service to all Christianity by reclaiming the rights and responsibilities of the individual Christian—the priesthood of all believers, from a Catholic Christian perspective—the Reformers so favored the personal as to diminish the communal. Catholicism remained convinced that, for all its sins and shortcomings, the Church is still the primary way that God comes looking for its members and through which they go looking for God. Although always an imperfect instrument, the Holy Spirit uses the Church as the first [S]acrament of Jesus to the world in mediating the [D]ivine/human encounter for Christians.[14]

As we said, many people hate "the Church," by which they mean the power structure, the magisterium. We have already seen the reasons for this. Deep polarization, an insensitive and repressive institutional hierarchy, an overblown papacy with its shameful history of medieval power, greed, warfare and domination, the out-of-touch dictates, a stagnant theology, a history of anti-Semitism and of excluding women, the suppression of theologians and free discussion, irrelevant pronouncements—all have undermined the credibility of the institutional Church. Still, I maintain, we need this ancient, historical Church, despite its failings and faults.

Yes, reform is needed—badly. Centralization—relatively new in the Church—is outrageous. The papal appointment of all bishops is a distinct, unwarranted novelty. The lack of a voice from the laity with respect to selecting bishops and pastors flies in the face of tradition. The exclusion of married men from the priesthood is arbitrary. The undervaluation of women begs for redress. The theological "one hat fits all" is arrogant. The need to control is demeaning. The silencing of voices is tyrannical. The list is long. Reform cries out to heaven. Still, for all that, like the prophet Hosea directed by Yahweh to remain with his unfaithful wife, we must stay connected to the apostolic tradition of the universal Church, and through it to Jesus, and be mature enough to look beyond the nonsense to the source of our religion.

This next speaker says it best, as he had said so many good things in his life. Frank Sheed was a husband, father, public speaker, defender of the faith, writer, publisher, and one privy to the faith and foibles of the Catholic [C]hurch. He wrote:

> We are not baptized into the hierarchy; do not receive the cardinals sacramentally; will not spend an eternity in the beatific vision of the pope. St. John Fisher could say in a public sermon, "If the pope will not reform the curia, God will." A couple of years later he laid his head on Henry VIII's block for papal supremacy, followed to the same block by Thomas More, who had spent his youth under the Borgia pope, Alexander Vl, lived his early manhood under the Medici pope, Leo X, and died for papal supremacy under Clement Vlll, as time-serving a pope as Rome ever had.

> Christ is the point. I, myself, admire the present pope but even if I criticized him as harshly as some do, even if his successor proved to be as bad as some of those who have gone before, even if I sometimes find the [C]hurch as I have to live with it, a pain in the neck, I should still say that nothing a pope could do or say would make me wish to leave the [C]hurch, although I might well wish that he would leave.

> Israel, through its best periods as through its worst, preserved the truth of God's oneness in a world swarming with gods, and a sense of God's majesty in a world sick with its own pride. So

with the [C]hurch. Under the worst administration we could still learn Christ's truth, receive his life in the sacraments, be in union with him to the limit of our willingness. In awareness of Christ, I can know the [C]hurch as his mystical body, and we must not make our judgment by the neck's sensitivity to pain.

Three people close this chapter with brief remarks. Fr. Bryan Hehir wrote that if you accept the Church as an institution seriously you'll experience it both as a blessing and a burden:

> There are times when the institution bears down on you. There are times when it sets limits on what you think most needs to be done. There are other times when you are deeply grateful that it has survived 2,000 years and that it is present in an institutional form in a world that is tough to change. I believe that our faith teaches us that, and I believe this is our hope.[15]

Beyond all the intellectual reasons for sticking with the institution we call the Church—despite the limitations, the practicalities, the bureaucracies, and the efficiencies of all institutions, beyond the pull of the dead weight of the past and the sturdy anchor of traditions that institutions exhibit—when it comes right down to it, we stick with it because of people. Like so many we have seen, the pull of community and the compelling faith of the "here comes everybody," messy pilgrims. It is the people who have their love-hate relationship with the Church who ultimately make the difference. As this poet who asks himself "Why am I a Roman Catholic?" answers:

> So why am I a Roman Catholic? Why do I remain a Roman Catholic? Just now, today, I don't have an answer. I have people. But those people are not always particularly lovable. They're people. Indeed, sometimes, they can be maddening. But I have a little love, and I know I need more. And sometimes the [C]hurch can be maddening. But I have little faith, and I know I need more. And I know where to go to get more of all that. Put simply because I am weak, I need these people this

[C]hurch in the person of Jesus. And, as a wise man once said to me, "This is all I will ever need."[16]

Indeed it is. And finally, T.S. Eliot, a poet of another age:

Why should men love the [C]hurch?
Why should they love her laws?
She tells them of life and death
and all they would forget.
She is tender where they would be hard
and hard where they would like to be soft.
She tells them of evil and sin
and other unpleasant facts.[17]

24

INCLUSIVE/EXCLUSIVE

In his book, *Reconciling Faith and Reason*, Thomas Rausch, SJ, out-
lines a few of the practical problems facing us in this third millennium:

> How will the Church find a new language for its faith, one
> that will bring the liberating message of the Gospel to millions
> of the poor and suffering who make up the majority of the
> world's people? How can the Church reconcile its faith and
> doctrine with scientific knowledge? Who decides on questions
> of doctrine?
>
> What does the Church say to those who feel excluded from
> its life? What about women in the Church? Can they be called
> to ordained ministry? How can the Church learn to pray and
> name God in a more inclusive way? What does the Church
> say to those who are homosexual, not by choice, but from an
> orientation determined very early in their lives, perhaps even
> before birth? Are they to be told that the physical expression
> of their lives in a committed, exclusive relationship is sinful?
> What does it say to those whose marriages fail, and who seek
> new unions?
>
> What does the Christian community say to the vast majority
> of human beings who belong to other religions? Is there sal-
> vation for those outside the Church? Are they excluded from
> God's grace if they do not make an explicit confession of faith
> in Jesus? Is grace to be found in their religious traditions?

What grounds for dialogue exist between the different faiths? What about human life questions such as abortion, the death penalty, the possibilities of genetic engineering? Do Christians have an obligation towards the environment?[1]

I think that if there are two words that might describe an effective approach to these questions from a brave new Church, they are the polar words of inclusive and exclusive. Let us start with the notion of inclusiveness.

Being inclusive

First, there is God. We dearly need to widen our concept of that word itself because our point of vision of both ourselves and our cosmos has dramatically and drastically changed in the past decades. For many, God is still defined as a person, a male father figure located in the skies, not doing much but overseeing his creation. But in our new consciousness we simply know that God cannot be "up there" in the skies for, in our expanding universe, there is no "up there." There is only out. And God is out, yet not even out, but within and with all. That is, God is the pervasive, animating force of all that is, the center of all reality, the horizon of our experience, the Mystery who is and is always in the background, the Source of beauty and truth, the Spirit. The simple and limiting concept of a father-figure God in the sky won't do anymore.

Over the centuries, we have used many figures of speech to try to catch something of the wide mystery of God. Common Biblical terms are Spirit, King, Father, Warrior, Mother. Religion has added more: Source, Depth, Power, Presence, Mystery, Matrix, Transcendence, and so on. Of all these images, we have tended to canonize just one: the Father image. Perhaps this is because it is the image found in the Old Testament, and because Jesus called God his Father. And the deep tradition of using this term must be honored, for it is the foundation of our fundamental belief in the Trinity and Incarnation. The use of Creator, Redeemer, and Spirit or similar formulas to substitute for Father, Son, and Holy Spirit, or to avoid using the word "Father" distorts sound theology. There is a real danger of undermining revelation if we jettison that term. We simply want to point out that if we use this image only and exclusively we soon forget that it is just an image. We then concretize God as the male person with the white beard, like Michelangelo's God on the ceiling of the Sistine chapel.

An exclusive Father image is not only false and misleading, but also, on the practical level, difficult for those who have had a bad father experience. A male-only image tends to reinforce patriarchy and omit the experience of women. As we face the future, then, we need to use better God-talk and more inclusive images, such as Friend, Lover, Spirit, Mystery, Godself. A brave new Church needs to have a more inclusive name for God, for sometimes I suspect that the "loss of faith" experienced by many people has more to do with the images of God than it does with the Mystery of life as people actually experience it.[2]

A brave new Church enters the post-Christian era more inclusively ecumenical, for we have learned that we share with all faith traditions the hunger of the human person for God, a reaching for the transcendent. Recall that "In my Father's house there are many mansions" (Jn 14:2). With the great religious traditions—Judaism and Islam, for example—we share a belief in a personal God who loves humankind, is compassionate, and has revealed Godself to us. With mainstream Protestants, we are Christian, cherish the Bible, share the Nicene Creed and the Apostles' Creed, and profess Jesus as the Messiah and giver of life. So we move away from any sense of triumphalism, knowing the differences but celebrating the sameness. We are led into "dialogue and cooperation with the followers of other religions, and in witness of Christian faith and life, acknowledge, preserve, and promote the spiritual and moral goods found among these [peoples], as well as the values in their society and culture."[3]

A brave new Church enters the post-Christian era with the inclusiveness of ministry. If, as we saw, the second millennium was the millennium of the papacy (and bishops and clergy), the third millennium will be the millennium of the baptized. If Ignatius of Antioch could proclaim in the second century, "Where the bishop is, there is the Church," this century will proclaim, "Where the people are, there is the Church." We have seen in a previous chapter how the baptismal gifts of the laity have been reclaimed and validated, that there is no greater dignity than that of being baptized. Further, the clergy are but baptized persons with the charism of ministering to the baptized to help them link liturgy and life. Cardinal Suenens got it right when he gave the homily at a Mass for Pope John XXIII, then recently deceased:

> The greatest day in the life of Pope John was not the day he became pope, not the day he was ordained a bishop, not the day he was ordained a priest. The greatest day in the life of Pope John was the day he was baptized into Christ Jesus. There is no greater Christian dignity than that of being a baptized person.

It is taken for granted that shared and collaborative ministry is the norm for living and expressing the Christian life, and that the parish is and will be forevermore one of inclusive ministry. It is a communal enterprise, a mixture of gifts and charisms that makes up the faith community. Our challenge is not only to offer a community of shared gifts, but also to scatter those gifts, energized by the liturgy, into the marketplace.

A brave new Church enters the post-Christian era with an inclusive embrace of the whole world as one living organism, God's creation, which is both interconnected and a reflection of God's glory. Within this embrace is a respect for the earth and its resources and especially a commitment to social justice, wherever it operates, which seeks to lift up the lowly and marginal.

Finally, a brave new Church moves into the post-Christian era guarding and celebrating the gift of women, seeking parity in ministry and in their relationships with men, offering a platform for their voices to be heard.

Exclusive

But if, as Catholics, we share so much in common and seek to be inclusive, we must also remember and celebrate what makes us exclusive, in the sense of being unique. And what makes us so is the precise combination and configuration Catholicism gives to the religious truths we share with other faiths. Richard McBrien gives a good summary:

> How can one distinguish Catholicism from other theological, doctrinal, spiritual, liturgical, moral, and institutional expressions of Christianity on the basis of characteristics which Catholicism presumably shares with one or another Christian church? It is true: There is no one characteristic, apart from the Petrine doctrine, which sets the Catholic Church apart from all other churches. On the other hand, a case can be made that nowhere else except in the Catholic Church are all of Catholicism's characteristics present in the precise configuration in which they are found within Catholicism.[4]

To use one example, others find the church important, but we Catholics really underscore the importance of the Church in our lives (say, in contrast to the individualism of Protestantism). Perhaps the best definition of our distinctiveness comes, of all places, from the pen of a Protestant theologian who summarizes five characteristics of Catholicism. He sees Catholicism in terms of

- the people as community

- the reality of tradition

- the grace of caritas

- the sacramental sense of the living presence of God

- the rationality of the traditional faith.[5]

That is a great summary, and an even better agenda for us to follow. Let's take a look at each of these elements.

Community. Above all, we have always had the sense that salvation is a communal affair. This is what we must preach and live and worship in a world of fierce individualism, where so many have dropped out of communal worship seeking only a "Jesus and me" piety or a New Age self-improvement agenda. We must be steadfast in our sense of connectedness and in our common breaking of the bread at Mass. Be faithful, for as we have noted in a previous chapter, so many people, so many converts, are drawn to this sense of Eucharistic community, to a welcoming parish. Through the shared gifts of all, through collaborative ministry and, above all, where liturgy and faith, worship and life connect, community will not only be evident, but compelling.

The reality of tradition. This embraces the huge storehouse of wisdom and lived experience of the saints, the depository of councils and writings, and the treasury of art and poetry. There is so much hidden in our attic, so to speak, that remains unknown and unused. We Catholics have an enormously rich tradition, one that includes what we have called a "thick" Catholicism, along with the sacramentals and devotions that shadow a deeper mystery, that help us sing, touch, and feel something more behind the movements, chants, and rhythms of popular prayer and devotions.

The grace of caritas. Our sense of regard for the human race and the human experience reminds us that behind the "slings and arrows of outrageous fortune" is Someone who cares and Someone who makes all things new again, and so is the basis for a benevolent view of the human condition. The Catholic understanding of human nature, as Bernard Lonergan put it, is one of "realistic optimism." We must encourage a sense that life is meaningful and worthwhile and has a purpose. The answer given by the old Baltimore Catechism to the question, "Why did God make us?" is still valid (masculine pronoun notwithstanding): "God made us to know him, love him, and serve him in this life and be happy with him forever in the next."

The sacramental sense of the living presence of God. To a Catholic, this says there is more to be found in the ordinary and everyday events of our lives. The words from a poem by Gerard Manley Hopkins, SJ are our theme: "The world is charged with the grandeur of God." We must encourage people's appreciation for what is beautiful and pleasing, holding fast to our optimistic view of people and life and to our sense that the mystery of God is in all of creation. We continue to maintain that there is always "the More" to be discovered in the everydayness of life.

The rationality of the traditional faith. This honors the intellectual life, brings reason to bear on faith, and helps us to gain an appreciation of who we are through study, reflection, and evangelization. In a world of sound bites, our Catholic tendency for rationality is more needed than ever, for it is part and parcel of who we are. Indeed, it is regrettable that some colleges have jettisoned the liberal arts for more trendy agendas.

As the brave new Church faces the post-Christian era, perhaps the best place to stand might be beside the apostle Paul, who was facing the post-pagan era.

We have this treasure in clay jars, so that it may be made clear that this extraordinary power belongs to God and does not come from us. We are afflicted in every way, but not crushed; perplexed, but not driven to despair; persecuted, but not forsaken; struck down, but not destroyed; always carrying in the body the death of Jesus, so that the life of Jesus may also be made visible in our bodies. (2 Cor. 4:7–10)

Amen.

25

THE SPIRIT OF FRANCIS

At precisely 8:12 p.m., March 13, 2013, Cardinal Jean-Louis Tauran appeared at the basilica balcony of St. Peter's in Rome and made the formal announcement, "I announce to you a great joy: we have a pope! The most eminent and most reverend lord, Jorge Mario, Cardinal of the Holy Roman Catholic Church Bergoglio, who has taken the name of Francis."

Francis: a name that immediately conjured up the poor man of Assisi, the one who heard a voice in the tumbled-down Church of San Damiano saying, "Go, rebuild my church, which, as you can see, is falling into ruin." Was there a prophetic message here, a hopeful one? Could this man who rode the bus to work, lived in a simple apartment, and cooked his own meals rebuild a Church much in need of reformation?

In no time at all, he chose eight cardinals from around the world to assist him in reforming the Roman Curia. He jettisoned the royal robes of his predecessors, wears a simple white cassock, uses the term "brother cardinals" rather than "your lordships," and soon made public a wish list of bishops and priests whose pastoral qualities exceed their loyalty or orthodoxy and who, in Bertrand Russell's phrase, would not so reflexively sacrifice people to doctrine. His much heralded and much commented July 2013 trip to Brazil revealed a pope willing to revitalize the Church.

There are signs, then, that this new pontificate, so concerned for the poor, impatient with bureaucracy and sensitive to the need for reform, might inaugurate sweeping changes that line up the official Church with the gifts and needs of the rest of the Church, the People of God. In view of what has been written in this book, let me suggest a list of possible pastoral changes that may begin the reform. We have already suggested changes in rule of celibacy and the choosing of bishops. This is my additional (controversial) list. Others have theirs.

Shared and collaborative ministry

One of the criticisms of the Vatican bureaucracy is its high-handed unilateral decisions. There is little input beyond its boundaries. The papal office, as we have seen, for over a thousand years a minor entity in the Church where bishops made their own local decisions, had steadily absorbed all else. Collegiality evaporated to the vanishing point over the centuries. Alien voices—women, minorities, local pastors—were not heard or heeded. This is the time for a new balance, the creation of new official forms or the revitalization of old ones, to seek input, to recognize regional differences and traditions. The magisterium needs to dialogue with more than itself.

But, for most of us, the practical issue is our own dioceses and parishes. At one time, let it be said, heroic bishops and priests helped the "PIGS" immigrants (Poles, Irish/Italians, Germans, Slovaks) assimilate to America. The people, largely illiterate, desperately trying to assimilate to the new country and earn a living were concomitantly the object of widespread vicious anti-Catholicism. There was little time for leisure, schooling or theological distinctions. With such bias ecumenism was impossible. The local priest—an undisputed authority figure—helped them with the more urgent survival matters and gave them a sense of home away from home. They created parishes that gave them identity and comfort. They created ethnic liturgies and celebrations, instructed them in their faith—

a militant "true" one, to be sure, ("us against them" in the face of bias)—and taught them their simple catechisms.

They taught them, as they must, in simple, direct, straightforward ways. There was no need, no time for nuances. Theological qualifications would only confuse the people. In siege times, it was better to give the people one way, one theory, one custom as absolute truth and practice and not confuse them. Rather, the priests used their energies in helping them look to the future, a future of financial stability, careers and, above all, the key that would get them there, education.

So, in America, one of the glories of the age was that the local Church, at great sacrifice, gradually built schools (local public ones were rift with anti-Catholicism), colleges, and universities. The glory and the shame was that by and by the Church was successful. Glory because it built an educational system second to none and educated millions of immigrants and moved their children to mainstream America. Shame, because the clergy *forgot* they were successful. With more education and more assimilation came wider perspectives. The laity moved to middle class. In recent decades, general education has become the norm. Catholics entered positions of leadership and authority. They dealt with consensus decision making. They knew how to run corporations. They were exposed to new thinking, new theologies, new Biblical studies. Today, in the average parish, you may have a significant part of the congregation more educated than the pastor. You may have those with degrees in comparative religion, management, and Scripture. When the clergy forgot they were successful and still treated the laity like illiterate children to be talked down to, to be kept in the dark, they found out that the top-down way of leadership was passé, resented and ineffectual—not to mention spiritually suffocating. As the United States Bishops wrote in their underrated document, "Called and Gifted: The American Catholic Laity" (1980):

> One of the characteristics of lay men and women today is their growing sense of being adult members of the Church.

> Adulthood implies knowledge, experience and awareness, freedom and responsibility, and mutuality in relationships.... Thanks to the impetus of the Second Vatican Council, lay women and men feel themselves called to exercise the same mature interdependence and practical self-direction which characterize them in other areas of life.

Besides, their Church has told the laity in no uncertain terms that they are the Church. They have rights. They are not passive members at the bottom of the discarded pyramid model that has been hammered by Vatican II into a circle. The call to holiness is universal, not particular to the clergy and religious. In short, the parish is a matter of shared and collaborative ministry, a matter of co-laborers. Authority must be exercised in a collegial manner through a consensus decision-making process, with councils and boards. The Church may not be a democracy, but it is a community. So, the first field of renewal is transparency and a deep sense of co-responsibility and collaboration both on the curial and local levels. We have the mandate. We have the principles. We need the will.

Divorce and remarriage in the Church

Divorce is, sadly, commonplace. The usual figure is around 40% or more. That's a lot of grief, displacement and, frequently, financial ruin. Children are mightily affected. Social studies show, for example, that young children of divorce are not only more likely to suffer from anxiety, loneliness, low self-esteem, and sadness, they also experience long-lasting setback in interpersonal skills and math test scores.

Catholics divorce almost as much as the general population. For them the problem comes when they remarry. Then, if they cannot obtain an annulment, they are cut off from the Church in that they cannot receive the sacraments. They either leave, find another church that accepts them, or stick it out in a kind of ecclesiastical limbo. The Church is right to hold fast to the ideal of a lifelong, faithful marriage and is right to promote serious marriage preparation, but is its penalty for divorced Catholics too severe? After all, even repentant murderers are welcomed back to the sacraments.

On the pastoral level in the day-to-day care for divorced people, many priests leave the question of remarriage and church participation up to the couples' careful and thoughtful consciences provided they fulfill the following conditions: 1) they acknowledge that their first marriages are irretrievably lost. There's no hope of a reconciliation; 2) they have sincerely tried to go through the Church, but wound up with no official recourse to change their status—the annulment, say, is on indefinite hold for some reason or another; 3) they are sincerely desirous of participating in the life of the Church and; 4) they show solid signs that the second marriage, even though it cannot be celebrated by the Church, will in all other respects be a Christian marriage. Under these conditions, divorced Catholics should be admitted to the sacraments and a compassionate Church should make this official.

Gay marriage

Gay marriage, pretty much a given today, poses a special problem to the Church. First of all, we need to affirm some of the things that gay marriage symbolizes: universal health care, the right not to be bullied, the right to employment without being harassed, the dignity of every human being. These things belong to our tradition regardless of the politics involved. Second, we need to understand that society sees marriage as a civil contract, a matter of individual freedom and equality (which translates "the same as"), autonomy and rights. The Church's teaching of chastity, fidelity, lifelong unity, openness to children and community is way out of sync with the modern secular attitude. We need both to make clear and defend the difference and provide a rationale for a stance that is pastoral yet firm.

Some have suggested that, given the current divide, perhaps it's time for the Church to get out of the civil marriage business. It came very late to it. For centuries the Church accepted as legitimate, binding, and valid any marriage properly celebrated. Only after the first millennium, for practical reasons, did the Church demand that Catholics get married before a priest and two witnesses. Today, in our secular society, the young have opted out of Church and view marriage as a TV "happening", and an expensive one at that—the average wedding runs about $65,000. The participants are often woefully ignorant of Church etiquette. Often the faith element is so anemic that, as one wag said, the bride and groom could pick up their annulment papers on the way out. One thinks of the multi-million-dollar wedding of the reality star Kim Kardashian on TV, with its four million viewers, a cake costing $20,000 (a sum that would feed a village in the fourth world many times over)—and divorce, two and a half years later.

Clergy of all faiths dislike weddings for this reason. By getting out of the civil marriage business (clergy, remember, are agents of the state), the Church can be open to share its teaching on marriage and let couples whose faith is strong, before or after their civil marriages, seek a sacramental celebration of their marriage in Church. For some it might mean coming to church with their family and a few close friends and celebrating the Nuptial Mass to be followed by a small brunch and later have the civil marriage with all of its requisite hoopla. This would also forestall the issue of gay marriage in Church. The Church, which has a distinct view of the nature of marriage as a union between one man and one woman, would be neutral to gay marriage in its civil form but on religious principle deny a religious ceremony to gay unions without prejudice.[1]

Contraception

The fact is that, for millennia, avoiding or embracing pregnancy, because it is inextricably connected to sex, is an elemental fact of human life. Therefore there is a certain element of hubris present when those who make universal and binding pronouncements on both are celibate. While they make laws, the married must make decisions. We don't have to go as far as one man who declared that Canon Law ought to be revised to state that no man is qualified to become a bishop who has not slept every night for nine months with the same pregnant woman—then he can speak about marriage, sex, and humanity with some credibility. But he has a point.

They, the bishops, are right, of course, in some significant ways. Contraceptive intercourse can be relentlessly selfish, with pleasure as its only aim—witness the prevalent and demeaning hookup culture and ubiquitous mainstream pornography—and that, in the process, objectifies women, forgoes deep relationships and promotes the horrors of abortion. But is pleasure the only alternative to contraceptive sex? As Jo McGowan writes, "Adults understand that good sex, with or without contraception, goes deeper than pleasure. It is complex and demanding. And pleasure isn't necessarily a part of it. Any human encounter requiring honesty and surrender has the potential for both revelation and pain. The communication, healing and strengthening that good sex ensures is foundational to a marriage."[2]

Yes, sexual license, as we witness every day, is destructive. It threatens the social order, spreads disease, and commodifies people. So does sex that produces too many children beyond the resources and abilities of the parents or sex that threatens a mother's health or life. It's a tricky thing, but most people feel that there is room for committed married couples to sincerely form their consciences about contraception. The Church should help, not hinder, them. Too bad it ignored the Papal Commission on Birth Control set up by Pope John XXIII, where gifted and talented Catholic laypeople offered a concept of sex beyond mere conception to a sense of a deeper bonding, affirmation, and support. This attitude was in sharp contrast to the official Church that identified the morality of sexual intercourse with its physical aspects. The Commission ultimately suggested a change in policy while the Congregation for the Doctrine of the Faith (CDF), alarmed over the prospect of changing a "doctrine" and losing credibility, persuaded the Pope (Paul VI) to reject the findings of the married and accept the findings of the celibate.

The fact is that, by and large, the ban on and arguments against contraception have been widely rejected by both laity and clergy and remain so. For example, a recent study (2011) of Australian priests (closest in attitudes to their American counterparts) reveal for the first time that a mere 19% of respondents agreed that it is a sin for married couples to use artificial birth control. For most lay-people, it's a non-issue. That must form some kind of a *sensus fidelium*. Besides, from the beginning, the moral absolute of *Humane Vitae* has not been beyond challenge, as the works of many moral theologians testify. In any case, let there be more dialogue, more conversation, more openness to the consciences of sincere couples.

General Absolution

For a period in the 80's, it was permitted to give General Absolution, a privilege customarily reserved for soldiers going into battle. My memory is of a packed church, a common liturgy of hymns, scriptural readings and reflection, a public examination of conscience, a communal litany of sorrow and repentance and general absolution. In short, a lovely, sincere act of community reconciliation, something akin to ancient times.

In the first centuries reconciliation was very much a strict public affair, with public penitence, public confession, public reconciliation. And it was strict. Three sins, for example—apostasy, murder and adultery (all community-damaging sins)—could be forgiven only once. There was no second forgiveness. It was a harsh system, and many people put off reconciliation until death. In the seventh and eighth centuries it was the Irish monks who first introduced what we might call private confession: a one-on-one encounter where sins could be forgiven more than once. At first forbidden by the official Church, the sheer popularity of this form eventually made it the norm. There were benefits, but the community sense was woefully lost.

The Church soon took control, and by the time of Trent it had effectively removed any sense of a personal encounter of the Prodigal son or daughter with a forgiving Father, any sense of the communal effects of sin, and made it—what we called confession—a strict juridical private exercise in a small dark closet with precise legal steps to follow. Older Catholics will recall them: 1) Examine your conscience, 2) be sorry for your sins 3) have a firm purpose of amendment, 4) tell your sins—number, time and circumstance—to the priest, and 5) be willing to do the penance the priest gives you. These were the sure steps to obtain the goal—absolution—one way or another. (We soon learned that it was best to seek out priests who were hard of hearing or for whom English was a second language.) This was private confession in its most limited sense. The communal impacts of sin and forgiveness, any sense of wounding or being reconciled with the believing community, were lost.

Vatican II tried to revive the fuller liturgical, personal, and communal aspects by changing the title "Confession" to "the Sacrament of Reconciliation." It hasn't worked, as those long lines of confession of my childhood days have dwindled to a trickle of the disappearing gray-haired. But I can testify to this: with careful catechesis, the Communal Confession with general absolution was a powerful celebration of community confession, repentance, and reconciliation. It did not put the emphasis on the legal enumeration of number, times, and circumstance any more than the Prodigal Father did for his wayward son who tried to speak his rehearsed litany of faults but was immediately silenced by hugs and kisses. But it did make a community whole.

The bishops (alas, so many were never parish priests) became concerned that this was a case of cheap grace: just come in with the crowd, go through the ceremony and wind up with absolution. So they banned general absolution. Though one presumes that they must have known their history, they were uneasy that any or all of the sixteenth-century five steps were omitted, as if every one was essential. But I and others can testify that this was never the case. There was never any cheap grace. The catechesis was thorough, the liturgy was moving, and people who would never have been reconciled came in droves. They were sincere and joyous. It brought many back. A more pastoral Church must restore General Absolution.

Evangelization

For many years now, Church leaders, from the popes on down, have been talking about a new approach to evangelization, a new style of apologetics. They have expressed the urgent need to reach out to non-Catholics and catechize the faithful in a land of woeful religious illiteracy and saturated media literacy.

The problems are profound. For one thing, with religion ejected from the public square, there really is no forum to reach the people, much less the youth who, plugged in 24/7 to their gadgets, get their information and values from celebrities. The Bishops, in spite of the proven popularity of Bishop Sheen on commercial television, could never bring themselves to find a spokesperson they could agree upon, never could quite see the potential, not only of television, but also of the ubiquitous technology that rules today. The bishops must get around to investing heavily in TV spots, even-handedly admitting failures and yet highlighting the rich tradition of the Church's teaching, charity, and compassion. Every diocese should spend a considerable amount of its budget on a tech staff that can creatively connect with the people, especially the young. We need more Madison Avenue savvy.

Another problem that constricts evangelization is that the public image of the Church comes through a less-than-sympathetic press that keeps recycling stories of predatory clergy, negligent bishops, and what they consider Neanderthal teaching on sex, same-sex marriage, and abortion. Likewise, Catholic schools, as we have noted, are closing at record rates, dwindling the numbers we can reach. The Catholic press, often quite excellent, has a limited audience. Then, too, this must be said: our approach has not always been open. Internally, we are so wedded to an official party line, so committed to churchy language, so quick to parrot official Church answers, that we have no tradition of dialogue, only the certainties of monologue: "The Church says. End of discussion." As one man put it, "When I ask a priest a question, he readily gives me 'the teaching of the Church'. When I ask a rabbi a question, he replies by saying, 'Let's sit down and talk about it.'" *The Catechism of the Catholic Church* is a rich resource, but a poor textbook.

Finally, we must keep in mind that in about forty years—maybe sooner, if the immigration laws go through—Hispanics will be 30% of the population, and our cultural presentation of the faith must keep this in mind.

There is much at stake and it is this: the inclusive parish, committed to servant leadership and shared and collaborative ministry and, most of all, supported, not dominated, by a hierarchy under the charism of a pope with, if not always the name, but the spirit of Francis, will be a welcome sign that the Brave New Church is here, waiting to make its impact.

ENDNOTES

Preface

1. Trevor, Meriol. *Prophets and Guardians*. New York: Doubleday, 1969; p. 110.

2. Fox, Thomas C. *Sexuality and Catholicism*. New York: George Braziller, 1995; p. 166.

3. Quoted in *First Things*, March 2000; p. 108. See also, *Christian Identity in a Fragmented Age*, by Paul Lakeland (Minneapolis, MN: Fortress Press, 1997).

Part I: The Twelve Challenges

Chapter 1: Secularism and the Assault on Faith

1. Delbanco, Andrew. "Are You Happy Yet?" *New York Times Magazine*, May 7, 2000; p. 44.

2. The Center of Applied Research in the Apostolate (hereafter CARA), vol. 5, no. 3, Winter 2000.

3. Brueggemann, Walter. Quoted in the Foreword, *Journal for Preachers*, vol. XXIII, no. 4, Pentecost 2000; p. 1.

4. Crosby, Michael. "Living Compassionately in a Consumer Culture," *New Theology Review*, May 2000; p. 20.

5. Biddick, Bruce. Found in the "Business and Technology" section, *US News and World Report*, March 27, 2000; p. 44.

6. Wolf, Michael. "Why Your Kids Know More About the Future Than You Do," *New York Magazine*, May 17, 1999; p. 30.

7. Aird, Enola G. "Lamentations of a Rachel in the Digital Age," *Theology Today*, January 2000; p. 562.

8. Rolheiser, Ronald. *The Holy Longing*. New York: Doubleday, 1999; p. 31.

9. Chittister, Joan. "In Search of Belief," *National Catholic Reporter* (hereafter NCR), December 31, 1999/January 7, 2000; p. 11.

10. Appleby, Scott. "Catholicism in American Society at the Dawn of the 21st Century." Lecture given at The 2000 Archbishop Gerety Lecture Series, held March 1, 2000 at Seton Hall University, New Jersey (hereafter, Gerety Lecture).

11. Aird, op. cit., p. 563.

Chapter 2: The Suspicion of Institutions

1. Waxman, Sharon and William Booth. "Stuck in a '60s Groove: Boomer Nostalgia Is Bad Trip for Others," *Washington Post*, February 7, 1999; A1.

2. Wayne, Leslie. "Trial Lawyers Put Money into Democrats' Chests," *New York Times*, March 23, 2000; p. 1.

3. For a good look at political money corruption see the books, *The Money Men* by Jeffrey Birnbaum, and *Outside Money* by David Magleby.

4. Tarloff, Erik. *New York Times Book Review*, April 23, 2000; p. 13.

5. See the article, "The Kept University" by Eyal Press and Jennifer Washburn, in *The Atlantic Monthly*, March 2000; 39ff. Also see the book, *Beer and Circus: How Big-Time College Sports is Crippling Undergraduate Education* by Murray Sperber (New York: Henry Holt & Co, 2000).

6. The Prenuptial Contracts section of the Mowchuk.co, Website.

7. Breen, Stephen P. *Asbury Park Press*, March 14, 2000.

8. Allan, John L., Jr. "Real Disregards Ideal," *NCR*, January 5, 2001.

9. Cited in *Emerging Trends*, November 1999.

10. Knox, David and Caroline Schacht. *Choices in Relationships: An Introduction to Marriage and the Family,* fourth ed. Minneapolis, MN: West Publishing, 1994; pp. 4-5, 11, 20-23. Then there's Nancy Sanders, a Philadelphia psychologist who lists marriage as "a failing anachronism" and states that "society can no longer support what we think of marriage." For the long-terms effects of divorce and a defense of marriage see *The Unexpected Legacy of Divorce* by Judith S. Wallerstein, Julia M. Lewis and Sandra Blakelee (New York: Hyperion Press, 2000) and *The Case for Marriage* by Linda J. Waite and Maggie Gallagher (New York: Doubleday, 2000).

11. Dean, Kenda Creasy. "Proclaiming Salvation: Youth Ministry for the Twenty First Century Church," *Theology Today,* January 2000, p. 435.

12. *New York Times,* April 2, 2000 (section 9).

13. *New York Times,* April 25, 2000; p. B5.

14. Brooks, David. *Bobos in Paradise: The New Upper Class and How They Got There.* New York: Simon and Schuster, 2000; p. 135.

15. Ibid, p. 227.

Chapter 3: Religious Illiteracy

1. Konig, Cardinal Franz. "The pull of God in a godless age," *The Tablet,* 18 September 1999; pp. 1248ff.

2. This information was distributed at Beloit College, in Wisconsin.

3. McBrien, Richard. "Trying to Catechize a Generation that Can't Define 'Biretta,'" *NCR,* March 24, 2000; p. 18.

4. Simmons, Rose. "Rappers' Lyrics Revel in a Word Generations Have Tried to Erase," *Asbury Park Press,* February 18, 2000; p. 18.

5. Farrell, Michael. *National Catholic Reporter,* May 19, 2000.

6. Hahn, Scott. *Rome Sweet Rome.* San Francisco: Ignatius Press, 1993; p. 14.

7. Burghardt, Walter J., SJ. *Long Have I Loved You.* Maryknoll, NY: Orbis Books, 2000; p. 350.

8. Appleby, The Gerety Lecture.

9. Dalferth, Ingolf U. "I Determine What God Is," *Theology Today*, April 2000; p. 5.

10. *Newsweek*, April 22, 2000.

11. Bourgeois, Paul. "Redfield's Latest Yarn a Waste of Paper," *Fort Worth Star-Telegram*, January 2000; p. M1.

12. Hart, Thomas. *Spiritual Quest*. Mahwah, NJ: Paulist Press, 1999; p. 62.

13. Imbelli, Robert. In Book Symposium, *Commonweal*, February 11, 2000; p. 22.

Chapter 4: The Loss of "Thick" Catholicism

1. Massa, Mark. *Catholics and American Culture*. New York: Crossroad Publishing, 1999; p. 18.

2. Borchard, Therese Johnson. "Devotions which Endure," *Priests & People*, June 2000; p. 229. Borchard is also the author of *Our Catholic Devotions* (New York: Crossroad Publishing, 1998).

3. Massa, op. cit., p. 232.

Chapter 5: Anti-Catholicism

1. "Larry King Live," March 22, 2000.

2. "Postscript on Bob Jones," *Catalyst*. Journal of the Catholic League for Religious and Civil Rights, April 2000; p. 1.

3. Steinfels, Peter. "Of Bob Jones U., American Culture and Anti-Catholicism," in Beliefs, *New York Times*, March 4, 2000.

4. Lockwood, Robert, ed. *Anti-Catholics in American Culture*. Huntington, IN: Our Sunday Visitor Press, 2000; p. 86.

5. The plight of these people is documented in the powerful film *The Hidden Gift*, produced by the Windshover Forum, 719 Lomita Street. El Segundo, CA 90245. Also check their Website: www.petersvoice.com/sudan.html.

6. *Catalyst*, vol. 27, no. 2, March 2000.

7. See John Leo, *US News and World Report*, April 3, 2000; p. 14. Note also Woody Allen, who admits "I'm Jewish, but I'm not religious in any significant way; I don't have respect for any major religions." Yet somehow, in a recent movie titled *Picking Up the Pieces*, he manages to mock Catholicism—not the thousands of other religions out there that he doesn't have respect for. The movie is about a butcher who carves up his wife, whose hand (with a stiff middle finger) is discovered by a blind woman who is then cured. She declares it to be the hand of the Blessed Virgin and goes to a money-grubbing priest who is having sex with a prostitute and who then advertises the hand as capable of enlarging breasts and penises. Along the way we also learn that Mary Magdalene was Jesus' whore and that Mother Teresa has "sex slaves."

8. Mariani, Paul. "Descend on Us in Fire," *America*, March 4, 2000.

9. Chapter 6: Catholic Culture Wars

10. See Gertrude Himmelfarb's *One Nation, Two Cultures*. New York: Knopf, 1999.

11. Massa, Catholics and American Culture, p. 18. In his book, *Reconciling Faith and Reason: Apologists, Evangelists, and Theologians in a Divided Church* (Collegeville, MN: The Liturgical Press, 2000), Thomas Rausch, SJ, tells of how he was given the script to follow at a Mass for women religious from which the words "Father" and "Kingdom" were banished and the Mass ending was not the blessing "in the name of the Father, Son and Holy Spirit" but "May our God, Creator, Redeemer, and Lifegiving Spirit bless us." He remarks, "But one needs to move very carefully when dealing with the historical symbols of our faith. By eliminating (however inadvertently) the mutual relationship between Father and Son, this formula seems to eliminate the distinction of persons, and thus, the doctrine of the Trinity. Even more, it depersonalizes God" (p. 1).

12. Burghardt, *Long Have I Loved You*, p. 40.

13. When I say, "who many scholars claim is not historically attested to outside the Bible," I am referring to the fact that the scanty sources giving evidence for the existence of Jesus outside of the New Testament—the

Church Fathers, the letter of Tacitus, the writing of Josephus, the Babylonian Talmud, the alleged "Acts of Pilate," and the like—are all hotly contested as Christian interpolations. See books like *He Walked Among Us* by Josh McDowell and Bill Wilson (Nashville, TN: Thomas Nelson, 1988), which favor the authenticity of such texts, and books such as *The Jesus Myth* by G.A. Wells (LaSalle, IL: Open Court, 1999), which deny it. See also Catholic scholar John Meier's book, *A Marginal Jew: Rethinking the Historical Jesus* (New York: Doubleday, 1991). See also the letter from Andrew L. Sihler to the editor of the *New York Times Book Review* (June 11, 2000; p. 4), where he disputes a review of Thomas Cahill's book, *Desire of the Everlasting Hills*, which challenged Cahill's statement in the book that "there is not a shred of historical evidence outside the Bible itself to support the existence of Jesus." Sihler's letter proceeds to cite reasons why he supports that statement.

14. See also the article by Archbishop Rembert G. Weakland, OSB, "What Happened to the Common Ground Initiative?" in *New Theology Today*, August 2000.

15. Copain, Paul, ed. *Will the Real Jesus Please Stand Up?* Grand Rapids, MI: Baker Books, 1998; p. 148.

16. Appleby, Gerety Lecture.

17. McBrien, Richard. *Catholicism*, rev. ed. New York: Harper & Row, 1984; p. 1190.

Chapter 7. Pluralism

1. Schuth, Katarina. *Seminaries, Theologates, and the Future of Church Ministry*. Collegeville, MN: The Liturgical Press, 1999; p. 208ff.

2. U. S. Bishops Hispanic Affairs Committee. "Hispanic Ministry at the Turn of the New Millennium." See also Santos, John Philip, *Places Left Unfinished at the Time of Creation* (New York: Viking Penguin, 2000) and Davis, Mike, *Magical Urbanism: Latinos Reinvent the U.S. Big City* (New York: Verso Publications, 2000).

3. Schaffer, Pamela. "Scholars Say Religious Institutions Ignore Growing 'Latino Reality,'" *NCR*, March 17, 2000.

4. For the record, Catholics worldwide constitute less than eighteen percent of the total world population. Other Christians make up fifteen percent; Muslims, eighteen percent; Hindus, thirteen percent; Buddhists, seven percent; the rest includes all the other denominations, such as Jews, Sikhs, and Zoroastrians.

Furthermore, we might mention the stunning fact that as we enter the third millennium, Christianity is fast becoming a non-Western religion. As those who profess it in Europe and North America are declining, Christian churches in other countries continue to grow; already more than half the world's Christians live in Africa, Asia, Latin and Caribbean America, and the Pacific region. If the present trends continue, at some point in the future this figure could escalate to two-thirds. After being an almost exclusively Western religion for so long, so tightly associated with Europe that the two were interchangeable, Christianity is moving to other cultures.

Chapter 8: Contending with Scandal

1. Horgan, John. "Catholic Ireland: Sex, Lies and Accountability," *Commonweal*, March 10, 2000; p. 9-10. Italics mine. For more on Ireland's religious decline, see the fascinating book, *Goodbye to Catholic Ireland: How the Irish Lost the Civilization They Created* by Mary Kenny (Springfield, IL: Templegate Publishers, 2000).

2. See "Santa Rosa," by Arthur Jones; *NCR*, March 3, 2000. See also Jason Berry, *Lead Us Not into Temptation*, rev.ed. (Illinois Press).

3. See *Bless Me, Father, for I Have Sinned: Perspectives on Sexual Abuse Committed by Roman Catholic Priests.* Dr. Thomas Plante, ed. (Westport, CT: Greenwood Publishing Group, 1999).

4. Cozzens, Donald B. *The Changing Face of the Priesthood.* Collegeville, MN: The Liturgical Press, 2000; p. 125.

Chapter 9: The Priest Shortage

1. Young, Lawrence. *Sociology of Religion*, 59/98.

2. *New York Times*, February 2000.

3. *New York Times*, April 24, 2000.

4. Brown, Patricia Leigh. "'Sudden Wealth Syndrome' Brings New Stress." *New York Times*, March 10, 2000.

5. Cozzens, *Changing Face of the Priesthood*, p. 133-135.

6. Roger Cardinal Mahony. "As I Have Done For You," *Origins*, vol. 29, no. 46; May 4, 2000.

7. Greeley, Andrew M. "In Defense of Celibacy?" *America*, September 10, 1994; p. 10.

8. Friedl, Francis P. and Rex Reynolds. *Extraordinary Lives*. Notre Dame, IN: Ave Maria Press, 1997; p. 10

Chapter 10: Gay Clergy

1. Perri, William D. *A Radical Challenge for Priesthood Today*. Mystic, CT: Twenty-Third Publications, 1996; p. 77.

2. See *NCR*, "Editor Takes Aim at Sipe," Kansas City Star, April 21, 2000; p. 20. See also the exchange of letters in First Things, August/September 2000; pp. 10-11.

3. Cozzens, *Changing Face of the Priesthood*, p. 100.

4. Wills, Garry. *Papal Sin: Structures of Deceit*. New York: Doubleday, 2000; p. 200.

5. Ibid., p. 195.

6. Pastor Ignotus. *The Tablet*. April 24, 1999; p. 553.

7. Boswell, John. "Homosexuality and Religious Life: A Historical Approach," in *Homosexuality in the Priesthood and Religious Life*. Jeannine Gramick, ed. New York: Crossroad Publishing, 1989; p. 9.

8. Fuller, John, SJ. "Priests with AIDS," *America*, March 18, 2000; p. 8.

Chapter 11: Women and Men

1. See the article by Steven A. Holmes in the *New York Times*, December 15, 1996, section 4.

2. Address for the Jubilee Day for Women, *Origins*, vol. 29, no., 43, April 13, 2000; p. 705.

3. Ehrenreich, Barbara. "Maid to Order," *Harper's Magazine*, April 2000.

4. See "The War Against Boys," by Christina Hoff Sommers, *The Atlantic Monthly*, May 2000. We see other biases in figures and statistics that are regularly trotted out but never proved. For example, a 1987 Canadian report titled "The War Against Women" was based on a survey which showed that many men beat up on women. Accordingly, the government commissioned a $10 million inquiry into what must be done. What was kept quiet was that this same research showed that women beat up on men at an equal rate, but this was not publicized because the authors of the survey said that they were primarily interested in male-to-female violence at the time. See also, *A Return To Modesty* by Wendy Shalit. See also the article, "The Male Minority," by Daren Fonda, in *Time* (December 11, 2000), which cites the worrisome statistic that males now make up just forty-four percent of undergraduate students nationwide, and that number is expected to decline to forty-two percent by the year 2010. This has some colleges scurrying to recruit males.

5. Gates, Anita. "Dumb as Posts and Proud of It," *New York Times*, April 9, 2000. See also the article in the *Wall Street Journal*, "If Boys Just Want to Have Fun, This May Bring Them Down," by Ann Zimmerman. In it the author notes that, with their newfound assertiveness, girls today feel it is pay-back time. This is reflected in the growing popularity of T-shirts that carry boy-bashing slogans. For example: "I make boys cry"; "Boys will be boys" stenciled above a picture of a donkey's hindquarters; "Boys make good pets"; "So many boys, so little minds"; and "Boys 'R Toys." Of course, this is a response to the offensive T-shirts often worn by boys, along with their traditional vulgarity and putdowns of girls. You can hardly blame the girls for reacting this way; it's understandable. Still, not to make a big thing of it, it's a bit sad and disconcerting to hear Christian women relish the theme of revenge in the gender wars.

6. Arnold, Patrick M. *Wildmen, Warriors and Kings: Masculine Spirituality and the Bible*. New York: Crossroad Publishing, 1992; pp. 15-16. See also *On Men: Masculinity in Crisis*, by Anthony Clare (Chatto & Windus).

7. Heffern, Rich. "On the March to a Different Model of Maleness." *NCR*, December 3, 1999; p. 40.

8. Hodge, Roger D. "Onan the Magnificent," *Harper's Magazine*, March 2000.

9. Pope, Harrison and Katherine Phillips. *The Adonis Complex: The Secret Crisis of Male Body Obsession*. New York: The Free Press, 2000; pp. 51-53.

10. Johnson, Elizabeth. "Feminism and Sharing the Faith: A Catholic Dilemma." Warren Lecture Series in Catholic Studies (29).

11. See Sommers, Christina Hoff. *Who Stole Feminism: How Women Have Betrayed Women*. New York: Simon and Schuster, 1994.

12. Steinfels, Margaret O'Brien. "Obstacles to the New Feminism: Look Before You Leap," *America*, July 6–13, 1996.

13. Bausch, William. *The Parish of the Next Millennium*. Mystic, CT: Twenty-Third Publications, 1997; pp. 261-263.

14. Podles, Leon. *The Church Impotent: The Feminization of Christianity*. Dallas, TX: Spence Publishing Co., 1999. See also the issue of the magazine *Priests & People*, August/September 2000, which is dedicated to "Men in the Church."

15. Sullivan, Andrew. "The He Hormone." *New York Times Magazine*, April 2, 2000. This whole article is very much worth reading. See also Melanine Phillips, *The Sex-Change Society: Feminised Britain and the Neutered Male* (The Social Market Foundation).

Chapter 12: The Crises of Authority and Identity

16. O'Malley, John. The Millennium and the Papalization of Catholicism," *America*, April 8, 2000, pp. 8ff.

17. Wills, *Papal Sin*.

18. Sipe, A.W. Richard, "Perilous Choice to Ignore AIDS Issue," *NCR*, March 31, 2000; p. 9.

19. *Origins*, 1/28/99. See also, Archbishop John R. Quinn. *Reform of the Papacy: The Costly Call to Christian Unity*. New York: Crossroad Publishing, 1999.

20. *Constitution on the Church in the Modern World*, no. 43.

21. Burghardt, *Long Have I Loved You*, p. 411.

22. Huebsch, Bill. "A View from the Pews: Vatican II and the Priesthood," *Touchstone*, Fall 2000; p. 6. For another view of the current state of the priesthood, see Shaw, Russell. "The Priest's Confused Identity." *Crisis*, December 2000; p. 12ff.

23. Nahapiet, Janine. "Priests Renewing People," *Priests & People*, April 2000; p. 145.

Part II: Temporary Transitions

Chapter 13: The Fallouts

1. Martini, Richard. *Touchstone*, Fall 1998, p. 10.

Chapter 14: Current Approaches and Solutions

1. Sweetser, Thomas P. and Patricia M. Forster. *Transforming the Parish: Models for the Future*, rev. ed. Mahwah, NJ: Paulist Press, 1993; pp. 206-207.

2. *The Priest and the Third Christian Millennium: Teacher of the Word, Minister of the Sacraments, and Leader of the Community*. Washington, DC: United States Catholic Conference Publishing Services, 1999.

3. The National Catholic Parish Survey. See http://members.aol.com/cathparishsurvey/welcome.htm.

4. See, for example, my book, *The Total Parish Manual* (Mystic, CT: Twenty-Third Publications, 1994). See also Roger Cardinal Mahony's pastoral letter, "As I Have Done for You" (Chicago: Liturgy Training Publications, 2000).

5. See, for example, Lumen Gentium (25) and Decree on the Ministry and Life of Priests (4).

Chapter 15: Ministerial Confusion

1. Provencher, Norman. *Theology Digest*, Summer 1997.

2. Second of a four-part series on the U.S. Catholic Church in the *New York Times*.

3. *Origins*, July 1, 1999.

4. National Catholic Reporter-Gallup poll, *NCR*, November 29, 1999; hereafter referred to as NCR-Gallup.

5. Kathleen Reagan, "Prison Ministry: Are Catholics Being Locked Out?" *Commonweal*, September 8, 2000; pp. 11-12.

Chapter 16: Lay Ministry: Glories and Perils

1. *Celebration*, October 1999, p. 429.

2. *Theological Investigations*, vol. XIX. New York: Crossroad Publishing, 1983; p 71 and 79ff.

Part III: Responses

Chapter 17: A Married Clergy

1. See www.womenpriests.org. Also see Zagano, Phyllis. *Holy Saturday: The Argument for the Reinstitution of the Female Diaconate in the Catholic Church*. New York: Crossroad Publishing, 2000. A recent poll (Gallup News Service, June 15, 2000) found that most of the American public (71%) say they support women acting as pastors, ministers, priests, or rabbis, while less than a quarter (23%) are opposed. This is a significant change from a 1977 poll conducted by the same organization, which found only forty-two percent in favor of women as clergy.

2. Kelly, J.N. *The Oxford Dictionary of Popes*. New York: Oxford University Press, 1989.

3. Stravinskas, Peter M.J., ed. "Canon Law of Celibacy." *The New Catholic Encyclopedia*. Huntington, IN: *Our Sunday Visitor*, Inc., 1993.

4. Cited in *America*, November 27, 1999; p. 5.

5. Sloyan, Gerald. "The Return of an Old Tradition," *America*, April 15, 2000.

6. Norris, Kathleen. *The Cloister Walk*. New York: Berkeley Publishing Group, 1997; pp. 116–117.

7. Egan, Robert J., SJ. *Commonweal*, August 11, 2000; p. 23.

8. *New Oxford Review*, January 1999.

9. Throop, John R. *The Christian Ministry*, March-April 1999; p. 13 ff.

10. Weidner, Hallbert. *The Tablet*, September 9, 2000; p. 1189.

11. See this book, from which I have drawn these thoughts: Lobinger, Fritz. *Like His Brothers and Sisters*. New York: Crossroad Publishing, 1988. (Although written with an African village in mind, the ideas can be extrapolated to the larger Church.)

12. See, for example, the Gallup Survey of Catholic Opinion (May 15-17, 1992) on acceptance of a married clergy.

13. Sultana, Fiorella. *The Tablet*. September 5, 1998.

14. Lovasik, Ken. "Not for Hire," *Commonweal*, June 4, 1999; p. 31.

15. Brown, Raymond. *Priest and Bishop: Biblical Reflections*. Mahwah, NJ: Paulist Press, 1970; pp. 41-42.

Chapter 18: The Hungering and the Hope

1. Kerkhofs, Jan SJ. *Europe Without Priests*.

2. Cited in "The Pull of God in a Godless Age," by Cardinal Franz Konig. *The Tablet*, September 18, 1999; p. 1248.

3. See books like: Polkinghorne, John. *Belief in God in an Age of Science*. New Haven, CT: Yale University Press, 1998.

4. Berger, Peter. *The Desecularization of the World*. Grand Rapids, MI: Wm. B. Eerdmans Publishing Co., 1999; p. 13.

5. Cited in *Emerging Trends*, April 2000.

6. Report issued in January 2000.

7. From an article in *Newsweek*, March 27, 2000.

8. Armstrong, Karen. *The Battle for God: Fundamentalism in Judaism, Christianity and Islam*. New York: Knopf, 2000.

9. *Wall Street Journal*, March 31, 2000; W1.

10. *CARA*, vol. 5, no. 1 (Summer 1999).

11. From a grant given by the Lilly Endowment to the Loyola Institute for Ministry.

12. *Time*, March 27, 2000. People like Garry Wills, however, take the whole rationale of apology to task because the official language states that not the Church itself but "her sons and daughters" have been sinful. Wills points out that, on the contrary, the Church itself must be included as sinful since in its official documents and, most tellingly, in its liturgy (lex orandi, lex credendi) the Church officially—not just its sons and daughters—condemned the Jews. (See his book, *Papal Sin*.) On the other hand, Richard John Neuhaus points out that the prophets of Israel regularly denounced the sins of the people of Israel while, at the same time, insisting that they are the elect people of God. See also Carroll, James. *Constantine's Sword: The Church and the Jews, A History*. Boston: Houghton Mifflin Co., 2001.

13. Kevin and Marilyn Ryan, eds. *Why I Am Still a Catholic*. New York: Riverhead Books, 1998; p 17.

14. Speltz, Karen Ann. *The Catholic World*, March-April 1993.

15. "A Feminist Becomes a Catholic," *Priests & People*, January 2, 2000; p. 13ff.

16. Peter Cornwell, "Crag and Torrent," *Priests & People*, January 2, 2000; p. 23.

17. *NCR*, November 12, 1999.

18. *Publishers' Weekly*, November 15, 1999.

19. These thoughts I owe to the insightful op ed column of Brooks, David. "The Secular Society." *The New York Times*, July 9, 2103.

Chapter 19: Linking Liturgy and Life

1. The full homily can be found in *The Word In and Out of Season: Homilies for Preachers, Reflections for Seekers.* Mystic, CT: Twenty-Third Publications, 2000.

2. *Celebration*, October, 1999.

3. *America*, July 31, 1999.

4. McLellan, Daniel, OFM. "Ministry for a New Culture," *New Theology Review*, February 2000; p. 57.

5. Wiltshire, Susan Ford. *Athena's Disguises: Mentors in Everyday Life.* Louisville, KY: Westminster/John Knox Press, 1998.

Chapter 20: The Strength of the Cross

1. *The Tablet*, December 2, 1995.

2. Cahill, *Desire of the Everlasting Hills*, p. 174-175.

3. *The Tablet*, February 2000.

Chapter 21: The Spirituality of Ecclesial Lay Ministers

1. NALM, 5420 South Cornell Avenue, Chicago, IL 60615. Phone: 773-241-6050; NCCL, 3021 Fourth Street, NE, Washington, D.C. 20017. Phone: 202-636-3826; NFCYM, 415 Michigan Avenue NE, Washington, D.C. 20017. Phone: 202-636-3825; NACPA, 100 East Eight Street, Cincinnati, Ohio 45202. Phone: 513-421-3085.

2. Bausch, *Parish of the Next Millennium*, p. 124.

3. See *Today's Parish*, January 2000 issue on Adult Formation.

4. Pastoral letter, "As I Have Done for You," *Origins*, p. 747.

Chapter 22: The Postmodern Generation

1. *New York Times*, April 18, 2000.

2. Appleby, Scott. "American Culture and Catholicism: Maintaining Faith Identity Amidst Pluralism of Our Times," in *Formation in Faith: A Discussion on Religious Education and Spiritual Growth Within a New Generation of Believers*, ed. Francis J. Butler. Washington, DC: Foundations and Donors Interested in Catholic Activities, Inc., 1997; pp. 5-10.

3. David Samuels. "Rock is Dead: Sex, Drugs, and Raw Sewage at Woodstock '99," *Harper's Magazine*, November 1999; pp. 69ff.

4. Reed, Eric. "Ministering with 'My Generation,'" *Leadership*, Fall 2000; p. 52.

5. *America*, April 22, 2000.

6. *A Royal Waste of Time: The Splendor of Worshiping God and Being Church for the World*. Grand Rapids, MI: Wm. B. Eerdmans, 1999.

7. See this collection of essays that speak to the issues of young adults: Miscamble, Wilson D. *Keeping the Faith: Making a Difference*. Notre Dame, IN: Ave Maria Press, 2000.

Chapter 23: Pondering the Institutional Church

1. Dao, James. "Ads Now Seek Recruits for An Army of One," *New York Times*, January 10, 2001; p. 1.

2. Goodstein, Laurie. "Most Americans See Benefit in Religion, a Poll Shows," *New York Times*, January 10, 2001; p. 14.

3. Schaper, Donna, quoted in Context by Martin Marty, December 15, 2000.

4. *Priesthood*, p. 146.

5. *That They May Live*, ed. Michael Downey, p. 87.

6. *The Hesitant Pilgrim*, pp. xiv, xv.

7. Ward, J. Neville. *Five for Sorrow, Ten for Joy*. New York: Doubleday, 1973; p. 48.

8. *Commonweal*.

9. *Commonweal*, September 9, 1994.

10. *NCR*, March 31, 2000.

11. "A Modest Proposal: A Place for Women in the Hierarchy," *Commonweal*, June 14, 1996.

12. Burghardt, *Long Have I Loved You*, p. 355.

13. Rolheiser, *Holy Longing*, chapter 6.

14. Groome, Thomas. *Educating for Life*. Allen, TX: Thomas More, 1998; p. 177.

15. Quoted by E. J. Dionne in *Commonweal*, Nov. 11, 1999.

16. Tieman, John Samuel. *America*, July 17, 1999; p. 21.

17. Eliot, T.S. *The Rock*.

Chapter 24: Inclusive/Exclusive

1. Rausch, *Reconciling Faith*, p. 53-54.

2. Hart, *Spiritual Quest*, chapter 1.

3. Declaration on the Relation of the Church to Non-Christian Religions (2).

4. McBrien, *Catholicism*, p. 1189.

5. Groome, *Educating for Life*, p. 58.

Chapter 25: The Face of Francis

1. I am indebted to Michael Sean Winters' article, "No Longer One Nation Under God" in *The Tablet*, 6. July 2012. pp. 12-13.

2. Jo McGowan, "Simplifying Sex", *Commonweal*, April 9, 2012.

How Jesus Won the West
by Rodney Stark

Desire of the Everlasting Hills
by Cahill

Made in the USA
Lexington, KY
28 June 2015